FITNESS FOR LIFE
Middle School

Teacher's Guide

Guy C. Le Masurier
Dolly D. Lambdin
Charles B. Corbin

Human Kinetics

ISBN-10: 0-7360-6828-7
ISBN-13: 978-0-7360-6828-4

The Web addresses cited in this text were current as of January 2007, unless otherwise noted.

Acquisitions Editor: Scott Wikgren; **Developmental Editor:** Ray Vallese; **Assistant Editor:** Derek Campbell; **Special Projects Editor:** Anne Cole; **Copyeditor:** Patsy Fortney; **Proofreader:** Jim Burns; **Permission Manager:** Dalene Reeder; **Graphic Designer:** Robert Reuther; **Graphic Artist:** Denise Lowry; **Photo Manager:** Laura Fitch; **Photo Office Assistant:** Jason Allen; **Cover Designer:** Robert Reuther; **Photographer (cover):** Kelly Huff, Tom Roberts, © Image 100 LDT; **Photographer (interior):** ©Human Kinetics, unless otherwise noted; courtesy of Charmain Sutherland (p. 39); © Art Explosion (p. 94); courtesy of Scott Wikgren (pp. 128 and 142); © Brand X Pictures (p. 141); © Stockdisc (p. 209); © Eyewire/Photodisc/Getty Images (p. 210); © Image Source (p. 233); © Photodisc (p. 234); **Art Manager:** Kelly Hendren; **Illustrator:** Accurate Art, Inc.; **Printer:** Versa Press

Printed in the United States of America   10   9   8   7   6   5   4   3   2

Human Kinetics
Web site: www.HumanKinetics.com

United States: Human Kinetics, P.O. Box 5076, Champaign, IL 61825-5076
800-747-4457
e-mail: humank@hkusa.com

Canada: Human Kinetics, 475 Devonshire Road, Unit 100, Windsor, ON N8Y 2L5
800-465-7301 (in Canada only)
e-mail: info@hkcanada.com

Europe: Human Kinetics, 107 Bradford Road, Stanningley
Leeds LS28 6AT, United Kingdom
+44 (0) 113 255 5665
e-mail: hk@hkeurope.com

Australia: Human Kinetics, 57A Price Avenue, Lower Mitcham, South Australia 5062
08 8372 0999
e-mail: info@hkaustralia.com

New Zealand: Human Kinetics, Division of Sports Distributors NZ Ltd.
P.O. Box 300 226 Albany, North Shore City, Auckland
0064 9 448 1207
e-mail: info@humankinetics.co.nz

Contents

Lesson Plans for Chapter 8   Body Composition, Physical Activity, and Nutrition . . 209

Lesson Plans for Chapter 9   Planning for Physical Activity. 233

Fitness for Life: Middle School is a unique fitness and physical activity program designed specifically for middle school students. It is meant to be included as a part of the total middle school physical education curriculum. *Fitness for Life: Middle School* can be implemented as a nine-week unit (base plan), as a semester unit (extended base plan), or in multiple three- to six-week units at several different grade levels. The student text includes nine chapters (one for each week of a nine-week unit or one for every two weeks in a semester program). In the *Fitness for Life: Middle School* program, students do classroom activities, activity sessions, and outside-of-class activities. As described later in this preface, lesson plans and resource materials for the entire program are included.

What Is the *Fitness for Life: Middle School* Philosophy?

Fitness for Life: Middle School shares the **HELP** philosophy created for the high school version of *Fitness for Life* and used as the basis for the Fitnessgram and Physical Best programs. The program is designed to help middle school students learn about **h**ealth-related physical fitness and the **h**ealth benefits of healthy lifestyles including participation in regular physical activity and sound nutrition. The program is designed to involve **e**veryone (all middle school students), not just those with special physical talents. While activities that can be used for a **l**ifetime are featured, the many activities included in *Fitness for Life: Middle School* were chosen to get kids active now, both in and out of school. Finally, *Fitness for Life: Middle School* is meant to be **p**ersonal. Both classroom activities and physical activities are designed to help each student find activities that are personally appropriate and plan a personal physical activity program.

What Are the Objectives of *Fitness for Life: Middle School*?

Fitness for Life: Middle School has both general and very specific objectives. First, the program is designed to be sure that the middle school physical education program plays a significant role in helping each student to be fully physically educated as described by NASPE. The general goals are to help the student to become physically active, physically fit, and knowledgeable about the health benefits of physical activity; to value physical activity; and to develop skills that can be used for a lifetime of physical activity. Second, the program is designed to help students meet grade (6-8) specific objectives outlined in the NASPE standards for physical education. The specific standards used as the basis for this program are described in greater detail later in this *Teacher's Guide*.

Why Have a Special Middle School Program?

Middle school physical education, in our opinion, has often been neglected. Many materials have been prepared specifically for elementary and high school programs but are less often available specifically for middle school physical education programs. The authors undertook this project because we wanted to have a program specifically for middle school students and teachers. The program is based on objectives specifically for middle school and is meant to prepare students for high school programs such as *Fitness for Life*.

What Is Included in This *Teacher's Guide*?

It is our hope that you will find this *Fitness for Life: Middle School Teacher's Guide* to be an easy-to-use, informative resource containing a wide variety of standards-based physical education lessons that are engaging and fun. Each of the nine sections of lesson plans features five lesson plans, which reinforce and build on the content provided in the nine chapters of the *Fitness for Life: Middle School* student textbook.

The CD-ROM bound into the *Teacher's Guide* contains materials designed to support and enhance the lesson plans, including student worksheets, class resources, assessment rubrics, quizzes, answer keys, and classroom quotes. These reproducible materials are ready to be printed and used right away. They are also customizable, so teachers can adapt them as desired to suit any school, class, or student needs.

In addition, we encourage you to integrate the *Fitness for Life: Middle School* program with your own skill-based activity units that complement and reinforce the key content. The *Teacher's Guide* provides ideas for sample units, as well as specific units that can be found in other resources. You'll also find information on national content standards, program scheduling options, teaching frameworks, teaching strategies, and more.

Finally, the *Fitness for Life: Middle School* Web site provides extended discussions of topics in the student textbook, a test package of hundreds of questions that teachers can use to create their own quizzes, two Web-based educational computer programs that supplement the lesson plans, and other teacher resources.

You can read further details about all of these components and more in the six sections of this *Teacher's Guide* (pages 1 to 42) that precede the lesson plans.

Who Is Responsible for This Unique Program?

Fitness for Life: Middle School is a result of a team effort. Scott Wikgren, director of the Health, Physical Education, Recreation, and Dance division of Human Kinetics, was the driving force behind this project. He was responsible several years ago for bringing the very successful *Fitness for Life* high school program to Human Kinetics and has long felt that a middle school program was needed. He made it happen!

With Scott's assistance, an author team and a team of expert consultants was assembled. Together Scott and I chose Guy Le Masurier and Dolly Lambdin as co-authors for the project. Guy brings youthful enthusiasm, an excellent ability to put words on paper in a meaningful way, and a practical understanding of the needs of school-aged youth. Dolly Lambdin brings years of practical experience working with both students and teachers, a sound understanding of pedagogical principles and curriculum planning, and strong leadership. The consultants listed in the student textbook provided field testing, critiques of activities and book content, and practical suggestions for revisions and improvement. Many of the *Fitness for Life* instructors who participate in a program jointly sponsored by Physical Best and Human Kinetics also provided input. Names of these contributors are available on the *Fitness for Life* Web site at www.fitnessforlife.org/middleschool or on page xiv of the student textbook.

Finally, I (and my co-authors) cannot say enough about the excellent work done by our editors Ray Vallese and Derek Campbell. In many ways these two hard-working people, as well as Scott Wikgren, are really co-authors of the book in that they not only did excellent proofing and editing but contributed ideas and content used in the student text and *Teacher's Guide*. Both editors worked long hours and were diligent far beyond the call of duty. We cannot thank them enough for their hard work and attention to detail. We would also like to thank all of the other people at Human Kinetics who contributed to this team effort.

—Charles B. "Chuck" Corbin

Acknowledgments

First, I want to thank my wife for being the best friend a Guy could have. I want to thank Dolly Lambdin for her wonderful ideas and creative energy that continually inspired me through this process. I want to acknowledge several mentors who have influenced the way I think about physical education: Chuck Corbin, Bob Pangrazi, George Graham, and Scott Kretchmar. Finally, I want to thank Chuck Corbin for his unwavering support of my career and life paths.

—Guy Le Masurier

Many friends and colleagues have contributed to my understanding of teaching and physical education and so to this book. To my husband Larry go my grateful thanks for being my best friend and partner in life, for his listening ear and thoughtful responses, and for always being willing to do whatever is needed. My daughter Becca, who is studying to be an elementary physical education teacher, deserves my eternal gratitude for affirming me and raising the standards of my own teaching through her questions, reflections, and example. My son Andrew has taught me a great deal about quality physical education by being willing to share his experiences in color guard, school PE, and university classes in handball, dance, and fencing. My extended family (almost all teachers) has enriched my understanding of teaching through years of thought-provoking discussions during holiday get-togethers. I would also like to gratefully acknowledge my mentors, colleagues, students, and friends who have challenged and guided me and made my life as a teacher so rich and rewarding. Thanks go especially to Larry, Bill, George, Daryl, Patt, Sue, Kathy, Tere, Jim, Michele, Fran, Amanda, Rosie, Pam, Judy, Theresa, Deborah, Lynne, Leslie, Margie, Dale, Gloria, Barb, and Carol. Finally I would like to thank Chuck Corbin for inviting me along on this wonderful adventure and for all he has taught me through the process, Guy Le Masurier for the excitement and insight each of our discussions brought into my life, and our outstanding team at Human Kinetics for their enthusiasm, insight, and skill at seeing us through this incredible process.

—Dolly Lambdin

Pedagogical Foundations

A quality physical education program must be built on a strong foundation and conducted by dedicated teachers. Accordingly, *Fitness for Life: Middle School* was developed only after considering standards appropriate for middle school youth and sound guidelines for good teaching. These standards and guidelines are covered under the following headings:

* REAL Teachers
* National Association for Sport and Physical Education (NASPE) Standards

Welcome to *Fitness for Life: Middle School!* The authors are excited to bring you a middle school physical education program that will enhance and complement your existing program. In developing *Fitness for Life: Middle School,* we have tried to address national and state standards and the special needs of middle school students concerning peer and parental relationships, while concurrently teaching

health-related fitness concepts and selected biomechanical principles. Physical activity is the focal point of the *Fitness for Life: Middle School* program, and we have surrounded the activity component with diverse learning experiences that enable students to connect with, and reflect on, their personal fitness and preferences for physical activity.

REAL Teachers

If you have chosen this text, we believe you are what Cathrine Himberg calls a "REAL teacher" (Responsible Educator who Affects Lives). She, and her students at Chico State University, developed a Web page titled CASPER: Center for the Advancement of Standards-based Physical Education Reform (www.csuchico.edu/casper). On this site they provide information and examples of quality physical education, pinpoint problems and challenges within the profession, and identify changes that must happen for all children to experience a quality physical education program.

Dedicated teachers are critical in this crusade. Cathrine developed an oath for teachers inspired by the Hippocratic Oath and the Florence Nightingale pledge so that we could be reminded of our best teaching selves (see figure 1). You may want to take the oath yourself and help swell the ranks of those registered at the CASPER site who are committed to being "REAL teachers."

REAL PHYSICAL EDUCATION TEACHERS' PLEDGE

I SOLEMNLY PLEDGE TO WHAT I HOLD MOST DEARLY, THAT AS A TEACHER I WILL PRACTICE MY PROFESSION WITH HONOR AND INTEGRITY.

I WILL ABSTAIN FROM USING TEACHING PRACTICES CONSIDERED INAPPROPRIATE AND I WILL FOLLOW THE STANDARDS AND GUIDELINES FOR MY PROFESSION TO THE UTMOST OF MY POWER.

ALWAYS REACHING FOR EXCELLENCE, I WILL CONTINUE TO LEARN AND ENHANCE MY TEACHING SKILLS THROUGHOUT MY CAREER.

I WILL BE A POSITIVE ROLE MODEL FOR CHILDREN AND YOUTH AND DO ALL THAT I CAN TO HELP THEM ACQUIRE THE SKILLS, KNOWLEDGE AND DESIRE THEY NEED IN ORDER TO ENJOY A LIFETIME OF PHYSICAL ACTIVITY.

Figure 1 Teachers' pledge.
Courtesy of Cathrine Himberg.

National Association for Sport and Physical Education (NASPE) Standards

The national content standards developed by the National Association for Sport and Physical Education (NASPE) define what a student should know and be able to do as a result of a quality physical education program (see figure 2). These standards were not intended to be addressed separately. As such, we have developed lesson plans that address multiple standards specific to the middle school level (grades 6 through 8).

NASPE Standards

A physically educated person:

Standard 1: Demonstrates competency in motor skills and movement patterns needed to perform a variety of physical activities.

Standard 2: Demonstrates understanding of movement concepts, principles, strategies, and tactics as they apply to the learning and performance of physical activities.

Standard 3: Participates regularly in physical activity.

Standard 4: Achieves and maintains a health-enhancing level of physical fitness.

Standard 5: Exhibits responsible personal and social behavior that respects self and others in physical activity settings.

Standard 6: Values physical activity for health, enjoyment, challenge, self-expression, and/or social interaction.

Figure 2 NASPE standards.

Moving into the Future: National Standards for Physical Education, 2nd Edition (2004) reprinted with permission from the National Association for Sport and Physical Education (NASPE), 1900 Association Drive, Reston, VA 20191-1599.

The goal of physical education is to develop physically educated people who have the knowledge, skills, and confidence to enjoy a lifetime of healthful physical activity. Please read over the middle school student expectations related to the national standards (figure 3) closely, as this text addresses many of the specifics identified.

Student Expectations (at the End of Grade 8) Related to the NASPE Standards

Standard 1: Adolescents are able to participate with skill in a variety of modified sport, dance, gymnastics, and outdoor activities. Students achieve mature forms of the basic skills of more specialized sports, dance, and gymnastics activities. They use the skills in combination with other basic skills. Students demonstrate use of tactics within sport activities.

Standard 2: Adolescents exhibit increasingly complex discipline-specific knowledge. They can identify principles of practice and conditioning that enhance movement performance. They have higher levels of understanding and application of movement concepts/principles and game strategies, critical elements of activity-specific movement skills and characteristics representing highly skilled performance. Students know when, why, and how to use tactics and strategies within game play. They use information from a variety of sources, both internal and external, to guide and improve performance.

Standard 3: Adolescents are able to independently set physical activity goals and participate in individualized programs of physical activity and exercise based on personal goals and interests as well as on the results of fitness assessments. They select and utilize practice procedures and training principles appropriate for the activity goals they set. Students have an increasing awareness of the opportunities for participation in a broad range of activities that may meet their needs and interests. They participate regularly in moderate to vigorous physical activities in both school and non-school settings.

Standard 4: Adolescents participate in moderate to vigorous physical activities on a regular basis without undue fatigue. They participate in physical activities that address each component of health-related fitness, including cardiorespiratory endurance, muscular strength and endurance, flexibility, and body composition. Students know the components of fitness and how these relate to their overall fitness status. Students monitor their own heart rate, breathing rate, perceived exertion, and recovery rate during and following strenuous physical activity. They assess their personal fitness status for each component and use this information to assist in the development of individualized physical fitness goals with little help from the teacher. Students show progress towards knowing the various principles of training (e.g., threshold, overload, specificity) and know how these principles can be utilized in improving one's level of fitness.

Standard 5: Adolescents begin to understand the concept of physical activity as a microcosm of modern culture and society. They recognize the role of physical activity in understanding diversity and continue to include and support each other, respecting the limitations and strengths of group members. Students move from merely identifying and following rules, procedures, safe practices, ethical behavior, and positive forms of social interactions to reflecting upon their role in physical activity settings and the benefits of physical activity. They have well-developed cooperation skills and are able to accomplish group/team goals in both cooperative and competitive activities. Adolescents seek greater independence from adults and effectively work independently and in groups to complete assigned tasks. They make appropriate decisions to resolve conflicts arising from the powerful influence of peers, and they practice appropriate problem-solving techniques to resolve conflicts when necessary in competitive activities.

Standard 6: Adolescents seek physical activity experiences for group membership and positive social interaction. They recognize and appreciate skilled performance. Physical activities provide a positive outlet for competition with peers and a means of gaining the respect and recognition of others. Physical activity can increase self-confidence and self-esteem as students discover renewed enjoyment in participation. Physical activities can provide confidence as students start to take steps toward independence. Challenge is found both in experiencing high levels of competition and learning new and/or different activities. As students experience a greater awareness of feelings, the avenues of self-expression provided by dance, gymnastics, and other sport activities become increasingly important.

Figure 3 Student expectations related to standards.

Moving into the Future: National Standards for Physical Education, 2nd Edition (2004) reprinted with permission from the National Association for Sport and Physical Education (NASPE), 1900 Association Drive, Reston, VA 20191-1599.

Lesson Components

To make your delivery of the *Fitness for Life: Middle School* program easy and effective, this section begins with a brief explanation of how the student textbook and the *Teacher's Guide* are integrated. You'll also learn about the basic features in the textbook and the format of the lesson plans in the *Teacher's Guide*, along with practical teaching strategies and supplemental materials. The information is covered under the following headings:

* Integration of the Textbook and *Teacher's Guide*
* Textbook Lesson Features
* *Teacher's Guide* Lesson Plan Format
* Icons for Incorporating Technology and Effective Teaching Practices
* Supplemental Activities for Integration With *Fitness for Life: Middle School*

Integration of the Textbook and *Teacher's Guide*

The nine chapters in the *Fitness for Life: Middle School* student textbook are broken into three units with three chapters per unit. Each chapter has two lessons that are identified using the numbering system 1.1, 1.2, 2.1, 2.2, 3.1, 3.2, and so on, for a total of 18 lessons.

This *Teacher's Guide* presents five lesson plans for each chapter in the student textbook, for a total of 45 lesson plans. In each group of five lesson plans, two are classroom lessons directly addressing the two lessons from the student textbook, and three are activity lessons that reinforce the content. In each group of five, the lesson plans are arranged in this order: classroom, activity, classroom, activity, and activity (see figure 4). Thus, in chapter 1, lesson 1.1 is for the classroom, lesson 1.2 is an activity, lesson 1.3 is for the classroom, lesson 1.4 is an activity, and lesson 1.5 is a culminating activity.

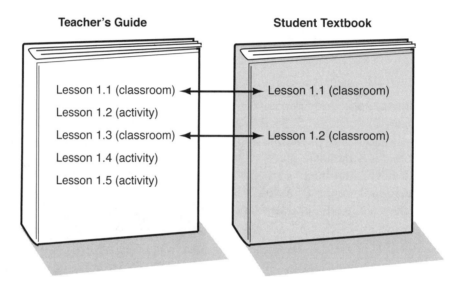

Teacher's Guide

Lesson 1.1 (classroom)

Lesson 1.2 (activity)

Lesson 1.3 (classroom)

Lesson 1.4 (activity)

Lesson 1.5 (activity)

Student Textbook

Lesson 1.1 (classroom)

Lesson 1.2 (classroom)

Figure 4   Textbook and *Teacher's Guide* integration.

Textbook Lesson Features

The following features are part of every lesson in the student textbook:

- ▶ **Vocabulary:** At the start of each lesson, students will find a list of the key words and concepts discussed in that lesson.
- ▶ **Questions:** Following the vocabulary, students will find questions that assess their current level of knowledge (prior to delivery of the basic content).
- ▶ **Basic content:** Following the questions, students will find the basic content of the lesson. Most section headings are posed as questions.
- ▶ **Fit Facts:** Scattered throughout the lessons, these short, interesting facts relate to health, fitness, and physical activity.
- ▶ **Web site links:** Scattered throughout the lessons, numerous Web pointers direct students to pages on the *Fitness for Life: Middle School* Web site (www.fitnessforlife.org/middleschool) where they can access additional information about relevant topics.

▶ **Lesson Review:** Following the basic content, students will find review questions (based on the section headings) that assess their new level of knowledge.

The following features are part of the first lesson in each chapter of the student textbook:

▶ **Moving Together:** This feature helps middle school students meet NASPE standards 5 (developing responsible social behavior; understanding diversity, cultural and societal issues) and 6 (valuing positive social interactions through activity and developing self-esteem) as described on page 4. Each "Moving Together" feature presents a scenario, poses questions for discussion, and offers guidelines for dealing with critical issues. Topics include effective communication, peer pressure, bullying, and so on.

▶ **Take It Home:** This feature reinforces the "Moving Together" feature by giving students opportunities to explore and engage in physical activity outside of class—at their school, in their neighborhood, and in their community.

The following feature is part of the second lesson in each chapter of the student textbook:

▶ **Biomechanical Principles:** This feature discusses basic biomechanical principles, encourages students to apply the principles in a variety of movement settings, and suggests ways to explore the principles through physical activity. Topics include levers, friction, resistance, and so on.

The following features are part of each chapter in the student textbook, applying to both lessons in that chapter.

▶ **In This Chapter:** The first page of the chapter presents a brief list of the main sections that will be covered.

▶ **Chapter Review:** The last page of the chapter offers review questions on the lessons.

▶ **Ask the Authors:** After reading both lessons in the chapter, students might still have questions. The last page of the chapter poses one sample question and encourages students to visit the *Fitness for Life: Middle School* Web site to find the answer—and to submit their own questions for the authors to answer online.

Teacher's Guide Lesson Plan Format

While there are two types of lesson plans (classroom and activity), all lesson plans in this teacher's guide have the same basic format.

Description of Lesson

This section provides a short description of the concepts covered in the lesson plan and the opportunities provided for student learning.

Performance Outcomes

This section lists specific performance outcomes addressed by the lesson plan that are related to the NASPE Physical Education Content Standards for grades 6 through 8.

Lesson Objectives

This section identifies the specific lesson objectives. The lesson plan includes a reminder to share the lesson objectives with students (see "Part 2: Lesson Launcher") and suggestions for how to assess student mastery of the objectives (see "Assessment").

Equipment

This section lists the equipment needed to conduct the class activities.

Reproducibles

This section lists any worksheets or resources needed for delivering the lesson and provides thumbnail images of each. All worksheets and resources are identified with a number that matches the number of their lesson plan.

▶ Worksheets are items designed to be handed out to students and completed, either during class or at home. Each worksheet number begins with the letter "W."

▶ Resources are items, such as activity station signs, designed to be used during class but not completed or written on by students. Each resource number begins with the letter "R."

You can print the worksheets and resources from the CD-ROM and use them as is, or you can customize them to better meet your specific needs. For instance, you can add your name (or the name of your class or your school), change the details of an example, replace photos with others that feature students or locations from your school, and so on. If you customize a reproducible file, please remember to save a copy of your customized version on your computer for future use. You can't save customized files on the CD-ROM.

Classroom Quotes

Each classroom lesson plan includes one or more quotes related to the content of the lesson. You can print all quotes from the CD-ROM and hang them around the room. Encourage students to find other quotes related to the chapter content. This allows students to share their unique perspectives and serves as a check for student understanding of the chapter content.

Setup

This section identifies preparations that you will need to make before delivering the lesson so that the lesson will run smoothly.

Delivering the Lesson

This section describes the lesson plan. Most lesson plans are presented in four parts. Some lesson plans are presented in five parts because they have more than one focus (to cover the "Moving Together" or "Biomechanical Principles" features in the student textbook).

PART 1: GATHERING INFORMATION (CLASSROOM LESSONS) OR INSTANT ACTIVITY (ACTIVITY LESSONS)

"Gathering Information" is the first part of each classroom lesson. It identifies the sections in the *Fitness for Life: Middle School* student textbook that students should read silently. If students are allowed to take their textbooks home, you can use the questions at the beginning and end of each lesson to have the students review their reading and provide responses.

"Instant Activity" (IA) is the first part of each activity lesson. The purpose of the IA is to get students moving as soon as they enter the activity area and warm them up for the lesson. The IA provides multiple opportunities to reinforce the concepts and importance of the warm-up and cool-down. The IA should be performed at a moderate level (e.g., walking and jogging rather than running) because there is not a warm-up before it. Because there will usually be some instructional time ("Lesson Launcher," instructions, or demonstrations) before the next activity, it is often not possible to use the IA as the warm-up time for the lesson focus activity. Therefore, each activity should be started at slow speed and gradually increased so that students can warm up before engaging at full speed. Dynamic stretching (e.g., arm or leg swinging) can and should be used as part of the warm-up before beginning the activity.

You should also take roll during the IA. Unfortunately, talking roll occupies a significant amount of the lesson in some physical education classes. You should have a goal of getting students physically active for at least 50 percent of class time. Incorporating an IA and taking roll during the IA is a great way to increase activity time in your class. Developing an efficient protocol for this important activity is essential. A good target is for roll check to take less than one minute of class time.

Keep the instant activities simple. At the beginning of the year, IAs should require little organization because time needs to be spent learning the basic class protocols. Once you have established the class protocols and students have become familiar with class routines, games, and equipment, the IAs can become more complex.

PART 2: LESSON LAUNCHER

This part of the lesson briefly introduces the topic to gain the students' attention and interest. As you become familiar with using the suggested Lesson Launchers, we encourage you to use your imagination and creativity to create your own.

PART 3: LESSON FOCUS

This part of the lesson provides step-by-step instructions for organizing the class and delivering the lesson content. If the lesson has more than one focus, part 3 will cover "Lesson Focus 1," and part 4 will cover "Lesson Focus 2."

PART 4: REFLECTION AND SUMMARY

For classroom lessons, this section provides suggestions for checking for student understanding and summarizing the lesson content. If the lesson has more than one focus, the "Reflection and Summary" section will be part 5.

For activity lessons, a designated cool-down is recommended. At the end of any vigorous activity it is important to have a protocol in which the students walk to gradually slow down before coming to a complete stop for further instructions. Static stretching for flexibility should be done at the end of class or after the body is fully warmed (i.e., sweating, feeling hot). Suggestions are provided for checking student understanding and summarizing the lesson content while students are quietly walking or stretching.

Take It Home

This section provides suggestions for encouraging students to be active with friends and family (the "support team"). Selected lesson plans have worksheets, which are homework assignments designed to reinforce concepts covered in class and encourage students to engage in physical activity with members of their support team.

Next Time

This section identifies the focus of the next lesson, whether it's a classroom lesson or an activity lesson. You can share this with the class at the end of the lesson.

Assessment

This section explains how you or the students will know that they have met the objectives for the lesson. The classroom lessons have been developed so that you have the opportunity to document evidence of student learning in a variety of ways, including discussions, student feedback, short presentations, role-playing, student data collection activities, and completed *Fitness for Life: Middle School* worksheets. Additionally, you should be able to check for student understanding during class by using a variety of techniques including verbal, performance, comprehension, and recognition checks (see the discussion on student comprehension, represented by the question mark icon, in the next section). For more information on assessments, please see "Portfolios and Assessment" on page 31.

Icons for Incorporating Technology and Effective Teaching Practices

Throughout the lesson plans you will encounter icons that identify opportunities for incorporating technology, reviewing class content, checking for student understanding, and observing student behaviors.

Throughout the *Fitness for Life: Middle School* program there are numerous opportunities to incorporate technology into the classroom, gymnasium, and activity areas. Whenever you see this icon in a lesson plan, you will find suggestions for incorporating technology into the classroom.

Whenever you see this icon in a lesson plan, you will find suggestions for reviewing key concepts in the *Fitness for Life: Middle School* program. As you deliver the program, you may find that there are many more situations in which you need to review the class content or class protocols.

Whenever you see this icon in a lesson plan, you will find suggestions for checking students' understanding of the class content, instructions, or demonstrations. You may find many more opportunities during the lessons in which a check for student understanding would be helpful. George Graham (2001) outlined four basic approaches to checking for understanding in his textbook *Teaching Children Physical Education* (Human Kinetics). They are as follows:

> ▶ *Recognition check:* A quick way to check for student understanding is to ask students to raise their hands, give a thumbs-up or thumbs-down, or hold up a response card (e.g., A, B, C, or D) to demonstrate their understanding of the concept, instruction, or demonstration.

> ▶ *Verbal check:* Ask students to tell you the concept or cue you are teaching.

> ▶ *Comprehension check:* Ask students to explain the concept. This demonstrates a deeper understanding than a verbal check.

▶ *Performance check:* Ask students to demonstrate the activity, skill, or principle. This approach is especially effective in physical education because you can see whether they understand the concept through physical demonstrations.

Adapted, by permission, from G. Graham, 2001, *Teaching children physical education,* 2nd ed. (Champaign, IL: Human Kinetics), 83.

 Whenever you see this icon in a lesson plan, it identifies a point in the lesson at which an observation of student behavior may be appropriate. By scanning the class, you can easily determine whether students are on task, working together, performing movements correctly, and following instructions. You will often see this icon when students are asked to work cooperatively in group settings. We believe that it is important for respectful communication (listening and talking) and inclusion of different points of view to be taught, required, and celebrated in physical education classes.

You can use the review, check for understanding, and teacher check strategies for assessing student learning and student participation. You may want to come up with a system on your roll sheet for identifying student understanding and student behavior for assessment purposes.

Supplemental Activities for Integration With *Fitness for Life: Middle School*

On the last page of each group of lesson plans, a section called "Supplemental Materials" provides suggestions for activity-based skill units and resources that could be used to reinforce the content of those lesson plans. One scheduling option is to intersperse regular activity-based skill units between *Fitness for Life: Middle School* lesson plans. Several suggestions on incorporating activity-based skill units are provided in appendix A (page 255). We encourage you to integrate your own favorite lessons or activity-based skill units with the lessons presented in this book. If you choose this option, please make sure that the new lessons or units reinforce the key concepts from each chapter.

Scheduling

This section provides a variety of methods for scheduling *Fitness for Life: Middle School* and suggestions for organizing the program. The information is covered under the following headings:

* Class Meets Daily
* Class Meets Every Other Day
* Class Meets Twice Per Week
* Scheduling a Classroom

As you learned earlier, the student textbook has nine chapters, and this *Teacher's Guide* provides five lesson plans for each chapter. This section describes a basic schedule to help you get started. You can adopt the basic schedule or use it as a foundation for adapting content to fit other scheduling plans. Alternative plans allow you to integrate *Fitness for Life: Middle School* lessons with existing programs. However, we encourage you to integrate activity-based skill units with the *Fitness for Life: Middle School* program to complement your existing program and to reinforce the important chapter concepts. Because the *Fitness*

for Life: Middle School lesson plans include classroom sessions, we provide some tips on scheduling a classroom for physical education.

As you know, it's imperative to introduce and practice class routines at the beginning of the semester. For this reason, many of the scheduling options include organizational lesson ideas (see pages 19 to 29) to use during the first few days of class. If your school calendar allows, run these lessons before you start the *Fitness for Life: Middle School* program.

Class Meets Daily

If your physical education class meets five days a week, you can implement any of the following *Fitness for Life: Middle School* program options.

Basic Plan (9 weeks)

Teach one lesson per day, covering one chapter of the *Fitness for Life: Middle School* student textbook each week. See figure 5.

Week	Student Text content	MONDAY	TUESDAY	WEDNESDAY	THURSDAY	FRIDAY
1	Ch. 1	1.1	1.2	1.3	1.4	1.5
2	Ch. 2	2.1	2.2	2.3	2.4	2.5
3	Ch. 3	3.1	3.2	3.3	3.4	3.5
4	Ch. 4	4.1	4.2	4.3	4.4	4.5
5	Ch. 5	5.1	5.2	5.3	5.4	5.5
6	Ch. 6	6.1	6.2	6.3	6.4	6.5
7	Ch. 7	7.1	7.2	7.3	7.4	7.5
8	Ch. 8	8.1	8.2	8.3	8.4	8.5
9	Ch. 9	9.1	9.2	9.3	9.4	9.5

Classroom lesson days are shaded.

Figure 5   Basic plan.

Basic Plan With Organizational Lessons (10 weeks)

Run the organizational lessons during the week before the program begins. Then teach one lesson per day, covering one chapter of the *Fitness for Life: Middle School* student textbook per week. See figure 6.

Week	Student Text content	MONDAY	TUESDAY	WEDNESDAY	THURSDAY	FRIDAY
Before program	—	—	—	Organizational lesson 1	Organizational lesson 2	Organizational lesson 3
1	Ch. 1	1.1	1.2	1.3	1.4	1.5
2	Ch. 2	2.1	2.2	2.3	2.4	2.5
3	Ch. 3	3.1	3.2	3.3	3.4	3.5
4	Ch. 4	4.1	4.2	4.3	4.4	4.5
5	Ch. 5	5.1	5.2	5.3	5.4	5.5
6	Ch. 6	6.1	6.2	6.3	6.4	6.5
7	Ch. 7	7.1	7.2	7.3	7.4	7.5
8	Ch. 8	8.1	8.2	8.3	8.4	8.5
9	Ch. 9	9.1	9.2	9.3	9.4	9.5

Classroom lesson days are shaded.

Figure 6   Basic plan (organizational lessons before program).

Basic Plan With Organizational Lessons (9 weeks)

If you don't have extra time before the program begins, you can fit the organizational lessons into the first week of the program, replacing lessons 1.4 and 1.5. See figure B.1 in appendix B (page 263).

Integrated Semester Plan (18 weeks)

Run the organizational lessons, and then alternate *Fitness for Life: Middle School* lessons with cooperative challenges or activity-based skill units (see appendix A, page 255). See figure 7.

Week	Student Text content	MONDAY	TUESDAY	WEDNESDAY	THURSDAY	FRIDAY
1	Ch. 1	Organizational lesson 1	Organizational lesson 2	Organizational lesson 3	1.1	1.2
2	Ch. 1	1.3	1.4	1.5	Cooperative challenges	Cooperative challenges
3	Ch. 2	2.1	2.2	2.3	2.4	2.5
4	Ch. 2	Skill unit 2	Skill unit 2	Skill unit 2	Skill unit 2	Skill unit 2
5	Ch. 3	3.1	3.2	3.3	3.4	3.5
6	Ch. 3	Skill unit 3	Skill unit 3	Skill unit 3	Skill unit 3	Skill unit 3
7	Ch. 4	4.1	4.2	4.3	4.4	4.5
8	Ch. 4	Skill unit 4	Skill unit 4	Skill unit 4	Skill unit 4	Skill unit 4
9	Ch. 5	5.1	5.2	5.3	5.4	5.5
10	Ch. 5	Skill unit 5	Skill unit 5	Skill unit 5	Skill unit 5	Skill unit 5
11	Ch. 6	6.1	6.2	6.3	6.4	6.5
12	Ch. 6	Skill unit 6	Skill unit 6	Skill unit 6	Skill unit 6	Skill unit 6
13	Ch. 7	7.1	7.2	7.3	7.4	7.5
14	Ch. 7	Skill unit 7	Skill unit 7	Skill unit 7	Skill unit 7	Skill unit 7
15	Ch. 8	8.1	8.2	8.3	8.4	8.5
16	Ch. 8	Skill unit 8	Skill unit 8	Skill unit 8	Skill unit 8	Skill unit 8
17	Ch. 9	9.1	9.2	9.3	9.4	9.5
18	Ch. 9	Skill unit 9	Skill unit 9	Skill unit 9	Skill unit 9	Skill unit 9

Classroom lesson days are shaded.

Figure 7 Semester plan.

Integrated Semester Plan II (18 weeks)

Some schools with five physical education classes share one classroom by having each class use it on a different day of the week. If your situation is similar, conduct the organizational lessons, and then break up the *Fitness for Life: Middle School* lessons with activity-based skill units so that you teach only one classroom lesson each week. See figure B.2 in appendix B (page 264).

Year Plan I (36 weeks)

Run the organizational lessons, then teach one week of *Fitness for Life: Middle School* lessons followed by three weeks of activity-based skill units. See figure B.3 in appendix B (page 264).

Teacher Tip

Some of you might be thinking, "Hey, this is physical education. Classroom sessions reduce activity time!" Let's face it, fully integrating academic content related to physical activity and fitness in the gymnasium is challenging. In a perfect world, academic content would be fully integrated with the appropriate physical activity experiences. But in the real world, it's much easier to hold discussions in a classroom environment. More importantly, we believe that it's crucial to spend time educating, exploring, and sharing fitness and physical activity concepts, biomechanical principles related to movement, and social diversity issues in physical activity settings.

We believe that the *Fitness for Life: Middle School* program is a key part of meeting national and state standards specific to adolescents (grades 6 to 8). In addition, we believe strongly that middle school students will benefit from a physical education program that reinforces movement experiences with academic content and tackles social issues related to physical activity participation.

Year Plan II (36 weeks)

Run the organizational lessons, then teach one or two lessons each week and run activity-based skill units on the other days of the week. See figures B.2 and B.4 in appendix B (pages 264 and 265).

There are many excellent possibilities for using the *Fitness for Life: Middle School* lessons over a full semester, a year, or even over the course of several years. Layouts for selected possibilities are illustrated in appendix B.

Class Meets Every Other Day

If your physical education class meets every other day, you can implement any of the following *Fitness for Life: Middle School* program options.

Semester Plan (18 weeks)

Follow the Basic Plan, as described earlier, every other day for 18 weeks. See figure B.5 in appendix B (page 265).

Year Plan (36 weeks)

Teach one lesson every other day for two weeks, and then run an activity-based skill unit every other day for two weeks. See figure B.6 in appendix B (page 265).

Class Meets Twice Per Week

If your physical education class meets only twice per week, it might be worthwhile to deliver the *Fitness for Life: Middle School* program over an entire year or over multiple years. For example, see figure B.7 in appendix B (page 266), which delivers unit I (chapters 1, 2, and 3) over eight weeks. Consider the following schedule options.

One-Year Program

▶ Fall of sixth grade (16 weeks): Teach unit I and unit II.
▶ Spring of sixth grade (8 weeks): Teach unit III.

Two-Year Program

▶ Fall of sixth grade (8 weeks): Teach unit I.
▶ Spring of sixth grade (8 weeks): Teach unit II.
▶ Fall of seventh grade (8 weeks): Teach unit III.

Three-Year Program

▶ Fall of sixth grade (8 weeks): Teach unit I.
▶ Fall of seventh grade (8 weeks): Teach unit II.
▶ Fall of eighth grade (8 weeks): Teach unit III.

If you want to follow this three-year articulation plan, be sure to consult with your colleagues first. If they deliver the full program in sixth or seventh grade, you'll end up with students who have already completed the program. Instead, look through all of the preceding schedule options to determine the best way to incorporate one unit of the program per year.

Scheduling a Classroom

For best results, the *Fitness for Life: Middle School* program requires a classroom setting for one or two days each week (depending on how the units are delivered; see the preceding schedule options).

Sharing a Classroom

If you have a classroom at your disposal, you're all set. However, if you must share a room with another class, start your lessons one day later so that the two classes won't need the room at the same time. See figure B.8 in appendix B (page 266).

If you must share a room with two or more other classes, consider following the once-a-week classroom format shown in figure B.2 (page 264) or the staggered classes shown in figure B.8 in appendix B (page 266).

Some of you might be thinking "How will I find a classroom for my physical education classes in my busy school?" Arranging for a classroom can be frustrating on certain days, but take a deep breath and consider the benefits of meeting with children to explore physical activity and fitness in an academic setting. One advantage to using a classroom once or twice a week is that it reduces the need for multiple classes to share valuable gymnasium or movement space. In schools in which there are five physical education classes using *Fitness for Life: Middle School,* one class can be scheduled each day in a classroom, leaving only four to share the other facilities instead of five. Additionally, students don't have to change clothes on classroom days. This saves valuable time and allows for more complete interactions with the lesson content.

So give it a try and tell your principal or school facilities manager about your need for a classroom. They might be thrilled that you're integrating reading and academic content into your class.

No Classroom

If no regular classroom is available for your physical education class, designate a specific area as your makeshift classroom. Don't set up in the gym because the activity going on around you will distract your students from the lesson. Instead, look for a different location, such as the following:

▶ Auditorium

▶ Library

▶ Cafeteria

▶ Academic classroom not in use at that time

▶ Some other space such as a dance room, weight room, locker room, or even a hallway

Whatever space you decide on, set it up to work well for you. Things such as a bulletin board and a white board can easily be added to any space and will help you establish a focal point for your lessons. Include visual aids that set the tone for your class. The *Fitness for Life: Middle School Teacher's Guide* CD-ROM contains relevant quotes for each classroom lesson plan that you can print and hang in your space.

Plan your classroom routines and seating expectations. Having everyone just sitting wherever they want can work with some groups, but it is usually better to use the same seating arrangement that you use in the gymnasium or some sort of group work clustering. It is important to think about student comfort in these makeshift areas. Sitting on the hard floor for the entire class period may make some bottoms sore, and will result in less-than-attentive behavior. In these situations, plan for several changes of position. Check to see whether exercise mats are available. If you can get access to an overhead or LCD projector with a good place to project, creating some visual focus points for the lesson will really help.

We have seen a wide, out-of-the-way hallway used nicely for classroom work. In this instance, a bulletin board was the focal point with visual aids surrounding the board reinforcing the unit concepts and classroom agreements. If you provide a stimulating environment, students will get into the spirit of discussing the course content and applying it to their lives.

Organizational Lessons

We call time spent at the beginning of the semester developing class agreements and protocols "putting money in the bank." A tremendous payoff comes during the rest of the semester when the class is well organized and everyone has agreed to basic expectations about how they're expected to treat one another, where to store their belongings, efficient and effective class routines, and so on. We are convinced that spending time at the beginning of the year getting to know students in the class, helping them get to know one another, and inviting them to care about the class and each other is time well spent. This section covers these topics under the following headings:

* Organizational Lessons
* Teaching Strategies for Organization

In this section we present organizational lesson ideas for the first few days of classes, as well as some important teaching strategies that should be used throughout the *Fitness for Life: Middle School*

program. These lessons and teaching strategies will beef up your "bank account" and pay dividends throughout the year.

Organizational Lessons

Beginning teachers sometimes jump right in on the first day of class setting up seating charts and delivering unit content, only to find that they have to start over the next day because students have been reassigned among classes. Seasoned teachers know how to make better use of the first few days of class. By leading the class in useful activities, you can build a community of learners and organize the group so that even if new students join the class later, the foundation remains effective.

Organizational Lesson 1

In addition to figuring out who is in the class, showing students the locker room, and so on, you can learn something about the students by inviting them to provide information in class. One option is having them fill in basic details on an information sheet (e.g., physical activity preferences, sports, music, unique talents, favorite classes). Another option is playing an icebreaker or mixer game to help the students get to know one another or simply have fun together.

Regardless, you can use this opportunity to set the ground rules for how students should treat one another in class. Students can participate in a discussion in which they develop a set of agreements about how they should act during class. This process can be quite effective, but it's also a challenging task. Your goal is to develop a community of respectful, responsible, fun-loving contributors who work to make it a good class for all involved.

Don Hellison, a physical education professional who works with inner-city at-risk youth, developed a vocabulary for helping people describe and reflect on their level of responsible behavior. His model has evolved into five levels of behavior:

- **Level 1: Respecting the rights and feelings of others.** The student is not interfering but not really working herself.
- **Level 2: Participation and effort.** The student is putting forth some effort.
- **Level 3: Self-direction.** The student is beginning to take responsibility for his own learning, thinking about what he needs, making a real effort, and doing his best.
- **Level 4: Caring about and helping others.** The student is taking responsibility for her own learning and trying to make the class a good experience for others.
- **Level 5: Going beyond.** The student carries level 4 behaviors into the rest of his life—at school, at home, and in the community.

Adapted, by permission, from D. Hellison, 2003, *Teaching responsibility through physical activity,* 2nd ed. (Champaign, IL: Human Kinetics), 17.

Talking to students about these levels of behavior and discussing what each looks like in practice (in other words, giving specific examples from a physical education setting) gives them a vocabulary and a way to think about their own behavior. It's important to be enthusiastic about your students as competent, responsible people and to remind them of the benefits you will all experience as a result of their respectful, responsible, fun-loving, positive attitudes. Make it a goal for each member of the class to move toward Hellison's level 3 or above. Introducing the levels to your students and periodically talking with them about which levels describe their behavior is a powerful method of moving toward more positive behaviors.

One way to initiate this discussion is to talk to students in the first class about standards for creating a great learning community (made up of level 3, level 4, and level 5 behaviors). There are many ways to have this discussion, but following are three possibilities.

DEVELOP A GROUP LIST OF BEHAVIORS

Ask students to think about responsible behavior for two minutes, and then list the behaviors identified by the students on a chalkboard or flip chart. After the group has created a good list, have a student copy it onto a poster board and, to create a good community, encourage students to commit to using these behaviors in class by signing the poster board.

CATEGORIZE BEHAVIORS WITH STICKY NOTES

Ask students to think about responsible behavior for two minutes, and then have students write specific behaviors on sticky notes (one per note). When everyone has identified several behaviors, have groups of six to eight students place their sticky notes on the wall and categorize their entries into groups. After each group has done this, have a few students combine the various categories from the different groups and name each category. This will teach them the sticky note categorizing protocol that you may want to use in future classes. Again, ask if they can commit to trying to use these behaviors.

SIGN CLASS AGREEMENTS

Create a contract or class agreement listing the behaviors that have been identified. Hand out copies to all students and ask them to sign the contracts to show their commitment to using those behaviors. (Alternatively, you can have several students or groups of students work together to write a contract, and ask the larger class to help refine it.)

Organizational Lessons 2 and 3

After reviewing and signing the final drafts of your class agreement, play icebreaker games to help students get to know each other and provide an opportunity for them to practice the behaviors outlined in the contract. Playing the games without attention to the established class behavior expectations is detrimental because inappropriate behaviors might get reinforced. Challenge the students to practice the desired behaviors during play and then reflect on how it went afterward.

In their book *Essentials of Team Building: Principles and Practices* (Human Kinetics), Daniel Midura and Donald Glover offer many great problem-solving games that would work well to practice respectful, responsible behaviors. Included here are brief variations of some of those games. When presenting these activities, it is important to identify them as challenges. Explain that success comes from meeting chosen criteria within specified rules. Clearly stating the success criteria of the activity as well as the rules and sacrifices (consequences of breaking a rule) before groups start to solve the challenge is important.

HUMAN PEGS

Lay out 10 polyspots in a pyramid with 4 across the bottom, then 3, then 2, then 1. See figure 8.

Have nine students stand on one polyspot each, leaving one vacant. If you can't form groups of nine students, use cones in place of missing students; there should be no more than two or three missing students in each game. Students take turns leapfrogging over another person, or just stepping around that person, and landing on an empty polyspot. The student who was jumped over leaves the game, causing

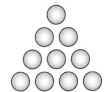

Figure 8 Human pegs cooperative activity setup.

another polyspot to become vacant. Play continues until only one student remains in the pyramid, or until no more jumps are possible.

All nine students are part of the same team, and their goal is to open up as many polyspots as possible. So there's no shame in being eliminated—in fact, it pushes the team closer to victory! Players who have been jumped form a circle around the spots and take turns helping to direct the next moves. The team that opens the most polyspots wins. Of course, the last student on a team can't be eliminated, so the best a team can do is to open all polyspots but one.

Other rules:

▶ Students can jump only in a straight line—no diagonal jumps.

▶ Students move only by jumping—no stepping to an adjacent polyspot.

▶ Teams can try the game more than once to improve their performance.

INDIANA'S CHALLENGE

Arrange the students into groups of six or eight and have each group form a circle. If possible, use tape to create circles on the floor to give each group a clear boundary. Provide one ball per group and one jump rope per pair in the group. Put the ball on top of an 18-inch (46-centimeter) cone in the center of the group. The goal is to find three ways to lift the ball without touching it with a body part and get it outside the circle. One of the three ways must be to lift the ball on the ropes and fling it outside the circle so that one of the group members can catch it.

UNTYING KNOTS

Arrange the students into groups of 8 to 12 and have each group form a circle. Provide one jump rope per student. Team members must connect with two other students by each holding the end of a rope. They cannot connect with the person on either side of them. Right hands must connect with another player's left hand and left hands with a different person's right hand. Groups must then work together to untie the knot without having anyone let go of his or her rope. The solution might cause the students to end up forming interlocking circles or even two separate circles.

JUGGLER'S CARRY

Arrange the students into groups, and give each group a number of large balls that is one fewer that the number of people in the group. Without using their hands, the students in each group must carry the balls across a space such as a volleyball court. If a group drops a ball, they must all return to the start and try again. (Challenge: Halfway across the space, have the students change positions within their group.)

Human Pegs and Indiana's Challenge adapted, by permission, from D. Midura and D. Glover, 2005, *Essentials of team building: Principle and practices* (Champaign, IL: Human Kinetics), 114-115, 118-119; Untying Knots adapted from Midura and Glover 2005 and T. Orlick 1978. Juggler's Carry adapted, by permission, from D. Glover and L. Anderson, 2003, *Character education: 43 fitness activities for community building* (Champaign, IL: Human Kinetics), 114.

Teaching Strategies for Organization

There are several organizational strategies or protocols that can help classes run smoothly and provide more equitable learning activities for everyone. Whether you are arranging students into groups or deciding who to call on, good strategies can make a big difference. This section describes organizational strategies that will be referred to in the lesson plans. Feel free to substitute other successful strategies that you might have developed.

Calling on Students

Research has shown that even very experienced, thoughtful teachers call on certain groups of students (often boys) and certain individuals (eager, focused, talkative, hand-wavers) more than others unless they devise a strategy to keep an even allocation. Try using the following protocols in your class.

EXPECT TO BE CALLED ON

Explain to the students that you want to have a classroom where everyone participates and contributes, but you know that sometimes the same people tend to speak up more often than others. To address this, introduce the protocol known as "Expect to be called on" (developed by Jim DeLine, a teacher in Austin, Texas).

Under this protocol, when you ask a question, give students anywhere from 10 seconds to 1 minute to discuss the answer with their partner or neighbor. At the end of the discussion period, they should be ready to talk about what they discussed. Students don't need to raise their hands; instead, they should simply expect to be called on. Ask three or four students for comments, calling on boys and girls in equal numbers.

This protocol helps to keep everyone on task and is a fairer method of encouraging class participation than calling on hand-wavers.

AND THE WINNER IS . . .

Whatever the seating arrangement, each student is assigned a color (for her row) and a number (for her column). For example, the third student in the first row might be assigned the combination "Red 3." Write the color–number combinations on index cards, poker chips, slips of paper, or some other item that students will find interesting. Put all the items in a box or hat and each time you ask a question, pull one out randomly as you say with a flourish, "And the winner is . . ." Consider keeping a seating chart on your clipboard so you can easily identify the student assigned to the color–number combination that was drawn.

Put the drawn item in another pile, rather than back into the box, so that you will draw different students for future questions. However, reach into the used pile occasionally so that students don't feel that they're done for the day after being called on once.

If you write the color–number combinations on index cards, you can make notes on the cards about each student's response (such as "Super example about muscular endurance—carrying backpack all day"). However, keep in mind that making notes each time distracts from the discussion and can make students feel as though they're constantly being evaluated, which might prevent them from taking risks with their comments. It's better to make your notes on the cards at the end of class or during the next student engagement activity.

Using Sticky Notes

Sticky notes (2-inch × 2-inch, or 5-centimeter × 5-centimeter) are a great way to get audience participation quickly and efficiently. Give each student a small stack of sticky notes to keep in his or her folder, or set a pad out at the start of each class next to a sign that indicates how many sticky notes each student should take for the day. The sticky notes can be used in many ways, but we'll outline two possibilities.

PARTICIPATION AND CLASSIFICATION

One strategy is to use sticky notes to gather and categorize thoughts. For example, ask students to write a physical activity they did yesterday on their sticky notes. Then ask groups to stick their notes to a large outline of the Physical Activity Pyramid on the chalkboard or a wall, placing each note in the proper category (lifestyle activity, active sport, and so on). Once all the sticky notes have been placed, discuss their arrangement and ask for more information about certain activities. You could do the same thing with favorite activities or activities that students are interested in but have not yet tried.

GRAPHING DATA

You can use sticky notes to make bar graphs of data (see figure 9). In some cases, you might want students to put their names on the sticky notes, too. For example, you might ask students to write their favorite physical activity on the sticky note. On the board, write a baseline with the categories you are discussing, such as categories from the Physical Activity Pyramid, types of active aerobics, competitive activities, or noncompetitive activities.

The students then stack their sticky notes to create a bar graph. You can then use the graph as a stimulus for class discussions, as well as a tool to learn about the interests of the class. In some cases you can even save the sticky notes as a form of data collection.

Dancing   In-line skating   Tae Bo

Figure 9 Bar chart created with sticky notes.

Start and Stop Signals

Whatever you decide to use for a start or a stop signal (such as music, a whistle, a bell, or even a crazy noisemaker), make sure it's not harsh or annoying. In addition, it's good practice to use a visual signal, such as raising your hand up, along with an audio signal to aid those who are farther away or have English as a second language.

It's also great to have a position that you want them to stop in so that you feel you have their attention, but the position has to be comfortable and not awkward or embarrassing.

"Take a knee" works well for getting students still and attentive sometimes (but certainly not in grass with sticker burrs), but don't use it too many times in any one class period. "Take a knee" is a good one to use as a safety protocol when someone is hurt because it stops students from moving around.

You can create some fun positions for students to be in for attending to you, and you can even allow for student choice or input, but don't use them when they are not needed. Stop positions work best in many cases. For example, sometimes kids are expected to always face the teacher in the ready position with hands on knees when they hear the whistle. Try doing this yourself. It's not comfortable for very long, so it should only be used as a temporary position. If used repeatedly in a lesson it gets old, so use it sparingly. So maybe when the whistle blows (outside) or when the music stops (inside), students need only stop and face you. When there is a safety concern, you can have a different protocol (e.g., three whistle blasts means that everyone immediately "takes a knee"). You may want to practice the safety concern signal a couple of times at the beginning of the year, but after that save it for the few situations when you need immediate attention from the students.

Explaining the reasons behind the class protocols goes a long way toward getting students to comply with the expected behavior. It also provides you with a good starting point for counseling a student who has not been following the behavior expectations in class.

Finally, it is important to practice the start and stop signal early in the year. Students need to practice the protocols just as much as you do. Practice using your signals during the instant activity portion of your lessons for the first few weeks of class. Don't move forward with the lesson focus until the students are responding to your signals. This practice also puts "money in the bank."

Formations

Another protocol that needs to be established at the beginning of the year is getting into different formations. Having students practice getting into different formations can be done during the organizational lessons, and really helps make future classes more efficient and effective. Give each formation a name, or better yet, establish different hand signals for formations so that you don't even have to say anything. Some examples of formations and instructions for getting into the formations are provided in the following sections. The *Fitness for Life: Middle School* lesson plans refer to many of these examples.

LISTENING POSITIONS

Having different signals for attention (one whistle or clap means stop, face the teacher, and listen) and for longer instruction (two whistles or claps mean come over closer for instruction or huddle) also helps. Some teachers use hand signals to indicate what level of attention is needed. When the whistle blows or music stops, students are to stop and turn to face the teacher. If the teacher is standing still, they can just stand still and listen. If the teacher's hand is placed on his or her head, the students know to come in closer into a huddle around the teacher. If the teacher's hands are folded across the chest, they are to come close and sit down. Practicing the protocols as an integral part of the activities of the first few days really helps classes run smoothly.

One teacher we know (Judy Howard) has a signal for a comfortable position. It may be lying down or lounging comfortably. She calls it "Hawaii." So if she blows the whistle and puts her hand on her head, they know to come in closer. When they get close, she says, "Hawaii," and they know they can lounge on the ground around her. Having fun protocols helps make the students more willing to do all the protocols.

SHRINKING SQUADS

Squad lines have been used since physical education began and have several useful characteristics. Sophisticated use of rows and columns provides many simple grouping strategies, which are discussed later. However, being spread out across the gym in squad lines, although useful to give each student space to perform some activities, is not a good format for "talk time" (i.e., when you are giving anything but the briefest of directions to students). Those at the back are too far away, and if you ever try sitting there yourself when someone is talking, you quickly realize how hard it is to pay attention.

Thus, the "shrinking squads" protocol is worth teaching for those times when you want to give instructions, and also want to take advantage of the row and column grouping strategies available with squads. Basically, you just shrink the squad lines down to a small area, maintaining the same formation and having the students sitting nearer to each other rather than spread out in the gym. You may need to talk with the students about not bothering each other when they sit close. If you are having a short discussion or your instructions are going to take a few minutes, it actually helps if you sit on a folding chair when talking rather than standing over them (unless you need to perform a demonstration). This provides a more personal environment for communicating with students. This is not to be mistaken for encouragement to sit on the side when the students are active!

CIRCLES

Although it takes a while to establish the protocol, sitting in a circle during discussions really changes the dynamics from each person talking to the teacher to it being a class discussion. When establishing circle protocols, an important standard to set is that it is everyone's job to ensure that the circle works for everyone. That is, when you ask the class to sit in a circle, everyone must be part of the circle; each student must be a member of the class community. So when students sit down, it is their responsibility to make sure everyone will fit into the circle. If someone sits down behind them they should scoot back a little so there is room for that person to join the circle. Again, using this protocol at the beginning of the year and being consistent about not allowing double rows is important for building this useful community protocol.

Of course, if the class is too large, the circle becomes too large for people to hear each other during discussions. In cases when the class is too large, use the shrinking squads formation or a double circle with the inside sitting and the outside standing. Kids sitting randomly behind each other or spread out across the gym ensures that a discussion will not be worth having.

Groups and Teams

One of the challenges in physical education is dividing students into groups or teams for various activities. Many teachers like to allow students to create their own groups, and many students like this format as well. Although occasionally this is a great thing to do, if you watch closely, almost always there are kids who are left out of the process or denied group membership by one group or another. Teachers often respond by placing students with a partner or group, but the damage is already done in terms of that student's comfort in the class.

One of the goals for the teacher should be to develop a class community in which every child feels supported and part of the class. To accomplish this, it is imperative to talk to the students about this goal and work on getting their buy-in to it being part of building a strong community. Have several ways to mix up the groups so students don't feel they will always be with one group. When you decide on groups, it takes the responsibility off the students and allows them to get to know other students in the class. This should build students' comfort levels for working with different partners and groups. Once the class has really become a community (i.e., where all members are accepted), having students determine groupings becomes much less of a popularity issue and more of a community endeavor. Teachers who talk to their students about the class as a community and have simple strategies for getting students into groups end up having a class in which everyone is included and supported.

Almost everyone uses some sort of a squad formation for seating in the gym. It helps spread kids out during exercises and allows you to see quickly where there are missing students. If the squad formation is more fully developed by using a column (color) and row (number) designation, it can be very efficient in grouping students for activity. Having the students wear colored jerseys, wristbands, or bandannas corresponding to their color makes it easy to see at a glance that everyone is in the right place.

In a squad system in which students wear the color of their squad (e.g., jersey, wristband, bandanna) and know their row number within the squad, you can group them in different ways. For example, in a class of 24 students, you might have four colors (i.e., squads) and six numbers (i.e., 1, 2, 3, 4, 5, and 6). A class of 36 might have six colors and six numbers, and larger classes might have enough students for six colors and eight numbers. To form groups for station work or practice drills, alternate using colors and numbers so that the same kids are not always in a group together. Using the class of 24 as an example, consider the following:

▶ To form groups of four, have students group by numbers (e.g., all 1s together, etc.).

▶ To form groups of six, use the colors (i.e., squads).

▶ To form groups of three, use three numbers in each color (1, 2, and 3 together; 4, 5, and 6 together in each color).

▶ To form groups of two (partners), pair the same number in two colors.

▶ To divide the class in half, use two colors in each half. (Note: this gives you three possible arrangements: red/yellow and blue/green; red/blue and yellow/green; red/green and blue/yellow). You could also have the 1s, 2s, and 3s in one group and 4s, 5s, and 6s in the other, or odd numbers in one group and even numbers in the other.

The key is to divide the class in different ways and at different times so that everyone works with a variety of partners. If you know students' abilities beforehand (i.e., you had them in sixth or seventh grade), you can even strategically place them in their position in the columns and rows so that sometimes the groups are heterogeneous in terms of skill (maybe columns) and other times homogeneous in terms of skill (rows). You must remember to use this wisely so that it does not become a stigma within the groups.

Safety

One of the most challenging organizational jobs of the teacher is to ensure that students are properly supervised both in the locker room and in the gymnasium. It is not OK for the teacher to be in the locker room while students are gathering in the gym, nor is it OK for the teacher to be in the gym while students are getting dressed in the

Teacher Tip: Ask the Students

We have found that it helps to think about what a physical education class might feel like from the student's point of view (whistles constantly blowing, anxiety about performing well, anxiety about working with new partners, and being expected to pay attention when you're in the back row sitting on a dirty, dusty floor). It is not always possible to change these situations, but it helps to acknowledge certain situations and ask for suggestions for improvement (for example, students can volunteer to sweep the floor before class so it's cleaner for sitting). It's important to establish simple routines early such as what you do when you get to class, where to put your backpack, how to handle the need for the restroom, who will help with equipment, and so on. Whenever possible, getting student input helps. Identifying the goal of each activity or protocol and approaching it as a problem to be solved with students provides valuable perspective.

Throughout the *Fitness for Life: Middle School* lesson plans, we have included activities that achieve specific goals and are fun for the students. But they won't find all of our ideas fun. One of the ways to increase student buy-in is to teach one way of doing something (a warm-up activity, for instance) and then after a couple of days, say, "We need to do a warm-up before exercising vigorously. I've taught you three different warm-ups. How should we proceed? Should we just alternate among the three? Would you like to identify favorites and do those more often, or would you like to suggest another way to warm up we should try? I'm interested in your input. Please put your ideas in the suggestion box."

Having students write their responses and turn them in gives you a chance to see how everyone is feeling, not just the ones who are comfortable expressing their opinions out loud. Whenever possible, work to become the "guide on the side" who helps guide the students toward a healthy lifestyle. This appears to be a more powerful strategy than being the "sage on the stage" who merely lectures them about what they should do.

locker room. Teachers should work out a system that ensures safety for students in the transition from changing their clothes to arriving in the gymnasium. Following are a few suggestions:

1. Work out a plan with the other physical education teachers so each person is responsible for one area during the changing time. If you have one large gymnasium in which classes meet, this would require three teachers (i.e., one in each locker room and one in the gymnasium).

2. Work with the principal to schedule class aides, hall monitors, or other personnel to be assigned to help monitor at one of the sites for a few minutes at each change time. You may need to remind the administrator that this is a safety need. It's important to train any assigned monitors so they know the class rules and standards for behavior as well as appropriate ways of intervening when there are problems. Establishing protocols for instant activities really helps this transition time. This might be a great opportunity to build support for your program, because other staff get an opportunity to see the great things that are happening in physical education.

3. The least attractive option is to establish a protocol in which everyone leaves the locker room together. This may be your only option if you cannot procure the staff needed to supervise each post. This will require coming up with something interesting for some students to do while you wait for others. Providing some

motivation for everyone to get changed quickly would also be helpful. Ask the students for suggestions for motivational ideas.

Taking Roll

Unfortunately, taking roll in some physical education classes eats up a significant amount of lesson time. Because one goal of physical education is to provide high percentages of activity time to the students, physical educators need efficient methods of taking roll as students enter the activity area. Taking roll during the instant activity is a good idea. Regardless of your strategy, an efficient protocol that takes less than a minute of class time is recommended.

Dressing Out

For many middle school girls, changing into and out of physical education clothing presents problems. This is a more of an issue for girls than boys because of the enormous societal pressures on girls to look a certain way. In fact, no one tries to get presentable in less than 10 minutes. Would you go to a fitness club that gave you 5 minutes to change following your workout? Consider a problem-solving session with the girls in your class to establish a good situation for everyone. It may be a good idea to trade dress out time at the beginning of the class for time at the end (5 minutes to dress for class, 10 minutes to get dressed after class).

Portfolios and Assessment

Assessing student learning and participation is an important part of any physical education program. To effectively meet your assessment goals, a variety of assessment techniques are typically used, including student portfolios, student participation, and quizzes and tests. Information concerning these techniques is described under the following headings:

* **Student Portfolios**
* **Student Participation**
* **Quizzes and Tests**

The sections that follow describe each of these types of available assessments. In addition, assessment rubrics are included for portfolios and student participation. Teachers are encouraged to use all methods of assessment when determining student grades.

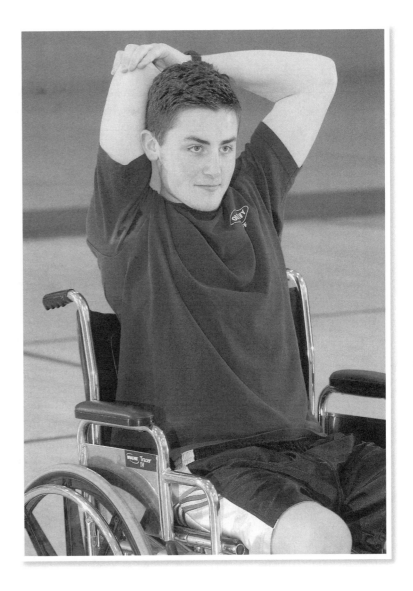

Student Portfolios

Physical education is a subject that lends itself well to authentic assessment. Authentic assessment aims to evaluate students' abilities in real-world contexts. In other words, students learn how to apply their skills to authentic tasks and projects. Authentic assessment does not encourage rote learning and passive test taking. Instead, it focuses on students' analytical skills, ability to integrate what they learn, creativity, ability to work collaboratively, and written and oral expression skills. It values the learning process as much as the finished product. Authentic assessment in the *Fitness for Life: Middle School* program includes the following:

- ▶ Self-assessment of physical fitness
- ▶ Setting goals for physical activity and keeping an activity log
- ▶ Applying biomechanical principles to improve skills and performance
- ▶ Engaging family members in physical activity outside of the classroom
- ▶ Writing reflections about physical activity experiences
- ▶ Creating modified games that promote full inclusion

Throughout the *Fitness for Life: Middle School* lesson plans we have incorporated individual, pair, and group learning experiences that allow for authentic assessment of student learning. The teaching strategies presented in this introduction are effective observational methods for authentic assessment of student learning and active participation (i.e., capturing the learning process). However, we also understand teachers' need to document student learning with methods other than observations of students. In response to this need, we have developed a series of worksheets that can be combined into the *Fitness for Life: Middle School* student portfolio. The worksheets provide students with an opportunity to apply their knowledge within and outside of physical education.

All worksheets are found on the CD-ROM. Each worksheet has a title and a corner code that identifies the lesson plan in which the worksheet is used, and the relative order of the worksheet in the plan. For example, the code "W4.1a" indicates the first worksheet in lesson plan 4.1, while the code "W4.1b" indicates the second worksheet used in that lesson plan.

You can print all the worksheets in advance and create portfolios for students to complete during the semester, or you can print the worksheets as they are used and have students add them to portfolios that grow as they progress through the program. Regardless of how the student portfolios are created, the worksheets provide an excellent opportunity for student assessment.

Worksheets are provided in class or in the "Take It Home" section of the lesson plans. For a breakdown of all worksheets, along with recommendations for when to distribute and collect each worksheet, see figure 10. Of course, you are free to decide on a system that works best for your classes.

We have provided a basic rubric for you to use to grade the *Fitness for Life: Middle School* student portfolio worksheets (figure 11). It is important that you share the grading criteria with students at the beginning of the year and each time you modify a rubric for an assignment or activity. The assessment rubric is also available on the CD-ROM and is customizable. Feel free to adapt it to reflect your own expectations for student work.

We also recommend the following Web sites to help you develop rubrics for the assessment of participation, oral presentations, and any other activities you may choose to evaluate. These sites provide a free and user-friendly service for creating and modifying rubrics.

▶ **teAchnology**: www.teach-nology.com/web_tools/rubrics/
▶ **University of Wisconsin at Stout:** www.uwstout.edu/soe/profdev/rubrics.shtml

Recommended distribution	Title	Recommended completion
1.1	Physical Activity Pyramid	1.5
1.4	Direction of Force	1.5
2.1	Your Support Team	2.5
2.3	Everyday Levers	2.5
2.5	Footbagging With the Family	3.1
3.1	Activitygram	In class
3.1	Making Changes	5.1 (check progress at 4.1)
3.3	Friction in Physical Activity	3.5
4.1	Tuning In	4.3
4.2	Perception of Exertion	In class
4.3	Stability	In class
4.4	PACER Test	In class
5.1	Community Clubs	6.1
5.3	Active Interviews	In class
6.1	Teamwork	6.5
6.4	Back-Saver Sit-and-Reach Test	In class
7.1	Respect and Protect Oath	In class (or 7.2)
7.1	Strength of Character	7.3
7.4	Muscular Endurance Self-Assessments	In class
8.1	Body Mass Index (BMI)	In class
8.1	Give Me a Commercial Break	8.3
8.2	Counting Calories	8.4
8.4	Pedometer Predictions	In class
9.1	Fitness and Physical Activity Summary	In class
9.1	Support Team Physical Activity Summary	9.3
9.3	Personal Physical Activity Plan	In class
9.3	Support Team Physical Activity Plan	9.5
9.4	Logging Physical Activity	Teacher's decision

Figure 10 List of worksheets in *Fitness for Life: Middle School.*

Worksheet Rubric

Student: _____ Teacher: _____

Date submitted: _____ Title of work: _____

	CRITERIA				
Categories	**4**	**3**	**2**	**1**	**Points**
Assignment completeness	All items attempted.	Most items attempted.	At least half of the items attempted.	Less than half of the items attempted.	
Accuracy	All items are correct.	Most items are correct.	At least half of items are correct.	Less than half of all items are correct.	
Demonstrated knowledge	Shows complete understanding of the questions, fitness concepts, and processes.	Shows substantial understanding of the questions, fitness concepts, and processes.	Shows some understanding of the questions, fitness concepts, and processes.	Shows no understanding of the questions, fitness concepts, and processes.	
Requirements	Goes beyond the requirements.	Meets the requirements.	Meets some of the requirements.	Does not meet the requirements.	
Legibility	Writing is fully legible. No spelling errors.	Writing is marginally legible. No spelling errors.	Writing is not legible in some places. Some spelling errors.	Writing is not legible.	
				TOTAL POINTS →	

TEACHER COMMENTS:

_____

_____

_____

_____

_____

_____

_____

_____

_____

_____

_____

Figure 11 Worksheet rubric.
From G. Le Masurier, D. Lambdin, and C. Corbin, 2007, *Fitness for life: Middle school teacher's guide* (Champaign, IL: Human Kinetics).

Student Participation

If students actively participate in the lessons, they will meet the experiential and interactive goals of the lesson. For this reason, assessment of student participation is encouraged. When assessing student participation, use of the Physical Education Participation Rubric (see figure 12) is encouraged. Assessment of student participation is valuable for both grading and providing feedback to the teacher (you) on areas that need additional focus.

Quizzes and Tests

A variety of quizzes are available for assessing student learning of material contained in the text and reinforced in the classroom and activity sessions. Questions for quizzes and tests were reviewed for content and reading level by three different experts. In addition samples of quizzes were reviewed by a middle school teacher for grade level content and appropriateness. You will find answer keys to these quizzes on the CD-ROM, as well as answer keys for the Chapter Reviews in the student textbook and for the Unit Reviews on the *Fitness for Life: Middle School* Web site.

Chapter Quizzes

A 20-item multiple-choice quiz is available for each of the nine chapters of the student text. These quizzes are available on the CD-ROM and are easily printed for copying for use in the classroom. An answer key is also provided. Quizzes can be used as part of the formal assessment process for each chapter, as a method of reinforcing and reviewing chapter content, or for preparing students for unit quizzes or a comprehensive test.

Unit Quizzes

A 35-item multiple-choice quiz is available for each of the three units of the student text. These quizzes are available on the CD-ROM and are easily printed for copying for use in the classroom. An answer key is also provided. Quizzes can be used as part of the formal assessment process for each unit, as a method of reinforcing and reviewing unit content, or for preparing students for a comprehensive test.

Comprehensive Quiz

A 75-item multiple-choice comprehensive test is available. The test is available on the CD-ROM and is easily printed for copying for use in the classroom. An answer key is also provided.

Custom Quizzes

The *Fitness for Life: Middle School* Web site allows access to a test bank that includes several hundred multiple-choice questions. The test bank includes all of the questions from the chapter quizzes, unit quizzes, and the comprehensive test described above. In addition the multiple-choice questions from the unit reviews (online) are included.

You can prepare custom quizzes or tests for lessons, chapters, groups of chapters, units, or for comprehensive tests. Questions are labeled by chapter and lesson so that you can select as many, or as few, questions as you choose. If, for example, you want 10-item or 30-item chapter quizzes rather than the existing 20-item quizzes you may construct them yourself using the test bank. You need only select the questions

Physical Education Participation Rubric

Student: _____ Teacher: _____

Categories	CRITERIA				Points
	4	3	2	1	
Attendance and promptness	Student is always prompt and regularly attends classes.	Student is late to class once every two weeks and regularly attends classes.	Student is late to class more than once every two weeks and regularly attends classes.	Student is late to class more than once a week and/or does not regularly attend classes.	
Level of engagement in class	Student proactively contributes to class by offering ideas and asking questions more than once per class.	Student proactively contributes to class by offering ideas and asking questions once per class.	Student rarely contributes to class by offering ideas and asking questions.	Student never contributes to class by offering ideas and asking questions.	
Listening skills	Student listens when others talk, both in groups and in class. Student incorporates or builds off the ideas of others.	Student listens when others talk, both in groups and in class.	Student does not listen when others talk, both in groups and in class.	Student does not listen when others talk, both in groups and in class. Student often interrupts when others speak.	
Behavior	Student never displays disruptive behavior during class.	Student rarely displays disruptive behavior during class.	Student occasionally displays disruptive behavior during class.	Student always displays disruptive behavior during class.	
Preparation	Student is always prepared for class with assignments and required materials.	Student is usually prepared for class with assignments and required materials.	Student is rarely prepared for class with assignments and required materials.	Student is never prepared for class with assignments and required materials.	
				TOTAL POINTS →	

TEACHER COMMENTS:

_____

_____

_____

Figure 12 Participation rubric.

From G. Le Masurier, D. Lambdin, and C. Corbin, 2007, *Fitness for life: Middle school teacher's guide* (Champaign, IL: Human Kinetics).

you want from the test bank. You can also prepare lesson questions if you choose. An answer key is provided.

Quiz Overlap

The premade chapter quizzes, unit quizzes, and comprehensive test described in this section contain some overlap. For example, about 25 percent of the questions from the chapter quizzes are also included in the unit quizzes. This was done intentionally. Students can be informed that their performance on chapter quizzes will help them on unit quizzes or comprehensive exams. Likewise some of the questions in chapter or unit quizzes are contained in the comprehensive test. However, no questions appear in all three assessments—chapter, unit and comprehensive. Premade quizzes and tests do not contain questions from the unit reviews (online).

High-Tech Options

The lesson plans in this *Teacher's Guide* were developed so that virtually all schools could perform the lessons with their existing equipment. For schools that already have or can obtain high-tech equipment, learning can be enhanced by its use. Information concerning various high-tech options is described under the following headings:

* Student and Teacher Web Site for Accessing Additional Information
* Computer Programs for Review and Reinforcement
* Pedometers
* Video Clips

To make effective use of the Web sites for student and teacher use, a computer with an Internet connection is necessary. To use the computer programs for review and reinforcement, you will need a computer, computer projector, and an Internet connection. Other types of high-tech equipment that would be of value to enhancing learning include pedometers, heart rate monitors, a VCR or DVD player, and a television.

Student and Teacher Web Site for Accessing Additional Information

In the student textbook, each lesson contains a series of Web pointers that direct students to numbered topics on the *Fitness for Life: Middle School* Web site (www.fitnessforlife.org/middleschool). The Web topics provide further information on key concepts from the lessons. Students who have access to a computer can visit the site, click on the "Student Information" button, and click on the topic that relates to their reading.

For example, in lesson 2.2 in the student book, the section called "What Is Skill-Related Fitness?" discusses agility, balance, reaction time, and other components of skill-related fitness. The section includes a Web pointer that says "Click Student Info ▶ Topic 2.2." If students visit the Web site and click on Web topic 2.2, they will access a page that explores the concept of reaction time in more detail and provides links to simple reaction time games.

In addition, students who have other questions about the lessons can click on the "Ask the Authors" button to access a page of further questions and answers. The page addresses the "Ask the Authors" questions posed in the Chapter Review sections of the student book. It also provides a link through which students can submit their own questions to the authors via e-mail. The "Ask the Authors" page will be updated periodically with responses to selected questions.

The Web site also contains material for teachers. Simply visit the site and click on the "Teacher Information" button to access a page of updated resources and guidelines related to the *Fitness for Life: Middle School* program. The page includes links to a test bank of quiz questions (see "Quizzes and Tests," page 35) and to computer programs that you can use for review and reinforcement of key concepts.

Computer Programs for Review and Reinforcement

Mount Fitness and Tour de Fitness are computer programs designed to help students review content and to reinforce learning of concepts in the *Fitness for Life: Middle School* text and in classroom and physical activities. Both programs are available on the Teacher Information page at www.fitnessforlife.org/middleschool.

Mount Fitness allows students to answer multiple-choice questions from each chapter, each unit, or combinations of chapters and units determined by the instructor (students can use the Mount Fitness answer cards on the CD-ROM). Mount Fitness also allows teachers to introduce physical activity into the classroom.

The Mount Fitness software is designed to

▶ review and reinforce key concepts presented in each chapter by answering multiple choice questions,

▶ apply information by performing physical activities related to key concepts presented in each chapter, and

▶ involve all students in classroom physical activity and working with others to review, reinforce, and apply concepts learned in each chapter.

Tour de Fitness is an educational program that allows students to select letters to spell key phrases from the *Fitness for Life: Middle School* student textbook. Students click to spin a bicycle wheel and try to complete phrases that relate to fitness and physical activity. Key terms are reviewed and reinforced with definitions when the word puzzle is solved. In addition, you can choose to have students apply their knowledge by performing exercises related to the chapter from which key terms are selected. Students also learn strategy and tactics of game play. Tour de Fitness is designed for use either in the classroom or in the gym, after the students have studied the chapter materials.

Tour de Fitness is designed to

▶ review and reinforce key concepts presented in each chapter by solving word puzzles and getting feedback after the puzzle is solved,

▶ apply information by performing physical activities related to key terms presented in each chapter,

▶ involve all students in classroom or gym session that involves integrating physical activity with conceptual information (review, reinforce and apply concepts) learned in each chapter, and

▶ teach game strategy and tactics.

For more information on Mount Fitness and Tour de Fitness, see appendix C (page 267).

Pedometers

Pedometers are simple step-counting devices that are used in many schools and are a great example of technology that can motivate students and assess student performance. Setting step goals for class is a great way to motivate activity. Students enjoy the immediate feedback they get from the pedometers (e.g., seeing how many steps they can generate during activities, seeing if they can accurately predict the number of steps in activities). Once students become familiar with the pedometers and pedometer protocols, they can be incorporated into almost any activity. We have included the use of pedometers as a high-tech option in many of the activity lessons.

Establishing protocols for using the pedometers is critical. Before you use pedometers, number each with a permanent marker or engraving tool. Create an assignment sheet, hand the numbered pedometers out to students, and assign each student a specific number. That way at the end of class you can see at a glance whose pedometer has not been turned in if one is missing. During the first lesson, talk to the students about

▶ clipping the pedometer on the waist band so it is upright and in line over their right knee,

▶ attaching the safety strap to the waistband as well so if the pedometer gets knocked off it will not fall,

▶ resetting the pedometer to zero before starting to use it, and

▶ the "you shake it, I'll take it" rule. Shaking the pedometer can damage the working parts leading to inaccurate pedometers.

Have them put on the pedometers, reset to zero, and practice taking 100 steps and checking the pedometer to see how accurate it is. It should register between 90 and 110 steps. If it doesn't, adjust where it is placed on the waist band (either closer to the belly button or farther toward the hip) and try again. Have students find the hip location where they get the most accurate readings.

After becoming familiar with the pedometer protocols, students should be able to get them on quickly at the beginning of any activity lesson. Comparisons of activity levels can be made between lessons or among different activities. A step goal can be set for activity lessons, and if the goal is not met, discussions can center on how the activity could be changed to promote more activity next time.

Video Clips

More and more students are becoming capable of creating their own edited digital videos. They are certainly able to access video via the Web. We have provided ideas for video clips that you could ask students to create (or you could create yourself) or locate that could be used to launch a lesson (i.e., grab students' attention). These videos are not required for the lesson but would add an interesting touch and may help engage students with the content.

Introduction to Physical Activity and Fitness

Chapter 1 lesson plans provide a variety of individual and group activities for students to explore the concepts of physical activity, physical fitness, and the need for energy and force in human movement. The classroom and activity lessons emphasize effective communication skills for the purpose of building a respectful community of learners.

* 1.1 Introduction to Physical Activity (classroom lesson)
* 1.2 Exploring Physical Activity (activity lesson)
* 1.3 Introduction to Physical Fitness (classroom lesson)
* 1.4 Biomechanics, Energy, and Force (activity lesson)
* 1.5 Physical Activity Choices (activity lesson)

Introduction to Physical Activity

In this classroom lesson, students will become familiar with the Physical Activity Pyramid and have an opportunity to practice effective communication techniques (using the "Moving Together" and "Take It Home" features from the *Fitness for Life: Middle School* student textbook). They'll review the range of physical activities in which they currently participate, and they'll identify new physical activities that they can try.

Performance Outcomes Related to NASPE Standards

▶ Standard 3
  ▶ Have an increasing awareness of the opportunities for participation in a broad range of activities that may meet their needs and interests.
▶ Standard 5
  ▶ Have well-developed cooperative skills and are able to accomplish group or team goals in cooperative activities.
▶ Standard 6
  ▶ Recognize the role of physical activity in getting to know and understand others.
  ▶ Recognize physical activity as a positive opportunity for social and group interaction.
  ▶ Identify potential social and health benefits from participation in physical activity.

Lesson Objectives

▶ Students will describe why they need physical activity.
▶ Students will appropriately identify activities within the Physical Activity Pyramid.
▶ Students will identify and demonstrate effective communication techniques.

Equipment

▶ 1 *Fitness for Life: Middle School* student textbook per student
▶ 3 sticky notes per student (3- × 3-inch [8- × 8-centimeter])
▶ 1 pencil or marker per pair of students
▶ Chalkboard or flip chart (optional)

Reproducibles

- ▶ Resource 1.1, "Physical Activity Pyramid Headings"
- ▶ Worksheet 1.1, "Physical Activity Pyramid"
- ▶ Classroom Quotes

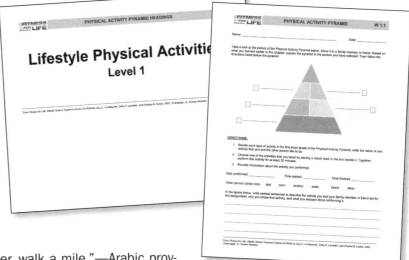

Classroom Quotes

You can print these quotes from the CD-ROM and hang them around your room.

- ▶ "After dinner, rest a while; after supper, walk a mile."—Arabic proverb
- ▶ "It is remarkable how one's wits are sharpened by physical exercise."—Pliny the Younger (ancient Roman philosopher)
- ▶ "Walking is the best possible exercise."—Thomas Jefferson (U.S. president)
- ▶ "A bear, however hard he tries, grows tubby without exercise."—A.A. Milne (author of *Winnie the Pooh*)

Setup

1. Print resource 1.1, the six "Physical Activity Pyramid Headings," from the CD-ROM. Hang them on the wall, chalkboard, or flip chart in the shape of a large pyramid.

2. Print worksheet 1.1, "Physical Activity Pyramid," from the CD-ROM. Make one copy for each student.

 tech

> Find, or have your students find, video clips of several types of physical activities (such as lifestyle, active aerobics, active sports, active recreation, flexibility, muscular strength, muscular endurance, and rest). Play the clips to launch your lesson.

Delivering the Lesson

The basic plan for delivering the *Fitness for Life: Middle School* program includes five lesson plans to cover the content for each chapter. This lesson begins the five-lesson sequence that corresponds to chapter 1 in the student textbook.

 review

> Pages 20 to 29 provide organizational lesson ideas that focus on management issues such as assigning lockers, developing agreements and expectations with the class, learning class protocols, and helping students to get to know each other. Proper coverage of these elements is essential for a successful class experience. Make sure you review them here.

Part 1: Gathering Information

1. Have students open their student textbooks. Talk about the text and help students become familiar with its format:

   ▸ Text
   - Three units, with three chapters in each unit
   - Each chapter includes two classroom-specific lessons that will be interspersed with activity lessons as follows: a classroom lesson, an activity lesson, a classroom lesson, an activity lesson, and a culminating activity lesson. (This is the basic schedule. For other ways to adapt *Fitness for Life: Middle School* to your school or course schedule, refer to "Scheduling" on page 13.)
   - Optional: Between chapters, present related activity units. See page 67 for sample activity units to use at the end of chapter 1. See the introduction for different options for working these activity units into your schedule.

   ▸ Lesson features
   - Fitness concepts
   - Lesson vocabulary and objectives
   - "Moving Together" feature that addresses important social aspects of playing together
   - "Biomechanical Principles" feature that addresses basic principles of human movement with opportunities for application and practice
   - "Take It Home" feature in which students explore a variety of physical activity concepts at home with family and friends; students typically complete related worksheets
   - Interesting Fit Facts about fitness and health
   - Links to extended discussions and resources on the *Fitness for Life: Middle School* Web site
   - Lesson review

   ▸ Classroom format
   - Read one lesson in the student textbook (half a chapter) at a time. Optional: Have students read at home or in class.
   - Do projects.
   - Share thoughts and results.
   - Talk about the reading.

2. Introduce the material.

   ▸ Ask students how many sides a pyramid has. Where is the biggest part?

   ▸ Ask students how much time they spend doing general daily activities during a typical 24-hour period.

   ▸ Explain that today they will read about physical activity and discuss different types of activities.

3. Have the students read "Introduction to Physical Activity," lesson 1.1 in the student textbook (chapter 1, pages 3 to 8).

Part 2: Lesson Launcher

1. Review the lesson objectives with students.

2. Have students read the opening section of "Moving Together: Communication" (chapter 1, page 7).

3. Tell the students to look over the discussion questions briefly, and then to read the "Guidelines for Effective Communication." Students should use the guidelines to come up with answers to the discussion questions.

4. Pose the discussion questions to the class.

5. Encourage students to use the guidelines when interacting with their partners in today's lesson.

Part 3: Lesson Focus

 review

Review class protocols about how to treat partners (what's OK, what's not OK, the importance of words, and the importance of body language), as well as how we can support each other. Explain that students will have many different partners or groups. Sometimes they'll choose someone nearby; sometimes other strategies will be used. Accepting each partner with a smile will make the class work well for everyone.

Physical Activity Pyramid

1. Reinforce the guidelines for appropriate partnering, such as having a positive attitude, welcoming your partner, and introducing yourself.

2. Set students up in pairs.

   ▹ If they're seated in rows, have two rows slide their desks together.

   ▹ If they're in a moving space, use one of the methods in "Groups and Teams" (pages 26 to 27) to set up partnerships.

 observe

Scan the room for positive verbal and nonverbal communication among students. Are partners getting together appropriately with positive body language and comments? If not, address this issue directly and immediately with students. Are pairs working productively (such as listening to each other)?

3. Give six sticky notes and a pencil or marker to each pair of students.

4. Direct students' attention to the Physical Activity Pyramid headings on the wall, chalkboard, or flip chart. For each pyramid section, have each set of partners identify an activity from that section and write the activity's name on one of their sticky notes.

5. Have each set of partners place their six sticky notes in the appropriate sections of the pyramid shape that you created.

 check

Ask students how many sticky notes each set of partners should place under the "Level 1" heading of the pyramid. (Answer: one.) Ask them how many activities they'll write on each sticky note. (Answer: one.) Ask them whether they should write only standard physical activities or whether they should be thoughtful and creative. (Answer: thoughtful and creative.)

6. Discuss why physical activity is important. Ask for, or provide, examples of disease and health limitations related to a lack of physical activity.

7. Celebrate all the different activities that students identified. Ask who has done any of the more unusual activities.

Part 4: Reflection and Summary

1. Compliment students on working together and using the communication skills discussed (listening, responding, and repeating; asking if they have questions; and giving their full attention).
2. Review why physical activity is important and the various ways we get daily physical activity.

Take It Home

▶ Hand out one copy of worksheet 1.1, "Physical Activity Pyramid," to each student. The worksheet requires students to make an activity pyramid for themselves and someone else and to perform an activity that they both want to do.

▶ Tell students when to return the completed worksheet to class. (Recommended: lesson 1.5.)

Next Time

Activity circuit with activities from the first three levels of the Physical Activity Pyramid

Assessment

▶ Comprehension check: Determine whether students are placing their activities in the right location of the Physical Activity Pyramid during class.

▶ Comprehension check: Have students describe why they need physical activity. The range of answers is large and will be personal (including reasons that are social, emotional, health-related, and spiritual).

▶ Performance check: Observe students participating and working effectively in groups (for example, actively listening to others, encouraging others, refraining from interrupting).

Lesson Plan 1.2 Exploring Physical Activity

In this activity lesson, students will participate in a circuit including the physical activities from each level of the Physical Activity Pyramid.

Performance Outcomes Related to NASPE Standards

▶ Standard 2
  ▸ Identify proper warm-up and cool-down techniques and reasons for using them.
▶ Standard 3
  ▸ Participate in health-enhancing physical activities both during and outside of school.
▶ Standard 4
  ▸ Participate in moderate to vigorous physical activities on a regular basis.
  ▸ Participate in activities designed to improve or maintain muscular strength and endurance, flexibility, cardiorespiratory endurance (cardiovascular fitness), and body composition.
▶ Standard 5
  ▸ Recognize the role of physical activity in understanding diversity and continue to include and support each other, respecting the limitations and strengths of group members.
  ▸ Reflect on their role in providing safe and positive physical activity settings.
  ▸ Demonstrate cooperative skills and accomplish group or team goals in cooperative and competitive activities.
  ▸ Work independently and in groups to complete tasks.
  ▸ Use time wisely given the opportunity to be active.
  ▸ Show concern for the safety of others.
▶ Standard 6
  ▸ Enjoy physical activity.

Lesson Objectives

▶ Students will practice positive communication and support skills (for example, giving attention when others are speaking, asking questions when needed, and providing encouragement to each other).

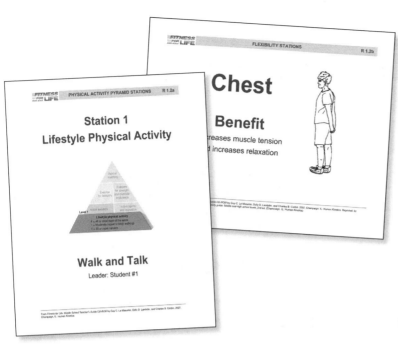

FITNESS
FOR LIFE   PHYSICAL ACTIVITY PYRAMID STATIONS   R 1.2a

Station 1
Lifestyle Physical Activity

Walk and Talk
Leader: Student #1

FITNESS
FOR LIFE   FLEXIBILITY STATIONS   R 1.2b

Chest

Benefit
reases muscle tension
d increases relaxation

▶ Students will describe and perform an appropriate warm-up and cool-down and explain why it is necessary.

▶ Students will perform activities from each level of the Physical Activity Pyramid.

Equipment

▶ 6 large cones (numbered 1 through 6)

▶ TV and DVD/VCR with aerobics or kickboxing tape

▶ 1 basketball for each student in one squad

▶ 2 items to designate "It" in tag, such as a jersey or a bandanna

▶ 6 to 8 small cones or ropes to mark the boundary for dribble tag

Reproducibles

▶ Resource 1.2a, "Physical Activity Pyramid Stations"

▶ Resource 1.2b, "Flexibility Stations"

Setup

1. Set up six circuit stations around the gym. At each station, place the appropriate "Physical Activity Pyramid Stations" card and related equipment. Place resource 1.2b, "Flexibility Stations," at the flexibility activities station.

2. Mark each station with one of the six large numbered cones.

 tech

Students can wear pedometers and record the number of steps they have taken at the end of class each day.

Delivering the Lesson

Part 1: Instant Activity

Team Follow-the-Leader

1. Organize students into groups of six, using one of the methods in "Groups and Teams" (see pages 26 to 27). Have each group line up. Explain that all groups will walk around the gym in a line, following the path of the leader—the first student in the line.

2. Instruct leaders to move at a pace that is appropriate for the whole group.

3. Each time the signal sounds, the leader steps aside and the line moves past with

a new leader. The former leader goes to the end of the line. Each time there's a new leader, call out a new, progressively more active locomotor skill (for example, power walk, skip, gallop, change lead foot, slide, change lead side, or jog).

 review

1. Expectations
   * Stop on signal (music stops, whistle, bell)
   * Importance of good body control; goal is to develop body control so you can move easily and efficiently; takes practice
   * Safety (always looking out for each other and own safety)
   * Class agreements (support each other, partners with everyone at some point, no verbal or body language put-downs)
2. Establish a boundary (for example, black line around basketball court, cones in large rectangle).
3. Talk about the importance of warming up before beginning an activity and the characteristics of a good warm-up.
   * Gradual
   * Long enough to warm muscles
   * Done in group that includes everyone at appropriate levels

Part 2: Lesson Launcher

1. Review the lesson objectives with students.
2. Ask the class to name the levels of the Physical Activity Pyramid. Explain that they will try activities from each of the levels.

Part 3: Lesson Focus

Physical Activity Pyramid Stations

1. Have students huddle in squad lines and thank each other for working together and choosing appropriate pacing in the warm-up.
2. Group students at the six stations according to their squads.
3. Introduce a signal and a procedure for changing stations. Example: "When the music stops, clean up the station, and when the music starts again, go to the next station clockwise."

check

Have students point or face clockwise to show that they know the direction in which they must proceed to the next station.

review

Review class agreements about encouraging each other regardless of gender, friendships, not knowing each other, and so on. Establish a class goal of becoming good workers (reading instructions, problem solving) who use time well to maximize activity and can work independently (without direct teacher supervision).

4. Stations
   ▶ *Lifestyle physical activity:* Students power walk in pairs around the boundary and discuss something they like (such as books, movies, music, and so on).

- *Active aerobics:* Students do three-minute sessions of cardio-kickboxing or an aerobics tape.
- *Active sports:* Students play dribble tag (dribble basketballs while playing tag).
- *Flexibility activities:* Students do a stretching routine.
- *Muscle fitness activities:* Students do wall push-ups, knee push-ups, full push-ups, or bench push-ups.
- *Sedentary living:* Students rest, take a water break, or do slow walking.

5. Have groups rotate through the activities. At each station a different member of the group becomes the new leader. (Stations are numbered 1 through 6, so whoever has that number in the squad is the leader at that station.) Discuss what a leader would do based on the communication/leadership reading (for example, read directions, encourage others, and ask needed questions). Discuss what good group members would do based on the reading ("Moving Together: Communication," page 7).
6. Have groups rotate through all stations.
7. After the last station, have everyone walk twice around the boundary as a cool-down.
8. If the equipment must be put away, ask the last group of students at each station to do it.

 observe

Scan to see whether students are staying on task, providing encouragement, having positive interactions, and performing activities safely. Reinforce these behaviors if you see them.

Part 4: Reflection and Summary

1. Compliment students for taking care of others' safety at the stations.
2. Compliment appropriate group interactions (for example, helping each other).
3. Ask students to compliment group members on their group interactions (for example, leaders who encouraged them).
4. Ask students these questions:
   - What is the importance of warm-ups and cool-downs?
   - Which activities were the hardest? Which were the easiest?
   - Which activities were the best for building strength? Which were best for building flexibility? Which were best for building cardiovascular endurance?
   - Which activities were the most fun?

Take It Home

Encourage students to do the activities with their family or friends.

Next Time

Energy and force in physical activity (May the Force be with you!)

Assessment

▶ Performance check: Observe students participating in the circuit activities and practicing positive communication and support skills (such as giving attention when others are speaking, asking questions when needed, and providing encouragement to each other) in their groups.

▶ Comprehension check: Student responses to the Reflection and Summary questions serve as a check for student understanding of the importance of warm-up and cool-down.

1.3 # Introduction to Physical Fitness

In this classroom lesson, students will review the Fitness-gram report, discuss the concept of the healthy fitness zone, and be introduced to the biomechanical concepts of energy and force.

Performance Outcomes Related to NASPE Standards

▶ Standard 2
  ▸ Identify the principle of appropriate direction of force (in the direction of the desired movement).
  ▸ Detect and correct errors in efficiency of movement and direction of force.
▶ Standard 4
  ▸ Know the components of fitness and how these relate to overall fitness status.
▶ Standard 5
  ▸ Exhibit (verbally and nonverbally) cooperation, respect, encouragement, and the ability to work independently.

Lesson Objectives

▶ Students will describe each of the components of health-related fitness and factors that affect fitness.
▶ Students will describe how a person can tell whether he or she is physically fit and the meaning of the healthy fitness zone.
▶ Students will describe the importance of energy and force in physical activity.

Equipment

▶ 1 *Fitness for Life: Middle School* student textbook per student
▶ Object (such as a chair or a box) to use in a demonstration of lifting methods
▶ Chalkboard or flip chart (optional)

 tech

　＊ Video clips of several types of physical activities (lifestyle, active aerobics, active sports and recreation, flexibility, strength and endurance, rest)
　＊ Two computer presentation programs (Mount Fitness and Tour de Fitness) are available for reviewing and reinforcing concepts. See page 40 for more information.

Reproducibles

▶ Resource 1.3, "Fitnessgram Report"
▶ Classroom Quotes

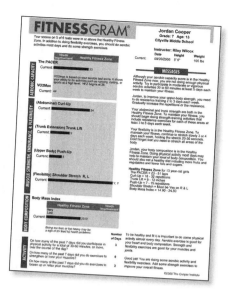

Classroom Quotes

You can print these quotes from the CD-ROM and hang them around your room.

▶ "Health is not simply the absence of sickness."— Hannah Green
▶ "By health I mean the power to live a full, adult, living, breathing life in close contact with . . . the earth and the wonders thereof—the sea—the sun."—Katherine Mansfield (author)

Setup

If desired, create an overhead or a slide of resource 1.3, "Fitnessgram Report," to show to the class during the lesson.

Delivering the Lesson

 review

Ask students to identify a level of the Physical Activity Pyramid and an activity at that level.

Part 1: Gathering Information

1. Explain to students that when we talk about physical fitness and health, there are several fitness aspects to consider. There are ways to check our fitness and see whether we are in a healthy zone.
2. Have the students read "Introduction to Physical Fitness," lesson 1.2 in the student textbook (chapter 1, pages 9 to 12).

Part 2: Lesson Launcher

1. Review the lesson objectives with students.
2. Explain to students that there are several parts of physical fitness, and that many things affect how physically fit we are. Heredity plays a role, so one of the big questions is: Did we pick good parents? But no matter what our heredity gave us, we can improve our physical fitness and get into a healthy fitness zone through practice.
3. Take the students through a movement routine that addresses the following components of health-related fitness:
   ▶ *Muscular endurance:* Up on toes 10 times, rest, up on toes 10 times, rest (or do the same reps of half-squats)
   ▶ *Strength:* Press hands together as hard as you can (isometric)

> ▸ *Flexibility:* Zipper stretch (try to interlock fingers behind your back)

> ▸ *Cardiovascular fitness:* March in place with high knees for 30 seconds and then check your heart rate

4. After they have completed the routine, ask students which component of physical fitness was their strongest and which was their weakest.

Part 3: Lesson Focus

Components of Health-Related Fitness

1. Have students look at the Fitnessgram report (on page 10 of the student textbook, or as an overhead or a slide). Talk about each assessment and what the healthy fitness zone means. Explain that they'll be testing themselves and producing a similar report that will help them set goals and know what to work on.

 check

Ask students to give a thumbs-up if sample specific scores on different fitness tests are in the healthy zone, and to give a thumbs-down if the scores are not.

2. Explain to students that fitness self-testing helps us know about specific components, but other things also affect our health and well-being. Force and energy are involved in every movement. Appropriate form makes the difference between safe and unsafe movements. Low-back pain (usually from poor sitting position, but sometimes a result of movements such as lifting incorrectly) is the number one reason adults miss work.

3. Using the object you obtained before class (e.g., chair, box), demonstrate poor and proper lifting technique. Then demonstrate an exaggerated sideways arm swing while walking. Explain how force in the direction of movement is most efficient. Discuss activities in which creating force is important and identify the direction the force should be provided.

 tech

Find and show a video of an inefficient runner or poor lifting.

4. Have students read "Biomechanical Principles: Energy, Force, and Movement" in chapter 1 of the student textbook (page 11).

5. Ask students to identify what happens in various physical activities when force is applied in the wrong direction. Examples: roller skating (you slide backward), tennis (the ball goes off the side of the racket), baseball (the ball is thrown too high or too low).

Part 4: Reflection and Summary

1. Compliment students on listening to each other, responding when called on, and offering thoughtful comments.

2. Ask students to identify components of health-related fitness and explain what the healthy fitness zone means.

Take It Home

Challenge students to engage in one of the health-related fitness activities (rising on their toes, pushing their hands together, doing the zipper stretch, or stepping in place) while they are idle (for example, while waiting for a bus, stopped at a red light, sitting during a commercial break, and so on).

Next Time

Physical activities that build fitness and require the effective application of force

Assessment

▶ Comprehension check: Class discussions serve as a check for student understanding of the concepts of energy and force in physical activity.

▶ Comprehension check: Correct responses to the Reflection and Summary questions serve as a check for student understanding of the components of health-related fitness and the meaning of the healthy fitness zone.

1.4 Biomechanics, Energy, and Force

In this activity lesson, students will focus on direction of force while participating in a continuous relay including the strength, muscular endurance, and cardiovascular fitness components of health-related fitness.

Performance Outcomes Related to NASPE Standards

▶ Standard 4
  ▶ Participate in activities designed to improve or maintain muscular strength, muscular endurance, flexibility, and cardiovascular fitness inside and outside of school.
▶ Standard 5
  ▶ Exhibit (verbally and nonverbally) cooperation, respect, encouragement, and the ability to work independently.
  ▶ Through verbal and nonverbal behavior demonstrate cooperation with peers who have different characteristics (such as gender, race, ethnicity, and ability).
  ▶ Participate with and show respect for peers of lesser skill ability.
  ▶ Assist and encourage group members by sharing positive feedback about skill performance during practice.
  ▶ Effectively work independently and in groups to complete assigned tasks.
▶ Standard 6
  ▶ Seek personally challenging physical activity experiences.

Lesson Objectives

▶ Students will be involved in moderate to vigorous activity for more than half of class time.
▶ Students will discover and apply the most effective techniques for production of force in the direction of desired movement.

Equipment

▶ 3 cones per group of six students
▶ 1 medicine ball per group of six students
▶ CD player and music

Reproducibles

▶ Resource 1.4, "Relay Stations"

▶ Worksheet 1.4, "Direction of Force"

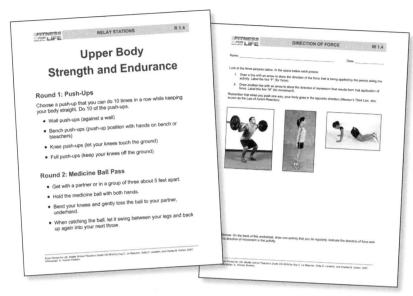

Setup

1. Make a copy of resource 1.4, "Relay Stations" and worksheet 1.4, "Direction of Force," for each student.

2. For each group of students, place three cones in a straight line about 10 yards (9 meters) apart from one another.

3. For each set of cones, place one lower-body "Relay Stations" sign on the cone at the left end, and place one upper-body "Relay Stations" sign on the cone at the right end.

Delivering the Lesson

Part 1: Instant Activity

Walk and Talk

1. Have students walk in pairs around the perimeter of the space taking turns answering the following questions:

   ▶ What are two components of health-related fitness?

   ▶ How can you tell if you have enough fitness?

2. Have students give their partners visual feedback on their answers using a thumbs-up or thumbs-down signal.

Part 2: Lesson Launcher

1. Review the lesson objectives with students.

2. Explain to students that health-related fitness involves strength, muscular endurance, cardiovascular fitness, flexibility, and body composition. Tell them they'll be working on flexibility at the end of the lesson after their bodies are well warmed up.

3. Explain that students will not be competing or racing. The object is to go at a pace at which they can attend to the direction of force as they do each activity.

4. Ask students to pay attention to their partners and give helpful feedback on body position.

Part 3: Lesson Focus

Continuous Relay

1. Divide students into groups of six. Assign each group to one of the sets of cones.

2. Demonstrate the order of the relay. Two players stand by each cone.

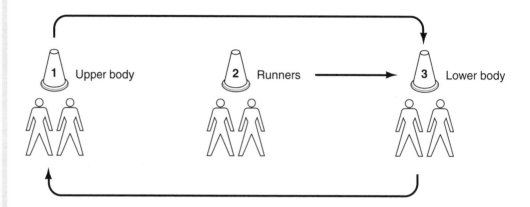

- ▸ Players by the cone at the left end (1) are the upper-body exercisers.
- ▸ Players by the cone in the middle (2) are the runners.
- ▸ Players by the cone at the right end (3) are the lower-body exercisers.
- ▸ Most exercises on the "Relay Stations" signs are to be done 10 times. Tell students that each one is called a rep (repetition) and that each group of 10 reps is called a set.

3. Start playing music to signal the beginning of the activity. The players at the end cones begin doing the Round 1 exercises for their station. Have all students switch places as follows:

- ▸ The runners in the middle run in place for 100 steps and then run to the right end cone (3), tag the cone, and start doing the lower-body exercises.
- ▸ The students who started at the right end cone run to the left end cone (1), tag the cone, and start doing the upper-body exercises.
- ▸ When the new students come to the cone, the students who started at the left end cone run to the right end cone (3), and the cycle continues. Each time students get to the cone, they should pick up on the exercises where they left off on their last visit to that cone.

4. Stop the music after 10 to 12 minutes. By that time, all students in each group should have completed all upper-body and lower-body exercises at least once (two exercises at each station).

 observe

> ＊ Observe students participating in the activities and working effectively in groups.
> ＊ Observe the use of force in each exercise (look for good examples and problems).

5. After students complete the stations, have them walk once around the activity area to cool down. If the station equipment won't be used again, have the last group to use it put it away.

6. Have students go through a series of stretching activities (including their necks, shoulders, trunks, hips, calves, and ankles).

Part 4: Reflection and Summary

Ask students to share their thoughts on the following:

▸ Which activities were hardest for you?

▸ What component of health-related fitness did the activities address?

▸ For which activities was it easiest to determine and align your force in the direction of your movement? For which activities was it hardest?

▸ Did you make any corrections in your movements that made the activities easier? Harder?

Take It Home

▸ Hand out worksheet 1.4, "Direction of Force." On the worksheet, have the students

  ▹ indicate the direction of force for each picture; and

  ▹ draw one activity that they do regularly (using stick-figure people), and indicate the direction of force and the direction of movement used in a particular skill (such as throwing or volleying).

▸ Tell students when to return the completed worksheet to class. (Recommended: lesson 1.5.)

Next Time

▸ Choice of physical activities that relate to the different levels on the Physical Activity Pyramid

▸ Remind students that worksheets 1.1, "Physical Activity Pyramid," and 1.4, "Direction of Force," are due next class (recommended).

Assessment

▸ Performance check: Observe students working effectively in groups.

▸ Comprehension check: Throughout the lesson, ask selected students questions about the application of force during the activities to check for student understanding.

▸ Performance check: Observe students participating and working effectively in groups (such as actively listening to others, encouraging others, and refraining from interrupting).

1.5 **Physical Activity Choices**

In this activity lesson, students will practice effective communication and support techniques as they participate in their choice of physical activities.

Performance Outcomes Related to NASPE Standards

▶ Standard 3
  ▶ Have an increasing awareness of the opportunities for participation in a broad range of activities that may meet needs and interests.
▶ Standard 5
  ▶ Exhibit (verbally and nonverbally) cooperation, respect, encouragement, and the ability to work independently.
▶ Standard 6
  ▶ Recognize the role of physical activity in getting to know and understand others.
  ▶ Recognize physical activity as a positive opportunity for social and group interaction.
  ▶ Identify potential social and health benefits from participation in physical activity.

Lesson Objectives

▶ Students will list and demonstrate effective communication techniques.
▶ Students will appropriately identify activities in the Physical Activity Pyramid.
▶ Students will identify how direction of force is used in a variety of physical activities.

Equipment

▶ Pinnies, scarves, or foam balls for the "Its" in the instant activity
▶ Equipment appropriate for the activity stations chosen. Suggestions include:
    ▸ TV and DVD/VCR with step aerobics and line dance video or DVD
    ▸ Basketballs
    ▸ Yoga video or DVD
    ▸ Medicine balls
    ▸ Resistance bands

 tech

    ✳ Heart rate monitors can provide feedback to students about the intensity of physical activity.
    ✳ Pedometers can provide feedback to students about the amount of steps accumulated in different physical activities.

Reproducibles

None

Setup

1. Set up eight physical activity stations: two for active aerobics, two for active sports and recreation, two for flexibility, and two for muscle fitness.

2. Suggested setup: Put activities from the same level of the pyramid along one side of the activity area so that it's easy for you to monitor student choices and easy for students to choose activities to work on.

    ▸ Level 2: Active aerobics
        – Step aerobics and line dance video
        – Walking or jogging
        – Tag game
    ▸ Level 2: Active sports and recreation
        – Shooting at the basketball basket
        – Four square
        – Dribble tag—tag while dribbling basketball
    ▸ Level 3: Flexibility (If students choose to start here, have them perform a short warm-up by walking around the area.)
        – Yoga stations—Here is a list of videos recommended by teachers that could be useful for this station:
            • *Yoga for Inflexible People*—Bodywise Interactive Yoga Series #6307326050, Baker & Taylor Inc. 800-775-1800
            • *Power Yoga for Flexibility*—Rodney Yee #1592504418, Baker & Taylor Inc. 800-775-1800
            • *Yoga for Beginners*—Gaiam, Patricia Walden #1930814828, Baker & Taylor Inc. 800-775-1800
            • *Pilates Workout for Dummies*—Andrea Ambados #6306559906, Baker & Taylor Inc. 800-775-1800

- *Ultimate Pilates*—Kathy Smith #0738924334, Baker & Taylor Inc. 800-775-1800
  – Stretching routine—After the warm-up, students perform and hold stretches for 20 seconds, working from the bottom of their bodies to the top. Have students stretch one side and then the other.
    - *Calves:* Lunge position with back heel on the ground; switch feet after stretching twice.
    - *Hamstrings:* Sit with one leg bent (so the knee is in front of the face and the foot is flat on the ground next to the other knee) and the other straight. Gently reach forward with both hands and try to touch as far down the straight leg as possible.
    - *Quadriceps:* Lie on your side with the top leg bent at the knee. Hold the ankle and pull the leg gently back behind the body. The bent leg should make a big circle—do not let the calf and the back of the leg touch each other.
    - *Side:* Reach one hand above the head and stretch to reach as high as possible.
    - *Shoulders:* Place one arm straight out in front of you. Reach across with the other hand to the far side of the straight arm and gently pull the straight arm across the chest.
▸ Level 3: Strength and muscular endurance
  – Medicine ball activities—With a partner, hold the medicine ball with two hands and try to do each of the following activities 10 times.
    - *Underhand toss:* Backswing between the legs and gently toss the medicine ball to your partner.
    - *Chest pass:* Pass the medicine ball with a slight arc to a partner.
    - *Biceps curl:* Partners take turns. Hold the ball in front of you with two hands, elbows bent at a 90-degree angle. Do a biceps curl, lifting the ball to the front of the chin.
  – Resistance band activities—Do each activity 8 to 12 times.
    - *Arm extensions:* Hold one end of the band in each hand, and put the band behind the back. Extend one arm at a time. Adjust where you are holding the band so that 10 extensions are just about right to make you tired.
    - *Biceps curls:* Hold one end of the band in each hand, and place the middle of the band under the feet. Bend the arm about 90 degrees with the elbows in close to the body. Flex the elbow so the hand is at your shoulder. Adjust where you are holding the band so that 10 reps are just about right to make you tired.
    - *Leg extensions:* Sit with the legs bent. Place one end of the band in each hand with your arms straight in front of you. Place the middle of the band under the feet. Extend your legs.
  – Calisthenics—10 jumping jacks, 10 curl-ups, 10 lunges, 10 push-ups, 10 half-squats, and so on

Delivering the Lesson

Part 1: Instant Activity

Walking Freeze Tag

1. Designate one-fourth of the students in the class as "It." Students who are "It" should wear pinnies or hold scarves or foam balls.

2. Students who are "It" try to tag other students. The goal is to get everyone frozen. Those who get tagged are frozen in place until they name three of the components of health-related fitness to a free partner who stops in front of them. While naming or listening, players cannot be tagged. Remind everyone to walk—no running.

3. After one minute, let other students have a turn being "It" until everyone in class has been "It."

Part 2: Lesson Launcher

1. Review the lesson objectives with students.

2. Explain to the students that you have been talking about the importance of different types of physical activity. You've also talked a good deal about how they can support each other in physical activity settings and how to work independently. Tell them that today they are going to spend as much of the period as possible trying different types of physical activities.

3. Explain that the goal is for each student to monitor his or her own behavior, stay on task, invite others to work together, and quickly move to a new task when the signal sounds.

4. Explain that students can choose which tasks they do, but they must choose one from each of the four categories (active aerobics, active sports and recreation, muscular fitness, and flexibility).

 review

Remind students how to encourage each other, and how to greet each other and take turns.

Part 3: Lesson Focus

Physical Activity Choices

1. Tell students that they will have time to work at four stations today.

2. When the signal sounds, have students move to an activity station of their choice.

3. At the next signal, have students stop the activity, put away their equipment at the station, and stand quietly while facing their next station.

4. If it looks like a station will be too crowded, ask some students to choose a different station so that everyone can continue to be active instead of waiting for turns.

 check

Ask students if they need to have one activity from each category. (Answer: yes.) Ask students what they should do when the signal sounds. (Answer: put equipment back and face next station.)

 observe

Scan for on-task behavior, sharing, encouraging each other, and mixing of groups.

Part 4: Reflection and Summary

1. Compliment students on working together and using the communication skills discussed (such as listening, responding, and repeating; asking when they have questions; and giving their full attention).

2. Ask students to answer the following questions:

    ▶ Which activities attracted the most people?

    ▶ Which type of activity did you like best? If you liked noncompetitive activities, make the letter "N" in sign language (fist with thumb between middle and ring finger). If you liked competitive activities, make the letter "C" in sign language (curve thumb and index finger). If you liked both kinds, make both letters.

    ▶ Can you explain how you used direction of force efficiently at a station?

3. Have students add completed worksheets 1.1, "Physical Activity Pyramid," and 1.4, "Direction of Force," to their *Fitness for Life: Middle School* portfolios.

Take It Home

Remind students to do some of these activities at home each day. Which ones could they do?

Next Time

Learning about and experiencing skills, skill-related fitness, and practice

Assessment

▶ Performance check: Observe student interactions (e.g., inviting each other to participate, resolving difficulties) and the stations students chose (i.e., did they choose from all four categories?) as a performance check for participation, effective communication, and cooperation.

▶ Comprehension check: Responses to the Reflection and Summary questions serve as a check for student understanding of the Physical Activity Pyramid and how direction of force is used in a variety of physical activities.

▶ Assess completed worksheets 1.1, "Physical Activity Pyramid," and 1.4, "Direction of Force," in students' *Fitness for Life: Middle School* portfolios. Use the worksheet rubric (available on the CD-ROM or on page 34) to assess student work, or modify the rubric to meet your specific objectives.

Supplemental Materials

If you choose to use the semester or year scheduling version of *Fitness for Life: Middle School* (see appendix B), there are excellent opportunities to insert activity-based skill units and to review and reinforce the concepts in each chapter using the *Fitness for Life: Middle School* computer programs: Mount Fitness and Tour de Fitness. You will find information about the two computer programs in appendix C. Listed below are suggestions of activity-based skill units that would go well with this chapter and resources that will help you develop great lessons.

As indicated in the "Scheduling" section (pages 13 to 18), integrating activity-based skill units with the *Fitness for Life: Middle School* lesson plans provides a great opportunity for reinforcing key concepts and for developing students' skills in a wide range of physical activities. The activity-based skill unit suggestions provided below were chosen specifically to complement chapter content. In addition, there are selected resources that can provide you with excellent lesson plans and lesson plan ideas. Approaches to teaching activity-based skill units can be found in appendix A.

COOPERATIVE CHALLENGES AND TEAM BUILDING

- ▶ **Key concepts to reinforce:** Communication, building a community, energy and force, physical activity, and health-related fitness
- ▶ **Resources:** *Essentials of Team Building* (Midura and Glover, 2005, Human Kinetics)

NEW GAMES

- ▶ **Key concepts to reinforce:** Communication, building a community, energy and force, physical activity, and health-related fitness
- ▶ **Resources:** *Best New Games: 77 Games and 7 Trust Activities for All Ages and Abilities* (Lefevre, 2002, Human Kinetics)

OMNIKIN

- ▶ **Key concepts to reinforce:** Communication, building a community, energy and force, physical activity, and health-related fitness
- ▶ **Resources:** Free lesson plans for Omnikin activities at www.omnikin.com

Learning Skills for Enjoying Physical Activity

2

Chapter 2 lesson plans focus on skills and skill development for physical activities. In order to build skills, students need to practice and participate in physical activities that develop skills. For this reason the classroom and activity lessons allow for student choice and address the issues of working effectively as leaders and participants in physical activity settings. In addition, students are introduced to lever systems and how the body uses lever systems to perform physical activities.

* 2.1 Learning Motor Skills (classroom lesson)
* 2.2 Skill-Related Fitness Stunts (activity lesson)
* 2.3 The Importance of Practice (classroom lesson)
* 2.4 Group Juggling (activity lesson)
* 2.5 Footbag Basics (activity lesson)

Lesson Plan 2.1 Learning Motor Skills

This classroom lesson provides students an opportunity to identify and discuss the skill-related fitness components associated with their favorite physical activities in group settings. Particular attention will be paid to working effectively as group leaders and group members.

Performance Outcomes Related to NASPE Standards

▶ Standard 2
  ▸ Identify skill-related fitness components required for a variety of physical activities.
▶ Standard 5
  ▸ Exhibit (verbally and nonverbally) cooperation, respect, encouragement, and the ability to work independently.
▶ Standard 6
  ▸ Analyze selected physical activity experiences for social, emotional, and health benefits.

Lesson Objectives

▶ Students will describe the skill-related fitness components associated with different physical activities.
▶ Students will actively listen to and encourage others (i.e., give positive feedback), participate, and refrain from interrupting others in small-group settings.

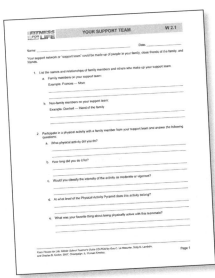

Equipment

▶ 1 *Fitness for Life: Middle School* student textbook per student
▶ Chalkboard or flip chart (optional)

 tech

Find and show video clips of people demonstrating skill-related fitness while performing a variety of physical activities.

Reproducibles

▶ Worksheet 2.1, "Your Support Team"
▶ Classroom Quotes

Classroom Quotes

You can print these quotes from the CD-ROM and hang them around your room.

▶ "Skill to do comes of doing."—Ralph Waldo Emerson (author)

▶ "When love and skill work together, expect a masterpiece."—John Ruskin (author)

▶ "Playing well with others is important—not being too flashy, just keeping good time and of course coming up with cool beats. A good snare drum, kick drum, high hat. Just getting good at the hand–feet coordination."—Chad Smith (professional drummer)

Setup

1. Write the following instructions on the board or a flip chart, and conceal them until needed:

    ▷ Share your favorite physical activity and why you like it.

    ▷ As a group, decide on one physical activity and record the following information:
    – Where does your physical activity fit on the Physical Activity Pyramid?
    – What components of health-related fitness are necessary for successful participation in that activity?
    – What components of skill-related fitness are necessary for successful participation in that activity?
    – What components of skill-related fitness are the most important for successful participation in that activity?

2. Make a copy of worksheet 2.1, "Your Support Team," for each student.

Delivering the Lesson

Part 1: Gathering Information

1. Ask students to name some skills required for playing tennis. (Possible answers: forehand, footwork, and serve.) Explain that to hit the ball, a tennis player needs to coordinate the movement of several body parts as well as coordinate the eye and hand to make solid contact with the tennis ball. Coordination, such as eye–hand coordination, is just one of the six skill-related fitness components students will explore today.

2. Have the students read "Learning Motor Skills," lesson 2.1 in the student textbook (chapter 2, pages 15 to 19).

Part 2: Lesson Launcher

1. Review the lesson objectives with students.

2. Have students read the opening section of "Moving Together: Full Participation" in the student textbook (chapter 2, page 18).

3. Tell the students to look over the discussion questions briefly, and then to read the "Guidelines for Full Participation". Students should use the guidelines to come up with answers to the discussion questions.

4. Pose the discussion questions to the class.

5. Encourage students to use the guidelines for full participation in today's lesson on skill-related physical fitness.

 review

Review some of the effective communication skills from last week (such as active listening, not interrupting, sharing the stage, and respecting others' opinions).

Part 3: Lesson Focus

Learning About Skills and Skill-Related Fitness

1. Organize students in small groups of three or four students.

2. Identify a group leader in each group.

3. Have the students in each group share their favorite physical activity and why they like it. As an option, have the students share an activity that they performed on worksheet 1.1, "Physical Activity Pyramid."

4. Direct the groups to decide on one physical activity and record the following information:

  ▸ Where does the physical activity fit on the Physical Activity Pyramid (such as lifestyle, active sport, flexibility)?

  ▸ What components of health-related fitness are necessary for successful participation in that activity?

  ▸ What components of skill-related fitness are necessary for successful participation in that activity?

  ▸ What components of skill-related fitness are the most important for successful participation in the activity?

5. Have the group leaders share their groups' findings. Facilitate the discussion and make connections with the health-related fitness components discussed in chapter 1 when possible.

 tech

Show a video of a variety of physical activities (one to three minutes) and ask groups to identify some of the skill-related fitness components illustrated in the activities. Go through steps 4 and 5 above.

Part 4: Reflection and Summary

1. Have students create an entry for their *Fitness for Life: Middle School* portfolio. On a sheet of paper, each student should identify the following:

  ▸ Their favorite physical activity

  ▸ How many times per week they participate in this activity

  ▸ Approximately how long (hours or minutes) they participate each time

  ▸ The components of skill-related fitness this activity develops

  ▸ Whether they participate alone or with someone (friend or family member)

  ▸ Why this activity is their favorite

2. Have students add their completed paper to their *Fitness for Life: Middle School* portfolios.

Take It Home

▶ Hand out worksheet 2.1, "Your Support Team." To fill out the worksheet, students will identify family members and others who are part of their "support team" or support network. Then they will participate in one activity with a family member and one activity with someone else, and answer questions about the activities.

▶ Tell students when to return the completed worksheet to class. (Recommended: lesson 2.5.)

Next Time

Skill-related fitness stunts circuit

Assessment

▶ Comprehension check: Use class discussions to check for student understanding of the skill-related fitness components associated with different physical activities.

▶ Comprehension check: Assess student responses to the Reflection and Summary exercise in students' *Fitness for Life: Middle School* portfolios.

▶ Performance check: Look for student behaviors such as active listening, encouraging others (for example, with positive feedback), participation, and refraining from interrupting others in small-group settings.

In this activity lesson, students will engage in activities that require the six skill-related fitness components: agility, balance, coordination, reaction time, power, and speed.

Performance Outcomes Related to NASPE Standards

▶ Standard 1
  ▹ Perform fitness stunts that require the six skill-related fitness components.
▶ Standard 2
  ▹ Through trial and error, identify strategies that improve performance on skill-related fitness stunts.
▶ Standard 5
  ▹ Exhibit (verbally and nonverbally) cooperation, respect, encouragement, and the ability to work independently.
▶ Standard 6
  ▹ Seek personally challenging experiences in physical activity experiences.
  ▹ Appreciate the aesthetic and creative aspects of skilled performance in others and themselves.

Lesson Objectives

▶ Students will participate in activities that require the six skill-related fitness components and explore challenges provided by the instructor.
▶ Students will actively listen to others, encourage others (i.e., use positive feedback), participate, and refrain from interrupting others in small-group settings.

Equipment

▶ 6 large cones (numbered 1 through 6)
▶ 4 exercise mats
▶ 6 volleyballs, basketballs, or playground balls
▶ 3 pinnies
▶ Floor tape (optional)

Reproducibles

Resource 2.2, "Skill-Related Fitness Stunts"

Setup

1. Set up six stations around the gym. At each station, place one of the "Skill-Related Fitness Stunts" signs, along with any equipment needed for the activity. Make sure you have enough space at each station for the activity.

2. Mark each station with one of the six large numbered cones.

Delivering the Lesson

Part 1: Instant Activity

Grouping Games

1. Ask the students if they can tell you what a mime is. (Answer: Mime or pantomime is a performance using gestures and body movements without words.) Ask them to name a game that uses pantomime. (Possible answer: charades.) Poll the class to see how many students have played charades.

2. Ask students to think about what animal they would like to be if they weren't a human and then act out (mime) this animal.

3. Have the students find and group themselves with others who are acting like them. They can consider some of the differences and similarities in their actions.

4. Now have the students mime their favorite physical activity and join with others who are miming the same activity. Ask them how they would classify their activity using the Physical Activity Pyramid (for example, as a lifestyle activity, an active sport, and so on).

5. Ask students to find others who have a birthday in the same month as they do, using mime. (Hint: Act out a holiday.) Put a couple of birthday months together so you end up with six equal groups for the skill-related fitness stunts circuit.

Part 2: Lesson Launcher

1. Review the lesson objectives with students.

2. Ask the class to name the six skill-related fitness components. Explain that they will be trying out activities that test each component of their skill-related fitness.

Part 3: Lesson Focus

Skill-Related Fitness Stunts Circuit

1. Have a group of students at each stunt station become the experts in that activity by reading the sign, trying the activity, and learning tips for success.

2. Jigsaw groups so one "expert" from each activity is in a group. One possible

method: Within their birthday-month groups, students line up in order by the day of their birthday (for example, 1, 4, 17, 23, 25, and 31). The first person in each line goes to station 1, the second person goes to station 2, and so on. This creates six new groups, and all groups will have one expert from each station.

3. Have the groups rotate through the activities every five minutes (or until each stunt has been explained and everyone gets to try it). At each station, the student who is the expert in that station becomes the group leader for that activity.

 review

Remind group leaders and group members about the guidelines for promoting full participation (see page 18 in the student textbook).

4. If time permits, have each group come up with a skill-related stunt to share with the other groups.

Part 4: Reflection and Summary

Ask students to share their thoughts on the following:

▸ What physical activities could help improve your performance on one of the skill-related fitness stunts?

▸ Based on your group work today, what did you learn about working with others?

▸ Who will share a compliment about a student who used one of the leadership principles that we talked about for promoting full participation (e.g., asking others to demonstrate, encouraging others, and participating at every station)?

▸ What were some hints you discovered for performing the skill-related fitness stunts better?

Take It Home

Encourage students to try these skill-related fitness stunts with their family or friends.

Next Time

Practice and improving skills

Assessment

Performance check: Observe students participating and working effectively in groups (for example, actively listening to others, encouraging others, and refraining from interrupting).

In this classroom lesson, students will learn about some effective strategies for practicing skills and the basic concept of levers.

Performance Outcomes Related to NASPE Standards

▶ Standard 2
  ▶ Explain how appropriate practice improves performance.
  ▶ Explain how inappropriate practice can hinder skill development.
  ▶ Identify the three types of lever systems.
▶ Standard 5
  ▶ Exhibit (verbally and nonverbally) cooperation, respect, encouragement, and the ability to work independently.

Lesson Objectives

▶ Students will be able to compare their personal practice experiences with effective characteristics of practice (i.e., positive feedback) and ineffective practice situations (i.e., paralysis by analysis, too much feedback).
▶ Students will be able to identify lever systems used in self-selected physical activities.

Equipment

▶ 1 *Fitness for Life: Middle School* student textbook per student
▶ Chalkboard or flip chart

 tech

  * Find and show video clips of athletes or musicians talking about practice.
  * Two computer presentation programs (Mount Fitness and Tour de Fitness) are available for reviewing and reinforcing concepts. See page 40 for more information.

Reproducibles

▶ Worksheet 2.3, "Everyday Levers"
▶ Classroom Quotes

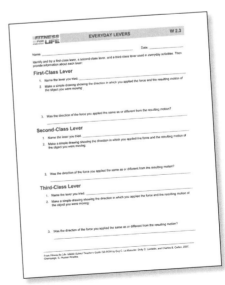

Classroom Quotes

You can print these quotes from the CD-ROM and hang them around your room.

▶ "Practice is the best of all instructors."—Publilius Syrus (Roman author, first century B.C.)

▶ "It's a funny thing, the more I practice the luckier I get."—Arnold Palmer (pro golfer)

Setup

1. On the chalkboard or a flip chart, create a large chart with X and Y axes to fill in information provided by students in the lesson.

2. Write the following notes on the board or a flip chart, and conceal them until needed:

   ▷ Feedback or tips that helped your partner improve at a skill (for example, step with the opposite foot)

   ▷ A situation in which your partner got too much feedback and experienced paralysis by analysis

3. Leave some space on the board or flip chart to write down student examples of levers.

4. Make a copy of worksheet 2.3, "Everyday Levers," for each student.

Delivering the Lesson

Part 1: Gathering Information

1. Ask students how they can improve their performance in physical activities. (Possible answers: by practicing, eating right, and getting enough sleep.) What thoughts come to their minds when they think about practice? Do they believe there is a right way and a wrong way to practice?

2. Have the students read "The Importance of Practice," lesson 2.2 in the student textbook (chapter 2, pages 20 to 24), in preparation for a discussion about practice.

Part 2: Lesson Launcher

1. Review the lesson objectives with students.

2. Explain to students that to get better at a skill, people need to practice. Many people get their practice by playing activities. Serious athletes and musicians need to practice specific skills to improve, because just playing is not enough.

3. Remind students that no matter how hard we practice, perfection is not guaranteed. Most professional athletes practice very hard and are not always successful. For example, a good batting average is .300. Ask students if they know what that means. (Answer: hitting 3 out of every 10 times.)

Part 3: Lesson Focus 1

The Importance of Practice

1. Arrange students into pairs using one of the methods in "Groups and Teams" (see page 26 to 27).

2. With their partner, have each student share a physical activity that they have practiced, how many years they have practiced that activity, and how they make practice enjoyable.

3. As a class, add up how many total years of practice the class has in different activities. Present this data in the chart you prepared so that it looks like the figure shown below. If you can't fit all the activities in the chart, group them by Physical Activity Pyramid level (active aerobics, active sports, active recreation, muscle fitness, and flexibility).

4. Reveal what you wrote on the board or flip chart during step 2 of Setup. Have students ask their partners to provide that information:
   ‣ Feedback that helped them improve at a skill
   ‣ Feedback that caused paralysis by analysis

5. Ask some of the students to share their helpful feedback and paralysis by analysis experiences with the class.

6. Ask if any students have a mental routine or use imagery when they practice.

7. Ask if any students imagine themselves performing skills in their daydreams or thoughts.

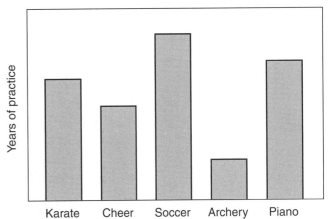

Part 4: Lesson Focus 2

Biomechanical Principles: Levers

1. Have students read "Biomechanical Principles: Levers" in the student textbook (chapter 2, pages 21 to 23).

2. Explain the concept of levers. Levers in the human body consist of a rigid bar (a bone), a fulcrum (a joint), an effort force (the pull of a muscle on a bone), and a resistance force (a load being moved or the weight of a body part). Provide examples of
   ‣ first-class levers (seesaw, scissors),
   ‣ second-class levers (wheelbarrow, nut-cracker), and
   ‣ third-class levers (sweeping with a household broom, forearm in biceps curl). Explain that third-class levers are the most common in the human body.

3. Use the biceps muscle and the flexion of the forearm at the elbow to demonstrate a third-class lever in the body.
   ‣ Although the biceps muscle is above

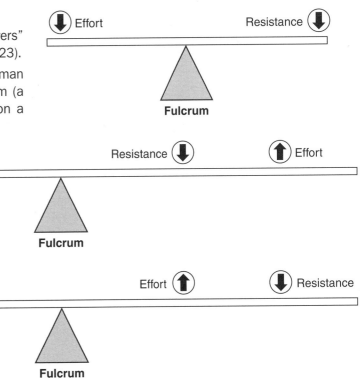

the elbow joint, the action of a contracting biceps muscle is to pull on the ulna bone (forearm). Thus, the effort is actually applied between the fulcrum and the resistance.

▸ Explain to students that understanding levers in the body is extremely complex because of the different forces exerted by muscles and the structure of joints. In fact, it's not uncommon for scientists who study human body mechanics (biomechanists) to disagree about the classification of lever systems in the body.

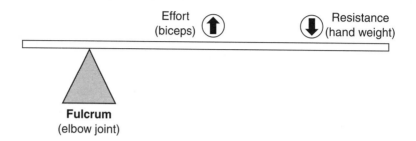

4. Have student pairs come up with a list of physical activity movements that require levers.

5. Ask students to share these with the whole class and try to classify the lever systems using the diagrams.

Part 5: Reflection and Summary

Pose the following questions to students:

▸ Why is feedback important for practice?

▸ What does "paralysis by analysis" mean?

▸ What are the most common kinds of levers in the human body?

Take It Home

▸ Hand out worksheet 2.3, "Everyday Levers." This worksheet requires students to identify and try first-, second-, and third-class levers used in everyday activities. Students will also indicate the direction of force applied and the direction of expected movement.

▸ Tell students when to return the completed worksheet to class. (Recommended: lesson 2.5.)

Next Time

Group juggling activities

Assessment

▶ Comprehension check: Student discussions serve as a check for their understanding of effective characteristics of practice (such as positive feedback) and ineffective practice situations (such as too much feedback).

▶ Comprehension check: Student discussions can serve as a check for their understanding of lever systems used for physical activities.

In this activity lesson, students will practice a variety of juggling activities while using effective practice techniques to improve (such as giving positive feedback to peers and focusing on one cue at a time).

Performance Outcomes Related to NASPE Standards

▶ Standard 1
  ▷ Perform stationary and moving juggling tosses and catches during group juggling activities.

▶ Standard 2
  ▷ Detect differences in the successful and unsuccessful execution of stationary and moving group juggling skills (for example, high tosses, following through to the target, and communication).

▶ Standard 5
  ▷ Exhibit (verbally and nonverbally) cooperation, respect, encouragement, and the ability to work independently.
  ▷ Assist and encourage group members by sharing positive feedback about skill performance during practice.

▶ Standard 6
  ▷ Seek personally challenging physical activity experiences.
  ▷ Enjoy becoming more skilled through effort and practice.

Lesson Objectives

▶ Students will discover and apply the most effective techniques for successful group juggling.

- Students will experience improvement in group juggling through practice.
- Students will encourage others by providing positive feedback on the successful execution of group juggling skills (such as following through to the target and making good tosses).

Equipment

- 4 cones
- 15 foam gator balls, volleyballs, or soccer balls
- Extra balls of different sizes (such as Wiffle balls, tennis balls, or playground balls) (optional)
- 5 crazy balls (optional)
- CD of juggling or circus music (optional)

Reproducibles

None

Setup

1. Place a selection of balls on the perimeter of the activity area or in a mobile ball bin that you can move around.
2. Using cones, mark a rectangle or square in which the instant activity will take place.

Delivering the Lesson

Part 1: Instant Activity

Jog and Toss
1. Ask students to list activities that require teammates to pass balls or objects to one another. How about an activity that requires passing balls to oneself?
2. Explain to students that today they will try partner juggling and team juggling. Juggling is an activity that takes a lot of practice. Tell students that they will practice juggling in pairs and groups and use their knowledge of effective practice to improve.
3. On your signal, students should find a partner and begin jogging side by side around the gym. While jogging, partners must toss a ball of their choice back and forth.
4. Challenge students to see if they can do a full lap without dropping the ball.
5. Challenge them to see how many times during one lap they can pass the ball without dropping it.

 observe

Remind students to stay in their personal spaces.

Part 2: Lesson Launcher

1. Review the lesson objectives with students.

2. Ask the class what techniques in the jog and toss activity helped them to be successful. Possible responses include:
   - ▶ Accurate toss: Requires a follow-through to the target.
   - ▶ Leading the partner: Requires them to see where the target is moving to.
   - ▶ Short tosses: Are easier to make accurately and to catch.
   - ▶ Medium-height tosses: Tosses that are too high or too low can be difficult to catch. A medium-height toss gives the catcher time to move to the ball and is low enough to make the catch easy.

 check

Ask students to identify an effective practice strategy discussed in the last class (positive feedback) and why it was helpful. What is an ineffective practice strategy (too much information or "paralysis by analysis"), and why is it ineffective?

3. Tell students that you expect them to use positive feedback with their group members to help them improve at juggling. When they give positive feedback to their partners, they should focus on the important elements of passing and catching, such as following through to the target, making good tosses, and leading their partners. For example:
   - ▶ "Good toss, Sheila—I like the way you followed through to your target."
   - ▶ "Nice toss, Braden—it was just the right height."
   - ▶ "Way to lead me with your toss, Danica."

Part 3: Lesson Focus

Group Juggle

1. Split students into groups of six to eight and have each group form a circle.

2. Without using any balls yet, have the students in each group practice a pattern for throwing a ball back and forth. Start by asking one student to name a person that he or she will throw the ball to, and then ask that student to name another person, and so on. Remind students that everyone must toss and catch the ball at least once, and that the group's success will depend on having a good pattern for throwing.

3. Ask the students to raise their hands when their group has established its pattern. Give one ball to each group.

4. After a few minutes, ask the students how many times it takes each group to complete the pattern without dropping the ball.
   - ▶ Challenge the groups to see how many times they can go through the pattern without dropping the ball.
   - ▶ Challenge the groups to see how many times the ball can go through the pattern in 30 seconds (or until the music stops) without being dropped.

5. Add a second ball to each group. The first person in the pattern throws the first ball. Once the ball has been caught and thrown by the second person, the first person starts the second ball.

6. Add a third ball, starting all three balls with the first person in the pattern.

7. Have each group try to move from one end of the gym to the other while completing the pattern. All students must touch the ball, and groups must return to their starting point if a ball is dropped. Start with one ball and build to three. Remind students about communicating with the person they are throwing to.

8. Interesting variations include the following:
   - Provide students with a variety of balls to make the tasks easier or harder.
   - Provide cooperative groups with a crazy ball to see how many successful catches they can make in a row.
   - Encourage students who have "mastered" the tasks to provide tips and encouragement to students who have not mastered them.

Part 4: Reflection and Summary

Ask students to share their thoughts on the following:

- Who can provide an example of someone who gave positive feedback?
- What techniques made it easy to complete the pattern successfully?
- How did practice help your group improve?
- What components of skill-related fitness were required for today's activities?
- What lever system was used at the forearm to throw the balls underhand? (Answer: third-class lever.) Demonstrate the underhand toss, focusing on flexion of the forearm at the elbow.

Take It Home

Encourage students to try juggling with a family member and to use their knowledge of effective practice to improve.

Next Time

- Footbag basics and other foot volleying games.
- Remind students that worksheets 2.1, "Your Support Team," and 2.3, "Everyday Levers," are due next class (recommended).

Assessment

- Performance check: Observe students providing positive feedback on the successful execution of group juggling skills (such as following through to the target and making good tosses).
- Performance check: Observe student improvement in group juggling through practice and the application of effective techniques for successful group juggling (such as following through to the target and making good tosses).

2.5 **Footbag Basics**

In a true test of agility and coordination, students will practice a variety of footbag activities in this activity lesson. These activities reinforce the importance of practice and highlight several components of skill-related fitness.

Performance Outcomes Related to NASPE Standards

▶ Standard 1
  ▶ Perform a variety of kicking techniques while footbagging alone, in pairs, and with a group.
▶ Standard 2
  ▶ Identify skill-related fitness components required for footbagging.
  ▶ Through trial and error, identify strategies that improve footbagging performance.
▶ Standard 5
  ▶ Remain on task in group activities without close teacher monitoring.
  ▶ Exhibit (verbally and nonverbally) cooperation, respect, encouragement, and the ability to work independently.
▶ Standard 6
  ▶ Identify potential social and health benefits from participation in footbagging.
  ▶ Seek personally challenging physical activity experiences.
  ▶ Appreciate the aesthetic and creative aspects of skilled performance in others and themselves.

Lesson Objectives

▶ Students will perform a variety of footbagging activities that require eye–foot coordination, agility, and balance.

▶ Students will identify the skill-related fitness components required for footbagging.

▶ Students will improve at footbagging through practice.

Equipment

▶ 30 balloons or balls of different sizes and textures (examples: balloons, beach balls, gator balls, soccer balls, foam balls, playground balls, Balzac balls) so you can vary the difficulty for students of different abilities

▶ 3 to 6 pickleball nets

▶ CD player and Brazilian or surf music (optional)

▶ Laptop, LCD projector, and link to the Web site www.footbag.org (optional)

Reproducibles

Worksheet 2.5, "Footbagging With the Family"

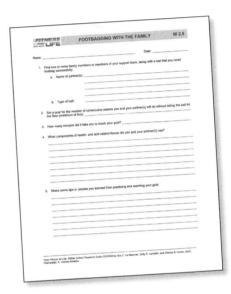

Setup

1. Place a selection of balls on the perimeter of the activity area or in a mobile ball bin that you can move around.

2. Blow up some balloons for beginner footbaggers.

3. Cue up some fun music (optional).

4. Set up pickleball nets (preferred), low barriers (benches), or badminton nets for footvolley or footbag tennis.

5. Make a copy of worksheet 2.5, "Footbagging With the Family," for each student.

Delivering the Lesson

Part 1: Instant Activity

Footbagging and Handbagging Warm-Up

1. Ask the class how many of them have heard of footbagging or hacky sack. Ask students to describe the object of footbagging. (Answer: to make as many consecutive foot volleys as you can; tricks are a bonus.)

2. Explain to the class that footbagging is extremely difficult and requires many components of skill-related fitness. It takes a lot of practice to become good.

3. On your signal, have students get a ball they think they can successfully hack, find their own space, and see how many consecutive foot volleys they can make without letting the ball touch the floor.

4. If students find this activity difficult, they can use their arms to volley the ball. Have them try to alternate between using their arms and using their feet (give a quick demo).

5. Challenge students to find a partner and see how many consecutive foot (and arm) volleys they can make in a row.

Part 2: Lesson Launcher

1. Review the lesson objectives with students.

2. Explain to students that footbagging is an ancient sport with its roots in North America and Asia. There is evidence of a game that native North Americans played using a sack made of animal hide that was filled with pellets or sand. Feathers were sometimes attached to give it a flight similar to a badminton birdie.

3. Tell students that footbagging is becoming a very popular sport for teenagers and adults around the world. There are several different footbagging competitions, including Footbag Freestyle (doing a routine of tricks) and Footbag Net (using a volleyball with your feet).

4. Tell students that today they will practice basic footbagging skills and play footbag games.

 tech

Show a video of footbagging available at the Web site www.footbag.org. (Click "videos" on the menu and select a clip from major national and international competitions. Consider showing the clip "33 feet," found at www.footbag.org/gallery/show/6943.)

Part 3: Lesson Focus

Footbag Basics

1. Demonstrate the four basic kicks: toe kick (top of toe), inside foot (instep), outside kick (outside of foot), and knee hit (top of thigh).

2. Explain that while music can make this class fun, when the music stops, students must freeze, look, and listen.

3. Allow students to choose a ball, balloon, or footbag and try the different kicks.
   ▸ Challenge them to see how many consecutive kicks they can do with each technique.
   ▸ Using balloons, they can try tricks such as the following:
      – Kick and spin (do one full spin and continue kicking before the ball hits the floor)
      – Kick, sit, stand, and kick
      – Kick and balance on their head (kick the balloon to head height and see how long they can balance the balloon before resuming the kicks)
   ▸ Challenge them to do kick routines with balloons, footbags, or balls. Have them try to use all the skills in a sequence (for example, toe, knee, instep, outstep).

4. Have students pair up and choose one ball to footbag with. Partners should stand one big step apart so they have room to footbag.
   ▸ Allow students to volley with arms if they need to.
   ▸ Challenge them to see how many passes they can make without dropping the ball.
   ▸ Challenge them to create a routine using different kicks and tricks. Partners can add clapping or songs while they wait for the ball.

5. Have each student pair join with another pair for casual circle play. Explain the rules:
   ▸ No hands (except when serving), no arms, and no shoulders. However, shoulders are widely accepted in most hack circles. You can also allow beginners to use their hands and arms.

- Unless you're playing alone, always serve the bag to someone else. Footbagging is traditionally a game of courtesy, hence "the courtesy toss": a light underhand lob usually toward the receiver's knee.

- Don't hog the bag until you drop it because that's no fun for everybody else. Being able to pass well is important to almost all footbagging games.

- Don't apologize for making mistakes. It happens to everyone, especially when people are learning, so apologies aren't necessary.

- Try not to give knee passes. Passes from the knee tend to go straight to the ground.

 review

Remind students to work together and communicate. Effective practice requires providing positive feedback.

 observe

Scan for a positive learning environment in which students offer encouragement and positive feedback. Do not tolerate negative behaviors, such as verbal and nonverbal put-downs.

6. Emphasize communication during casual play. The footbagger should call out the name of the person he or she is passing to in casual circle play.

7. Footbag games: Have all students play one game or set up a circuit of games that students can rotate through or choose.

   - *Four square footbag:* Played like four square with a "king" or "queen" court.

   - *Footbag net:* Played 2-on-2 or 4-on-4. Use a pickleball-size net or a badminton net. Played like volleyball, but with feet. Have students serve to the other team using a soft underhand toss from close to the net. For official rules, visit www.footbag.org.

   - *Footbag tennis:* Played 1-on-1 or 2-on-2. Play with a gator ball or a foam soccer ball. Play like pickleball, but with feet. Players are allowed to let the ball bounce once on their side before returning the ball. Players are allowed three contacts with their legs, chest, or head before returning the ball. For maximum play, have players serve using an underhand lob.

   - *Circle freestyle:* This is a noncompetitive game for groups of players who want to cooperate and try tricks while going for a high number of consecutive volleys.

   - *Battle hack:* This game can only be played with two or more people, and the rules are flexible depending on the situation and how everyone wants to play. The game involves a person kicking the bag a certain number of times to "activate" the bag. Players must agree beforehand how the bag will be activated (for example, three consecutive volleys, an outstep volley, or switching from a toe kick to a knee kick). Once the bag is activated, players attempt to contact or attack another player with the bag anywhere between the top of their knee and their neck. Make sure players don't hit the footbag hard enough to hurt somebody. If the player who has been attacked can't keep the bag in play, the attacker (kicker) scores a point. If the player who has been attacked keeps the bag in play, play continues. The bag can be passed at any time, but must be activated before attacking. Players can agree on bonus rules such as earning bonus points by using a trick kick or a kick combo.

Part 4: Reflection and Summary

1. Ask students the following questions:
   ▸ What components of skill-related fitness are required for footbagging?
   ▸ What components of health-related fitness are required for footbagging?
   ▸ What other benefits could someone get from participation in footbagging?
   ▸ What techniques or secrets did you discover during your practicing and playing that improved your footbagging skills?
2. Have students add completed worksheets 2.1, "Your Support Team," and 2.3, "Everyday Levers," to their *Fitness for Life: Middle School* portfolios.

Take It Home

▸ Hand out worksheet 2.5, "Footbagging With the Family." Encourage students to get a ball at home and try to get 5, 10, or 15 consecutive foot volleys with a family member or several family members. They should reflect on how long it took and the strategies they used to accomplish their goal.

▸ Tell students when to return the completed worksheet to class. (Recommended: lesson 3.1.)

Next Time

▸ Lifestyle physical activity and safety during physical activities

▸ Remind students that worksheet 2.5, "Footbagging With the Family," is due next class (recommended).

Assessment

▸ Performance check: Observe students participating in the activities and working effectively in groups.

▸ Comprehension check: Responses to the Reflection and Summary questions serve as a check for student understanding of the skill-related fitness components required for footbagging.

▸ Performance check: Observe student improvement at footbagging through practice.

▸ Assess completed worksheets 2.1, "Your Support Team," and 2.3, "Everyday Levers," in students' *Fitness for Life: Middle School* portfolios. Use the worksheet rubric (available on the CD-ROM or on page 34) to assess the worksheets, or modify the rubric to meet your specific objectives.

Supplemental Materials

If you choose to use the semester or year scheduling version of *Fitness for Life: Middle School* (see appendix B), there are excellent opportunities to insert activity-based skill units and to review and reinforce the concepts in each chapter using the *Fitness for Life: Middle School* computer programs: Mount Fitness and Tour de Fitness. You will find information about the two computer programs in appendix C. Listed below are suggestions of activity-based skill units that would go well with this chapter and resources that will help you develop great lessons.

As indicated in the "Scheduling" section (pages 13 to 18), integrating activity-based skill units with the *Fitness for Life: Middle School* lesson plans provides a great opportunity for reinforcing key concepts and for developing students' skills in a wide range of physical activities. The activity-based skill unit suggestions provided below were chosen specifically to complement chapter content. In addition, there are selected resources that can provide you with excellent lesson plans and lesson plan ideas. Approaches to teaching activity-based skill units can be found in appendix A.

FOOTBAGGING, FOOT VOLLEYING, OR HACKY SACK

- ▶ **Key concepts to reinforce:** Practice, skill-related fitness, inclusion, lever systems, support network (your support team)
- ▶ **Resources:**
  - ▷ www.footvolley.com
  - ▷ www.footbag.org
  - ▷ www.footbagging.com

SOCCER

- ▶ **Key concepts to reinforce:** Practice, skill-related fitness, inclusion, lever systems, support network (your support team)
- ▶ **Resources:**
  - ▷ *Teaching Sport Concepts and Skills: A Tactical Games Approach* (Mitchell, Olsen, and Griffin, 2006, Human Kinetics)
  - ▷ *Complete Physical Education Plans for Grades 7-12* (Kleinman, 2001, Human Kinetics)
  - ▷ *Quality Lesson Plans for Secondary Physical Education* (Zakrajsek, Carnes, and Pettigrew, 2003, Human Kinetics)

PICKLEBALL

- ▶ **Key concepts to reinforce:** Practice, skill-related fitness, inclusion, lever systems, support network (your support team)
- ▶ **Resources:**
  - ▷ *Complete Physical Education Plans for Grades 7-12* (Kleinman, 2001, Human Kinetics)
  - ▷ *Quality Lesson Plans for Secondary Physical Education* (Zakrajsek, Carnes, and Pettigrew, 2003, Human Kinetics)

TEAM HANDBALL

- ▶ **Key concepts to reinforce:** Practice, skill-related fitness, inclusion, lever systems, support network (your support team)

- **Resources:**
  - *Complete Physical Education Plans for Grades 7-12* (Kleinman, 2001, Human Kinetics)
  - *Quality Lesson Plans for Secondary Physical Education* (Zakrajsek, Carnes, and Pettigrew, 2003, Human Kinetics)

FLOOR HOCKEY

- **Key concepts to reinforce:** Practice, skill-related fitness, inclusion, lever systems, support network (your support team)
- **Resources:** *Quality Lesson Plans for Secondary Physical Education* (Zakrajsek, Carnes, and Pettigrew, 2003, Human Kinetics)

Lifestyle Physical Activity

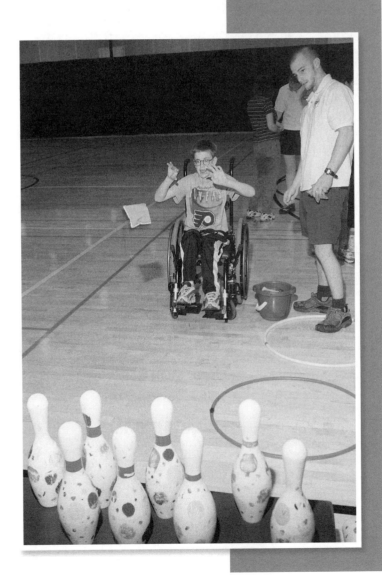

Chapter 3 lesson plans focus on lifestyle physical activities, safety in physical activity, and changing behavior to include more physical activity. Students are provided with opportunities to reflect on their physical activity levels, explore the consequences of increasing and decreasing friction in physical activities, as well as discuss their physical activity preferences with peers.

* 3.1 Lifestyle Physical Activity: Level 1 of the Physical Activity Pyramid (classroom lesson)
* 3.2 Safety in Physical Activity (activity lesson)
* 3.3 Benefits of Lifestyle Physical Activity and the Effects of Friction (classroom lesson)
* 3.4 Exploring Friction in Physical Activity (activity lesson)
* 3.5 Lifestyle Physical Activity (activity lesson)

Lifestyle Physical Activity: Level 1 of the Physical Activity Pyramid

In this classroom lesson, students will discuss the FIT formula for lifestyle physical activity and complete an Activitygram detailing their activity from the previous day.

Performance Outcomes Related to NASPE Standards

▶ Standard 3
  ▹ Have an increasing awareness of opportunities for participation in a wide range of activities that meet their needs and interests.
  ▹ Participate in health-enhancing physical activities both during and outside of school.
  ▹ Maintain a physical activity log (Activitygram).
▶ Standard 5
  ▹ Exhibit (verbally and nonverbally) cooperation, respect, encouragement, and the ability to work independently.
  ▹ Classroom climate: Move from identifying and following rules and safe practices to reflecting on their role in physical activity settings.

Lesson Objectives

▶ Students will describe what lifestyle physical activity is, what lifestyle activities they perform, and how they benefit from lifestyle activities.
▶ Students will identify the FIT formula for lifestyle physical activity.
▶ Students will identify appropriate safety practices related to physical activity.

Equipment

▶ 1 *Fitness for Life: Middle School* student textbook per student
▶ Chalkboard or flip chart (optional)
▶ Several pads of sticky notes
▶ Cartoon in which a child moves all about the neighborhood, leaving a trail that shows his or her path. (Visit the Web site www.familycircus.com for possibilities.)

* Find and show video clips of various lifestyle physical activities (such as walking the dog, doing housework, or doing yard work).

* Find and show a video clip of a student who is disabled or injured (for example, a quadriplegic from a diving accident or a tennis player with skin cancer) explaining the importance of safety guidelines.

Reproducibles

▶ Worksheet 3.1a, "Activitygram"

▶ Worksheet 3.1b, "Making Changes"

▶ Classroom Quotes

Classroom Quotes

You can print this quote from the CD-ROM and hang it in your room.

▶ "All growth depends upon activity. There is no development physically or intellectually without effort, and effort means work."—Calvin Coolidge (U.S. president)

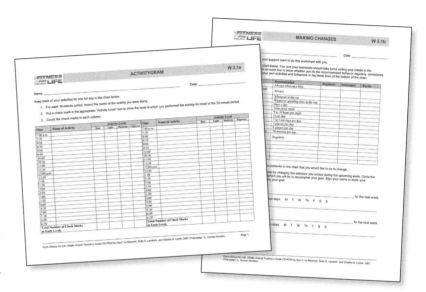

Setup

1. Write the FIT formula for lifestyle physical activities on the chalkboard or a flip chart.

2. For each student, make one copy of worksheet 3.1a, "Activitygram," and one copy of worksheet 3.1b, "Making Changes."

Delivering the Lesson

Part 1: Gathering Information

1. Ask students what they have done since they got up this morning. Every moment of the day we are doing some sort of physical activity. Some activities are light, while others are vigorous. Explain to students that you'll be talking about all kinds of physical activities today and how to do activity safely.

2. Have the students read "Lifestyle Physical Activity: Level 1 of the Physical Activity Pyramid," lesson 3.1 in the student textbook (chapter 3, pages 27 to 31).

Part 2: Lesson Launcher

1. Review the lesson objectives with students.

2. Explain to students that we all have different physical activity behaviors. Some people have patterns you can set your clock by, such as people who swim every morning. Others have erratic physical activity patterns, engaging in activity any opportunity they can get. Tell students that in this lesson, they'll be examining their own activity patterns.

 review

> Remind students of the class expectations (e.g., listen when someone else is talking, contribute to discussions, don't put others down).

3. Arrange students into pairs using one of the methods in "Groups and Teams" (pages 26 to 27).

4. Show students the cartoon of the child moving about his or her neighborhood, leaving a trail. Ask them to imagine what their own trails might look like on any given day.

5. Review the following sharing protocol: In each pair, students use rock, paper, scissors to choose who will talk first. That person will have 45 seconds to describe his or her day yesterday while the other listens. On your signal, the listener spends 15 seconds paraphrasing what the speaker said. Then partners switch roles.

? **check**

> Ask the students who will be talking first in each pair to raise their hands. Ask them to explain how long the whole process will take. (Answer: 45 seconds to talk, 15 seconds for the other to paraphrase, 45 seconds to talk, 15 seconds for the other to paraphrase—a total of 2 minutes.)

6. Give the signal for students to begin sharing their daily activities.

Part 3: Lesson Focus 1

Activitygram and Lifestyle Physical Activity

1. Discuss recall strategies (e.g., start at the beginning and walk through the day, or record major events and then fill in details).

2. Hand out worksheet 3.1a, "Activitygram," to each student, and read the directions together.

3. Have students complete the Activitygram by describing their activity for the previous day. Encourage partners to help each other by asking reminder questions. Examples: How did you get to school? Did you do anything after school? What time did you go to bed?

4. Have the students tally the number of minutes they spent in lifestyle physical activity. They should then identify the major type of lifestyle physical activity they participated in during the day.

5. Review the FIT guidelines for lifestyle physical activity. On the second page of the worksheet have students compare their activity levels to the FIT guidelines for lifestyle physical activities.

6. On the second page of the worksheet, students calculate the number of calories burned for one activity during the day and a replacement activity that would provide more active physical activity (such as taking the stairs instead of the elevator, or walking to school instead of riding). Have students calculate what effect that substitution would have if they did it for a year. Discuss the long-term effects of that change on weight, healthy fitness zone, and so on.

7. On the second page of the worksheet, have the students calculate how changes in a couple of activities changes calorie expenditure.

 ▸ Example 1: Changing from sitting (talking on the phone) for 30 minutes (4 calories) to walking the dog for 30 minutes (125 calories). Have students calculate what effect that substitution would have if they did it for a week (7 days), a month (30 days), and a year (365 days).

 ▸ Example 2: Using the elevator for three floors (1 calorie) to walking up three flights of stairs (15 calories). Have students calculate what effect that substitution would have if they did it for a week (7 days), a month (30 days), and a year (365 days).

 ▸ Discuss the long-term effects of that change on weight, healthy fitness zone, and so on. To determine weight loss from changing activities, have them divide the total calories by 3,500 calories burned to lose 1 pound (.45 kilograms).

Part 4: Lesson Focus 2

Safety

1. Have students read the opening section of "Moving Together: Safe Physical Activity" in the student textbook (chapter 3, page 30).

2. Tell the students to look over the discussion questions briefly, and then to read the "Guidelines for Safe Participation." Students should use the guidelines to come up with answers to the discussion questions.

3. Pose the discussion questions to the class.

4. Have students write down on a sticky note any of the guidelines they have followed in the last 48 hours (e.g., wearing a bike helmet, putting on sunscreen, or drinking water). Group the class responses on the chalkboard, flip chart, or wall.

5. Discuss which of the guidelines appear and which are missing from the class behaviors.

6. Discuss how to increase the use of the missing behaviors.

Part 5: Reflection and Summary

1. Ask students to provide a compliment to their partners regarding working together.

2. Ask students to identify the major safety guidelines.

3. Have students add completed worksheets 2.5, "Footbagging With the Family," and 3.1a, "Activitygram," to their *Fitness for Life: Middle School* portfolios.

Take It Home

 ▸ Hand out worksheet 3.1b, "Making Changes," to each student. This worksheet requires students to choose a member of their home team and set a goal for changing a behavior. Discuss the safety and lifestyle physical activity choices that they might consider.

 ▸ Tell students when to return the completed worksheet to class. (Recommended: lesson 5.1. In lesson 4.1, you can remind students of the due date for the worksheet.)

Next Time

Safety scavenger hunt

Assessment

▶ Assess completed worksheets 2.5, "Footbagging With the Family," and 3.1a, "Activitygram," in students' *Fitness for Life: Middle School* portfolios. Use the worksheet rubric (available on the CD-ROM or on page 34) to assess student work, or modify the rubric to meet your specific objectives.

▶ Comprehension check: Use class discussions as a check for student understanding of lifestyle physical activity, benefits of lifestyle activities, and appropriate safety practices related to physical activity.

▶ Comprehension check: When assessing the students' completed worksheet 3.1a, "Activitygram," check the second page of the worksheet to make sure they understand the FIT formula for lifestyle physical activity.

Lesson Plan **3.2** Safety in Physical Activity

In this activity lesson, students will engage in a scavenger hunt collecting appropriate safety practices for various activities.

Performance Outcomes Related to NASPE Standards

▶ Standard 2
   ▹ Identify proper warm-up and cool-down techniques and reasons for using them.
▶ Standard 5
   ▹ Move from identifying and following rules and safe practices to reflecting on their role in physical activity settings.
   ▹ Exhibit (verbally and nonverbally) cooperation, respect, encouragement, and the ability to work independently.

Lesson Objectives

▶ Students will identify appropriate safety practices related to physical activity.
▶ Students will be active at a moderate to vigorous level for at least 50 percent of class time.
▶ Students will actively listen to others, encourage others (i.e., use positive feedback), participate, and refrain from interrupting others in small-group settings.

Equipment

▶ 1 large cone per group of three students
▶ 10 polyspots (7 for the safety practices cards, 3 for jokes)
▶ 1 pedometer for each student (if available)
▶ 1 piece of paper and 1 pencil for each group (if using pedometers)
▶ CD player and upbeat music (the Beach Boys' "Surfin' USA" would be appropriate)

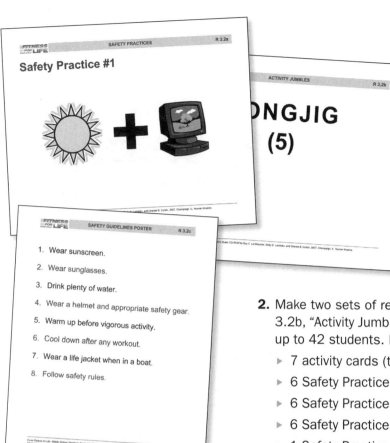

Reproducibles

▶ Resource 3.2a, "Safety Practices"

▶ Resource 3.2b, "Activity Jumbles"

▶ Resource 3.2c, "Safety Guidelines Poster"

Setup

1. Place the large cones in a circle around the edges of the playing area. Place the poly spots randomly on the floor in the middle of the playing area.

2. Make two sets of resource 3.2a, "Safety Practices," and resource 3.2b, "Activity Jumbles." Two sets will provide enough materials for up to 42 students. Each set should consist of the following:

   ▶ 7 activity cards (the scrambled activity names)
   ▶ 6 Safety Practices: Sunscreen cards
   ▶ 6 Safety Practices: Sunglasses cards
   ▶ 6 Safety Practices: Water cards
   ▶ 1 Safety Practices: Helmet card
   ▶ 5 Safety Practices: Warm-up cards
   ▶ 5 Safety Practices: Cool-down cards
   ▶ 1 Safety Practices: Life jacket card

3. Make up at least three joke cards, and mix them in with the Safety Practices cards for fun.

4. Put a stack of Safety Practices cards facedown on each polyspot. (Optional: Wait until after the warm-up so the cards don't get kicked around the gym.) You can place the cards in two different ways:

   ▶ Easy: Put the same set of cards on each polyspot. Groups will learn from watching each other find the cards.

   ▶ Difficult: Shuffle the cards so that each polyspot has a different set.

5. Hang resource 3.2c, "Safety Guidelines Poster," as an aid to be used during class. (Optional: Wait until the end of the lesson and show it as a review.)

Delivering the Lesson

Part 1: Instant Activity

Team Follow-the-Leader

1. Organize students into groups of six, using one of the methods in "Groups and Teams" (see pages 26 to 27). Have each group line up. Explain that all groups will walk around the gym in a line, following the path of the leader—the first student in the line.

2. Instruct leaders to move at a pace that is appropriate for the whole group.

3. Each time the signal sounds, the leader steps aside and the line moves past with a new leader. The former leader goes to the end of the line. Each time there's a new leader, call out a new, progressively more active locomotor skill (for example, power walk, skip, gallop, change lead foot, slide, change lead side, or jog).

↺ review

1. Expectations

   ✴ Stop on signal (music stops, whistle, bell)

   ✴ Importance of good body control; goal is to develop body control so you can move easily and efficiently; takes practice

   ✴ Safety (always looking out for each other and own safety)

   ✴ Class agreements (support each other, partners with everyone at some point, no verbal or body language put-downs)

2. Establish a boundary (for example, black line around basketball court, cones in large rectangle).

3. Talk about the importance of warming up before beginning an activity and the characteristics of a good warm-up.

   ✴ Gradual

   ✴ Long enough to warm muscles

   ✴ Done in group that includes everyone at appropriate levels

Part 2: Lesson Launcher

1. Review the lesson objectives with students.

2. Tell the class they will have great adventures today. Because safety is the topic of the day, they will need to determine the appropriate safety guidelines for their own activity.

Part 3: Lesson Focus

Safety Scavenger Hunt

The goal is to accumulate steps and for each group to collect all the "Safety Practices" cards that are appropriate for the activity on their "Activity Jumbles" card. However, the name of the activity is scrambled on each "Activity Jumbles" card, so each group must first unscramble the letters. Each "Activity Jumbles" card also has a number that indicates how many different "Safety Practices" are related to that activity.

This activity is great to do with pedometers as indicated below. If you don't have access to pedometers, simply start on step 3 and ignore the direction to have students subtract steps from their step count in step 8.

1. Explain what a pedometer is and how it works.

   ▸ A pedometer is a machine that counts steps and so gives a measure of activity.

   ▸ Students should wear it on their waistband (and attach the safety strap so it doesn't get lost).

   ▸ Many pedometers have a cover that covers the numbers. You open it to read the numbers, but must close it to have it count. Tell the students the pedometer only counts when the pedometer cover is in the closed position.

   ▸ Shaking a pedometer causes problems ("If you shake it, I'll take it").

▸ Explain that some research has indicated that people have fewer health problems when they are active enough to get 10,000 to 12,000 steps a day.

2. Have students try out the pedometers. They should take 10 steps, check the pedometer; then take 100 steps and check it again. If it is within 10 percent on either side, consider it OK. If not, have the student move it on the waistband (farther to the side or farther toward the belly button) to get a better registering of steps.

3. Split each group in half to form new groups of three students each. Have each group gather by a cone.

 observe

> Scan the class for positive body language and greetings when groups are getting together. Watch for careful handling of pedometers.

4. Show a stack of "Activity Jumbles" cards to the class. Have one person in each group (for example, the student with the most holes for laces in his or her shoes) choose one "Activity Jumbles" card for their group. Tell the group to unscramble the letters to determine the activity.

5. If you are using pedometers, have another person in the group get a pencil and paper for the group.

6. When the music starts, one student from each group walks or jogs to a polyspot, chooses a "Safety Practices" card, and tries to decipher the puzzle to determine whether the practice on the card relates to the group's activity. If it does, the student returns with the card to the group's home base. If it doesn't, the student leaves the card on the polyspot and travels to another, looking for an appropriate card. In the meantime, the other two students in the group must jog in place, do jumping jacks, do half squats, or otherwise move to collect steps on their pedometers.

 check

> Ask the students how many people from each group go out looking at one time. (Answer: one.) How many students jog or step in place? (Answer: two.) Ask them to point to where they would put a card that didn't go with their activity. (Answer: back on the polyspot where they found it.)

7. When the first student returns with a card that matches the group's activity, another student goes out to find another appropriate "Safety Practices" card. The "Activity Jumbles" card indicates how many "Safety Practices" cards must be collected. Once the group has found all the "Safety Practices" cards, the group sits down at its home base. (Optional: Have groups that finish do push-ups and curl-ups until the other groups finish as well.)

8. After 12 minutes, stop the music or blow a whistle. Have each team record their total steps on the paper and subtract 100 steps for each "Safety Practices" card that was not found. Have them subtract 50 steps for any "Safety Practices" puzzle that they couldn't decipher.

 observe

> Scan for students encouraging each other in their group to keep moving. Listen for praise behaviors when safety practices are decoded.

9. Have each team pair up with another team and walk around the boundary to cool down while describing their activities and the "Safety Practices" cards they collected.

Part 4: Reflection and Summary

1. Compliment students on working together to decipher the "Safety Practices" puzzles. Have them check their work against the "Safety Guidelines Poster" to make sure they have deciphered the clues correctly.

2. Ask if there are any additional safety practices they think are important in these activities.

3. Explain to students that there are two ways to give compliments—verbally and in writing. Introduce a box you call the "compliment box." If they don't want to give compliments directly, they can write them on index cards (either signed or anonymous) and put them in the box. Explain that you will deliver the compliments quietly. Explain that you will know they really understand the importance of valuing each other when they begin to be able to express it either through writing cards or giving verbal encouragement or compliments.

4. Ask students to share their thoughts on the following:

   ▹ What were the easiest safety practices to decipher?

   ▹ Which are the easiest to follow? Which safety practices do they do on a regular basis?

   ▹ Based on their work today, how well did their groups follow the class guidelines for how to treat each other? Refer to the class poster listing agreements made at the beginning of the semester. Do they have compliments for anyone in their group?

5. Have the students return all the cards by stacking the "Activity Jumbles" cards in one pile and the "Safety Practices" cards in another pile.

Take It Home

Encourage students to use safety practices with their family or friends.

Next Time

Lifestyle physical activities and friction

Assessment

▸ Performance check: Observe students participating in moderate to vigorous level of activity for at least 50 percent of class time.

▸ Performance check: Observe that students are working effectively in groups (by listening to each other, encouraging each other with using positive feedback, and refraining from interrupting others in small-group settings).

▸ Comprehension check: Responses to the Reflection and Summary questions serve as a check for student understanding of appropriate safety practices related to physical activity.

Lesson Plan 3.3 Benefits of Lifestyle Physical Activity and the Effects of Friction

In this classroom lesson, students will act out lifestyle physical activity scenes in which increasing and decreasing friction plays an important role.

Performance Outcomes Related to NASPE Standards

▶ Standard 2
  ▶ Understand and apply movement concepts (friction).
  ▶ Perform an activity and explain the significance of increasing or decreasing friction in that activity.
▶ Standard 5
  ▶ Exhibit (verbally and nonverbally) cooperation, respect, encouragement, and the ability to work independently.

Lesson Objectives

▶ Students will describe how lifestyle physical activity improves health and wellness.
▶ Students will describe the relationship between lifestyle physical activity and physical fitness.
▶ Students will describe times when more friction is needed and times when less friction is needed in movement activities.

Equipment

▶ 1 *Fitness for Life: Middle School* student textbook per student
▶ Chalkboard or flip chart
▶ Movie scene clap board (optional)

 tech

Two computer presentation programs (Mount Fitness and Tour de Fitness) are available for reviewing and reinforcing concepts. See page 40 for more information.

Reproducibles

- ▶ Resource 3.3a, "Movie Set Roles"
- ▶ Resource 3.3b, "Friction Scenes"
- ▶ Worksheet 3.3, "Friction in Physical Activity"
- ▶ Classroom Quotes

Classroom Quotes

You can print these quotes from the CD-ROM and hang them around your room.

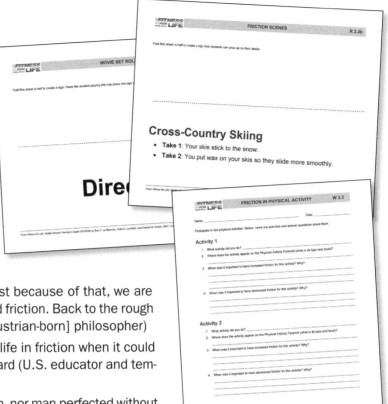

- ▶ "We have got onto slippery ice where there is no friction and so in a certain sense the conditions are ideal, but also, just because of that, we are unable to walk. We want to walk so we need friction. Back to the rough ground!"—Ludwig Wittgenstein (British [Austrian-born] philosopher)
- ▶ "The world is wide, and I will not waste my life in friction when it could be turned into momentum."—Frances Willard (U.S. educator and temperance activist)
- ▶ "The gem cannot be polished without friction, nor man perfected without trials."—Chinese proverb

Setup

1. Read through the "Friction Scenes" cards. If you wish, write notes or tips on each card to help students who might get stuck coming up with appropriate scenes.

2. Make copies of resource 3.3a, the "Movie Set Roles" cards (one set per group), resource 3.3b, the "Friction Scenes" cards (one set per group), and worksheet 3.3, "Friction in Physical Activity" (one per student).

Delivering the Lesson

Part 1: Gathering Information

1. Ask students how the things they do as part of their everyday lives improve their health and wellness. What systems of their body are affected? Does walking up the stairs improve their fitness?

2. Have the students read "Benefits of Lifestyle Physical Activities," lesson 3.2 in the student textbook (chapter 3, pages 32 to 35), to answer the questions you just asked. Tell them that after the reading, you'll be discussing the benefits of lifestyle physical activity.

3. When they finish reading the lesson, lead a five-minute discussion about the benefits.

Part 2: Lesson Launcher

1. Review the lesson objectives with students.

2. Ask if anyone in the class can explain the concept of friction. (Answer: Friction is a force that occurs when two surfaces rub against each other.) In everyday life, having more friction or less friction can help you perform many different activities.

3. Have students read "Biomechanical Principles: Friction" (chapter 3 of the student textbook, pages 33 to 34).

4. Discuss what types of physical activities need additional friction and what types need less.

 tech

Find and show video clips that show friction in different activities (some that would benefit from decreased friction, and some that would benefit from increased friction).

Part 3: Lesson Focus

Friction and Physical Activity

 review

Remind students of the class agreements for working in groups (for example, include everyone, listen to the person who's talking, give helpful feedback to improve performance, and participate and contribute).

1. Arrange the students into groups of four or five using one of the methods described in "Groups and Teams" (see pages 26 to 27). Make sure that students know the names of everyone in their group.

2. Explain that each group will act out a situation in which increasing friction is important.

3. Give each group one set of "Movie Set Roles," which indicate the roles to be filled. Each student chooses one of the following cards:

   ▶ *Director:* This student's role is to suggest how to stage the acting and to give feedback on the performance to make it better.

   ▶ *Performer 1:* This student's role is to act out a friction problem, without words.

   ▶ *Performer 2:* This student's role is to act out a solution to the problem, without words.

   ▶ *Narrator:* This student's role is to explain the scene to the audience.

   ▶ *Clapper:* This student's role is to use the clap board (or his or her hands, if no clap board is available) to start each performance and call out the number of the scene ("Take one!").

4. Give each group one "Friction Scenes" card. Explain that they will create a scene in which someone has a problem with friction. Point out that on a movie set, the cast and crew usually try each scene several times to get it right, so it's OK for the student groups to do the same.

5. Demonstrate the procedure to the class using the following scenario:

   ▶ Start by announcing the scene: "Take one—too much friction!" Clap your hands or the clap board. Mime having a hard time pushing a heavy box. At the end, yell "Cut!"

▶ Announce the scene: "Take two—solution to the problem!" Clap your hands or the clap board. Mime lifting up the edge of the box, sliding a piece of carpet underneath, and pushing the box more easily along the ground. (You can ask a student to be the narrator and describe what's happening to the class.)

 check

Make sure that all students know their roles. Ask directors to raise their hands, ask actors to high-five each other, ask narrators to stand up, and ask clappers to clap.

6. Allow students time to create their scenes and share them with the class. Sample scene:

▶ The narrator begins by telling the class, "We'll act out a person trying to walk on ice."

▶ During the first take, performer 1 acts out the problem. The narrator describes the scene to the class: "There's not enough friction on the ice, so the feet slip. Do we want to increase or decrease friction in this scene? Give me a thumbs-up for increase, or a thumbs-down for decrease."

▶ During the second take, performer 2 acts out a solution. The narrator describes the scene: "By putting on boots that have good treads, we increase friction between our shoes and the ice, so it's easier to walk without falling."

 observe

Scan for examples of groups working well together, students listening to each other and offering suggestions, directors suggesting improvements, and students trying those suggestions.

Part 4: Reflection and Summary

1. Compliment students and groups who were listening to each other, working together, and solving problems.

2. Ask students the following questions:

▶ Can you think of other lifestyle physical activities that are affected by friction?

▶ Do you want to increase or decrease friction during these activities? Show a thumbs-up for increasing friction, and a thumbs-down for decreasing friction.

Take It Home

▶ Hand out worksheet 3.3, "Friction in Physical Activity." At home, each student will participate in two physical activities. On the worksheet, they'll describe the activities, show where they fit in the Physical Activity Pyramid, and describe how increasing and decreasing friction affects each activity.

▶ Tell students when to return the completed worksheet to class. (Recommended: lesson 3.5.)

Next Time

Friction-related activities

Assessment

▶ Comprehension check: Student discussion can serve as a check for student understanding of how lifestyle physical activity improves health and wellness, and the relationship between lifestyle physical activity and physical fitness.

▶ Performance check: Student actions and responses to friction scenes will describe times when more friction is needed and times when less friction is needed in movement activities.

3.4 Exploring Friction in Physical Activity

In this activity lesson, students will experience the effects of increasing and reducing friction on pulling and pushing activities.

Performance Outcomes Related to NASPE Standards

▶ Standard 2
  ▶ Understand and apply movement concepts (friction).
  ▶ Perform an activity and explain the significance of increasing or decreasing friction in that activity.
▶ Standard 3
  ▶ Participate in health-enhancing physical activities both during and outside of school.
▶ Standard 5
  ▶ Move from identifying and following rules and safe practices to reflecting on their role in physical activity settings.
  ▶ Remain on task in a group activity without close teacher monitoring.
  ▶ Through verbal and nonverbal behavior demonstrate cooperation with peers who have different characteristics (e.g., gender, race, ethnicity, ability).
  ▶ Assist and encourage group members by sharing positive feedback about skill performance during practice.

Lesson Objectives

▶ Students will experience changes in friction.
▶ Students will discover and apply ways to increase and decrease friction.

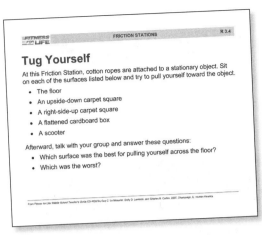

Within the image:

Tug Yourself

At this Friction Station, cotton ropes are attached to a stationary object. Sit on each of the surfaces listed below and try to pull yourself toward the object.

- The floor
- An upside-down carpet square
- A right-side-up carpet square
- A flattened cardboard box
- A scooter

Afterward, talk with your group and answer these questions:

- Which surface was the best for pulling yourself across the floor?
- Which was the worst?

Equipment

▶ 6 cotton ropes, 3/4 inch (1.9 centimeters) wide and 12 feet (3.6 meters) long

▶ 2 old, slippery basketballs that are hard to grip

▶ 2 new basketballs that are easy to grip

▶ 2 speed ropes

▶ 1 box of wet wipes

▶ 1 bottle of liquid dish detergent

▶ 4 carpet squares

▶ 4 to 8 shoe boxes

▶ 1 roll of duct tape

▶ 1 smooth, rubber soccer ball

▶ Paper plates

▶ Flattened cardboard box

▶ 1 scooter

Reproducibles

Resource 3.4, "Friction Stations"

Setup

Print out one set of the "Friction Stations" cards, and set up the four stations described on the cards. Alternate these with two to four active sports and recreation stations, such as dribbling, four square, dancing, or practicing an appropriate skill. In all, you should set up six to eight different stations.

Delivering the Lesson

Part 1: Instant Activity

Team Follow-the-Leader

1. Organize students into groups of six, using one of the methods described in "Groups and Teams" (see pages 26 to 27).

2. Have a short get-to-know-each-other time. For example, ask students to learn the names of everyone in their group and the names of their pets (if any).

3. Have each group line up. Explain that all groups will walk around the gym in a line, following the path of the leader—the first student in the line. Instruct leaders to move at a pace that is appropriate for the whole group.

4. Each time the signal sounds, the leader steps aside and the line moves past with a new leader. The former leader goes to the end of the line. Each time there's a new leader, call out a new, progressively more active locomotor skill (for example, power walk, skip, gallop, change lead foot, slide, change lead side, or jog).

1. Expectations
   * Stop on signal (music stops, whistle, bell)
   * Importance of good body control; goal is to develop body control so you can move easily and efficiently; takes practice
   * Safety (always looking out for each other and own safety)
   * Class agreements (support each other, partners with everyone at some point, no verbal or body language put-downs)

2. Establish a boundary (for example, black line around basketball court, cones in large rectangle).

3. Talk about the importance of warming up before beginning an activity and the characteristics of a good warm-up.
   * Gradual
   * Long enough to warm muscles
   * Done in group that includes everyone at appropriate levels

Part 2: Lesson Launcher

1. Review the lesson objectives with students.

2. Remind the students that in the previous lesson, they acted out situations in which increasing or decreasing friction helped them do an activity.

3. Explain that today, they'll experience the effects of friction by trying activities at different stations. At each station, they should consider whether increasing or decreasing friction might help them with the activity.

Part 3: Lesson Focus

Friction in Everyday Tasks

1. Using one of the methods described in "Groups and Teams" (see pages 26 to 27), rearrange the groups to create new groups with three to four students each.

Discuss how to make sure that all students have turns at each station. Give examples of encouraging remarks (such as "I went first last time; why don't you go first this time?"). Remind groups of the class goal to work independently without close teacher monitoring. Ask students to describe what great work would look like during today's activity. (Possible answers: reading instructions, sharing roles, respecting others, and using only kind words and body language.)

2. Start one group at each station. Students at the friction stations should try the activities at their station and consider factors that increase and decrease friction.

3. At your signal, all students leave their stations, jog once around the area in a clockwise direction, and go to a new station.

check

   * Have students point to the stations where their groups will start.
   * Have them point in the direction in which they will jog between stations.

Part 4: Reflection and Summary

1. Compliment students and groups for taking turns, working with each other, encouraging each other, and giving their full effort.

2. Ask students the following review questions:
   - Did friction make a difference in doing the activities?
   - Why do you think people wear special shoes for rock climbing? Why do they use resin on their hands? Why might belayers wear gloves?
   - Why do ice skaters and hockey players sharpen their skates?
   - Why do triathletes wear body suits when swimming?
   - What safety equipment uses friction to make participants safer? (Possible answers: a rope around your waist when belaying while rock climbing, boots on your feet in winter, and resin on your hands for a good grip.)

Take It Home

Encourage students to look for situations at home (e.g., opening slippery jar lids) where increasing or decreasing friction is helpful.

Next Time

- Lifestyle (moderate) physical activities.
- Remind students that worksheet 3.3, "Friction in Physical Activity," is due next class (recommended).

Assessment

- Performance check: Observe students participating in the activities and experiencing changes in friction.
- Performance check: Observe students discovering and applying ways to increase and decrease friction.

Lesson Plan **3.5** **Lifestyle Physical Activity**

In this activity lesson, students will get to know others in class by walking with partners and choosing moderate physical activities.

Performance Outcomes Related to NASPE Standards

▶ Standard 2
  ▶ Identify health-related fitness components required for walking.

▶ Standard 5
  ▶ Remain on task in group activity without close teacher monitoring.
  ▶ Through verbal and nonverbal behavior, demonstrate cooperation with peers who have different characteristics (such as gender, race, ethnicity, or ability).

▶ Standard 6
  ▶ Identify the potential social and health benefits of walking.
  ▶ Seek personally challenging physical activity experiences.

Lesson Objectives

▶ Students will be active more than 50 percent of class time.
▶ Students will identify the health- and skill-related fitness components required for walking.
▶ Students will identify and follow all appropriate safety guidelines.

Equipment

▶ 8 to 10 cones to mark a walking course and stations
▶ 3 soccer balls
▶ 8 cones to mark goals in small fields
▶ Scrimmage vests (pinnies) for a quarter of the class
▶ 6 jump ropes
▶ 3 footballs

▶ 2 four square balls and courts

▶ CD player with upbeat music

 tech

1 pedometer per student

Reproducibles

None

Setup

1. Set out the cones to make a walking track, or use a regular track if one is available.

2. Set up the small side fields and other activities close enough together to be easy to monitor but far enough apart to be safe. Place one large cone by the four square station and another by the jump rope station to identify them.

3. If you don't have four square courts, you can make portable courts by using blue tarps that are 12 feet by 12 feet (3.6 meters by 3.6 meters). Divide each tarp into four squares with lines of masking tape. Place the tarps on blacktop or a tennis court or sidewalk.

4. If you will be using pedometers, assign each one a number and the name of a student. Print the list so that each student can see which pedometer he or she should take.

Delivering the Lesson

Part 1: Instant Activity

Walking Freeze Tag

1. Designate one-fourth of the students in the class as "It." Students who are "It" should wear pinnies.

2. Students who are "It" try to tag other students. The goal is to get everyone frozen. Those who get tagged are frozen in place until someone who is free stands in front of them and they do five jumping jacks together. Students can't be tagged while doing jumping jacks. Remind everyone to walk—no running.

3. After one minute, let other students have a turn being "It" until everyone in class has been "It."

Part 2: Lesson Launcher

1. Review the lesson objectives with students.

2. Explain to students that walking is a great activity because it can be done anywhere, it can help them get places, and it allows them to enjoy the scenery on the way.

3. Explain that students will take a walk during the first half of the class. Students will find a partner who they think walks at about the same pace that they walk. Everyone will have a chance to pair up with several different partners.

4. Explain that during the second half of class, students will choose between continuous walking and playing a small-sided game.

Part 3: Lesson Focus 1

Walk and Talk

1. Give students 15 seconds to find someone who walks at the same pace that they walk (someone who seems to have legs of the same length).

 review

> Remind students of the class agreements about treating one another well. Tell them they'll change partners often and have many chances to practice those agreements. At the end of the class, all students should feel that they had good partners.

2. If you have pedometers, hand them out; otherwise, skip to step 3. Remind students how to use the pedometers and restate the rule against shaking them. ("If you shake it, I'll take it.")

3. Partners will walk the course you have designed. Let students know that it's OK to pass other walkers, but they must greet anyone they pass and wish him or her a good day. While walking with their partners, students must find out the following:

- A lifestyle physical activity the partner does at home
- One active sport or recreation the partner likes
- One thing the two of them have in common

4. After about two minutes, give the signal to change partners. All students stop walking and say good-bye to their current partners. Then each partner on the right moves up one pair so that all students now have new partners.

5. After two more minutes, give the signal to change partners again.

6. After two more minutes (a total walking time of six minutes), have students check the number of steps they have taken. Explain that if they know their step length and the number of feet per mile, they can determine how far and how fast they walked.

 observe

> Check students' body language and comments as they change partners. Check their effort and their on-task behavior.

Part 4: Lesson Focus 2

Activity Choices

1. Students can continue to walk in partners or play small-sided activities, such as the following:

- Soccer: 3-on-3 or 5-on-5
- Jump rope (short or long)
- Football patterns: 3-on-3 (quarterback and receiver against defenders; must get 10 yards in three plays). Players should change positions every three plays so everyone plays quarterback.
- Four square

2. Remind the students that the goals of these activities are to be active and support each other. Ask students for examples of how to do this in these activities.

3. Class cool-down: Have students walk twice around the activity area.

 observe

> Scan for students inviting each other to play, taking turns, making positive and supportive comments, and so on.

Part 5: Reflection and Summary

1. Compliment students on their treatment of partners, being on task, and their activity choices.

2. Ask students the following questions:

> ▸ What did your partner share as a lifestyle physical activity? As an active sport or recreation activity?

> ▸ What did you and your partner find that you had in common?

3. Have students add completed worksheet 3.3, "Friction in Physical Activity," to their *Fitness for Life: Middle School* portfolio.

Take It Home

Ask students to choose a place in their neighborhood that they could walk to within 10 or 20 minutes. Students should invite someone from their "support team" to accompany them on that walk at least once during the week.

Next Time

Active aerobics

Assessment

▸ Performance check: Observe students participating in activity more than 50 percent of class time, working effectively in groups, and following all appropriate safety guidelines.

▸ Comprehension check: Responses to the Reflection and Summary questions serve as a check for student understanding of health- and skill-related fitness components required for walking.

▸ Assess completed worksheet 3.3, "Friction in Physical Activity," in students' *Fitness for Life: Middle School* portfolios. Use the worksheet rubric (available on the CD-ROM or on page 34) to assess student work, or modify the rubric to meet your specific objectives.

Supplemental Materials

If you choose to use the semester or year scheduling version of *Fitness for Life: Middle School* (see appendix B), there are excellent opportunities to insert activity-based skill units and to review and reinforce the concepts in each chapter using the *Fitness for Life: Middle School* computer programs: Mount Fitness and Tour de Fitness. You will find information about the two computer programs in appendix C. Listed below are suggestions of activity-based skill units that would go well with this chapter and resources that will help you develop great lessons.

As indicated in the "Scheduling" section (pages 13 to 18), integrating activity-based skill units with the *Fitness for Life: Middle School* lesson plans provides a great opportunity for reinforcing key concepts and for developing students' skills in a wide range of physical activities. The activity-based skill unit suggestions provided below were chosen specifically to complement chapter content. In addition, there are selected resources that can provide you with excellent lesson plans and lesson plan ideas. Approaches to teaching activity-based skill units can be found in appendix A.

SOFTBALL, WIFFLEBALL, OR TENNIS

▸ **Key concepts to reinforce:** Safety, warm-ups and cool-downs, friction, rules, changing physical activity behavior

▸ **Resources:**
  ▸ *Teaching Sport Concepts and Skills: A Tactical Games Approach* (Mitchell, Olsen, and Griffin, 2006, Human Kinetics)
  ▸ *Complete Guide to Sport Education Model* (Siedentop, Hastie, and van der Mars, 2004, Human Kinetics)
  ▸ *Quality Lesson Plans for Secondary Physical Education* (Zakrajsek, Carnes, and Pettigrew, 2003, Human Kinetics)

GOLF

▸ **Key concepts to reinforce:** Safety, warm-ups and cool-downs, friction, rules, changing physical activity behavior

▸ **Resources:**
  ▸ *Teaching Sport Concepts and Skills: A Tactical Games Approach* (Mitchell, Olsen, and Griffin, 2006, Human Kinetics)
  ▸ *It's Not Just Gym Anymore: Teaching Secondary School Students How to Be Active for Life* (McCracken, 2001, Human Kinetics)
  ▸ *Quality Lesson Plans for Secondary Physical Education* (Zakrajsek, Carnes, and Pettigrew, 2003, Human Kinetics)
  ▸ *Complete Physical Education Plans for Grades 7-12* (Kleinman, 2001, Human Kinetics)

BOWLING

▸ **Key concepts to reinforce:** Safety, warm-ups and cool-downs, friction, rules, changing physical activity behavior

▸ **Resources:**
  ▸ *Teaching Sport Concepts and Skills: A Tactical Games Approach* (Mitchell, Olsen, and Griffin, 2006, Human Kinetics)
  ▸ *Quality Lesson Plans for Secondary Physical Education* (Zakrajsek, Carnes, and Pettigrew, 2003, Human Kinetics)

DANCING (LINE, COUNTRY, FOLK, OR SOCIAL)

▶ **Key concepts to reinforce:** Safety, warm-ups and cool-downs, friction, rules, changing physical activity behavior

▶ **Resources:**
- ▶ *Quality Lesson Plans for Secondary Physical Education* (Zakrajsek, Carnes, and Pettigrew, 2003, Human Kinetics)
- ▶ *Complete Physical Education Plans for Grades 7-12* (Kleinman, 2001, Human Kinetics)

BIKING OR MOUNTAIN BIKING

▶ **Key concepts to reinforce:** Safety, warm-ups and cool-downs, friction, rules, changing physical activity behavior

▶ **Resources:**
- ▶ *It's Not Just Gym Anymore: Teaching Secondary School Students How to Be Active for Life* (McCracken, 2001, Human Kinetics)
- ▶ www.bicyclinginfo.org/ee/ed_young.cfm

CRICKET

▶ **Key concepts to reinforce:** Safety, warm-ups and cool-downs, friction, rules, changing physical activity behavior

▶ **Resources:** *Teaching Sport Concepts and Skills: A Tactical Games Approach* (Mitchell, Olsen, and Griffin, 2006, Human Kinetics)

GARDENING

▶ **Key concepts to reinforce:** Safety, warm-ups and cool-downs, friction, rules, changing physical activity behavior

▶ **Resources:**
- ▶ Garden classes teach the principles of ecology (www.edibleschoolyard.org/cla_eco.html), the origins of food, and respect for all living systems. Students work together to shape and plant beds; amend soil; turn compost; and harvest flowers, fruits, and vegetables.
- ▶ www.edibleschoolyard.org/homepage.html

ARCHERY

▶ **Key concepts to reinforce:** Safety, warm-ups and cool-downs, friction, rules, changing physical activity behavior

▶ **Resources:** *It's Not Just Gym Anymore: Teaching Secondary School Students How to Be Active for Life* (McCracken, 2001, Human Kinetics)

FLY FISHING

▶ **Key concepts to reinforce:** Safety, warm-ups and cool-downs, friction, rules, changing physical activity behavior

▶ **Resources:** *It's Not Just Gym Anymore: Teaching Secondary School Students How to Be Active for Life* (McCracken, 2001, Human Kinetics)

WALKING (WITH PEDOMETERS)

▶ **Key concepts to reinforce:** Safety, warm-ups and cool-downs, friction, rules, changing physical activity behavior

▶ **Resources:** *Pedometer Power* (Pangrazi, Beighle, and Sidman, 2003, Human Kinetics)

Active Aerobics

Chapter 4 lesson plans engage students in active aerobic activities, self-assessments of cardiovascular fitness, and discussions about building confidence in physical activities. In addition to the physiological concepts of heart rate and target zone, students are required to reflect on their psychological responses to physical activity. Chapter 4 is a great opportunity to use heart rate monitors in physical education.

* **4.1 Active Aerobics: Level 2 of the Physical Activity Pyramid** (classroom lesson)
* **4.2 Active Aerobics Circuit** (activity lesson)
* **4.3 Benefits of Active Aerobics** (classroom lesson)
* **4.4 Fitnessgram PACER** (activity lesson)
* **4.5 Active Aerobics Choices** (activity lesson)

Active Aerobics: Level 2 of the Physical Activity Pyramid

This classroom lesson teaches students the meaning of active aerobics and how much activity is needed to improve cardiovascular fitness. Self-esteem is discussed, and students are encouraged to tune in to their bodies and their experiences.

Performance Outcomes Related to NASPE Standards

▶ Standard 4

   ▶ Explain the significance of target heart rate and aerobic activity to develop cardiorespiratory endurance.

▶ Standard 5

   ▶ Exhibit (verbally and nonverbally) cooperation, respect, encouragement, and ability to work independently.

▶ Standard 6

   ▶ Identify personally enjoyable physical activity experiences.

Lesson Objectives

▶ Students will give examples of active aerobic activities and identify the FIT formula for active aerobics.

▶ Students will learn some guidelines for increasing self-esteem.

▶ Students will identify ways to tune in to their bodies and surroundings.

Equipment

▶ 1 *Fitness for Life: Middle School* student textbook per student

▶ Chalkboard or flip chart (optional)

▶ 2 sticky notes per student (in two colors)

 tech

Find and show video clips of active aerobic activities (such as aerobic dancing, in-line skating, and so on).

Reproducibles

▶ Worksheet 4.1, "Tuning In"
▶ Classroom Quotes

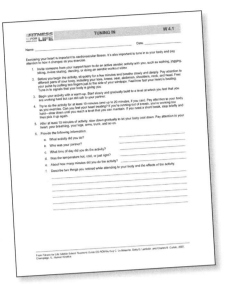

Classroom Quotes

You can print these quotes from the CD-ROM and hang them around your room.

▶ "Every day brings a chance for you to draw in a breath, kick off your shoes and dance."—Oprah Winfrey (TV personality)

▶ "Listen and attend with the ear of your heart."—Saint Benedict

▶ "Self-esteem is the reputation we acquire with ourselves."—Nathaniel Branden (psychologist)

Setup

1. Write the FIT formula for active aerobics on a blackboard or chart.
2. Make a copy of worksheet 4.1, "Tuning In," for each student.

Delivering the Lesson

Part 1: Gathering Information

1. Ask students if they ever actually feel their heart beating. What are some activities that increase their heart rate and make them breathe more deeply? Explain that to strengthen our hearts, we need to find those activities and do them on a regular basis. Do they know how often?

2. Have the students read "Active Aerobics: Level 2 of the Physical Activity Pyramid," lesson 4.1 in the student textbook (chapter 4, pages 39 to 45), to prepare for discussion.

Part 2: Lesson Launcher

1. Review the lesson objectives with students.

2. Have students read the opening section of "Moving Together: Building Self-Esteem" in the student textbook (chapter 4, page 42).

3. Tell the students to look over the discussion questions briefly, and then to read the "Guidelines for Improving Your Self-Esteem." Students should use the guidelines to come up with answers to the discussion questions.

4. Pose the discussion questions to the class.

 review

Review the importance of practice in building skills and confidence. Explain the importance of leaders involving others in decision making and providing positive feedback in encouraging full participation.

Part 3: Lesson Focus

Active Aerobics

1. Review the criteria for activities to be included in active aerobics.

2. Provide each student with two sticky notes of different colors.

3. On the darker sticky note, students should write the name of an active aerobic activity that they like or do a lot. On the other sticky note, they should write the name of an active aerobic activity that they would like to learn about or try.

(?) check

> Ask the students to list the characteristics of active aerobics. They should make sure that the activity they suggest gets their heart rate up so that they're working hard but still can talk easily. The activity should not be a sport (active sports are covered in the lesson plans in chapter 5).

4. Have the students place their sticky notes on the wall. While the class is discussing the FIT formula for aerobic activity, have two or three students cluster the sticky notes into groups and give each group a name. If several notes list the same activity, the students can make a histogram of those notes (placing one above the other in a column on the wall) so the class can see which activities are the most popular.

5. Identify from the groupings one or two activities to include in the next lessons.

6. Ask students to discuss how their body would feel if they were being active at the right level for active aerobics. How would it change if they were not being active enough? How would it change if they were working too hard?

7. Lead some deep breathing exercises—slowly breathe in to a count of 2, hold to a count of 2, breathe out to a count of 2, and hold to a count of 2. Have students do this 10 times while focusing on feeling the air coming in and going out of their lungs. Tell them that if their mind starts to wander, bring it back gently to feeling their breathing.

Part 4: Reflection and Summary

1. Compliment students on putting appropriate activities on sticky notes and on specific helpful behaviors during class.

2. Review the importance of keeping their heart rate at a level at which they're working hard but still can talk to a friend during active aerobics.

3. Review the idea of target heart rate—that it's the best level at which to exercise their heart.

4. Check back with students about their progress on worksheet 3.1b, "Making Changes."

Take It Home

▶ Hand out worksheet 4.1, "Tuning In." This worksheet requires students to choose an active aerobic activity to do with someone on their support team (such as walking, jogging, biking, in-line skating, dancing, or doing an aerobic workout video). Before, during, and after the activity, students should pay attention to the feelings and sensations within their body. Afterward, they should fill out the worksheet with information about the activity.

▶ Tell students when to return the completed worksheet to class. (Recommended: lesson 4.3.)

Next Time

Active aerobic activity circuit

Assessment

▶ Comprehension check: Use class discussions as a check for student understanding of active aerobic activities and the FIT formula for active aerobic activities.
▶ Comprehension check: Use class discussions as a check for student understanding of some guidelines for increasing self-esteem.

Lesson Plan 4.2 Active Aerobics Circuit

In this activity lesson, students will engage in active aerobic activities that keep their heart rate in their target zone for 20 minutes.

Performance Outcomes Related to NASPE Standards

▶ Standard 1
  ▶ Perform aerobic activities that require balance and agility.
▶ Standard 3
  ▶ Have an increasing awareness of opportunities for participation in a wide range of activities that meet their needs and interests.
  ▶ Participate in health-enhancing physical activities both during and outside of school.
▶ Standard 4
  ▶ Self-assess heart rate before, during, and after vigorous physical activity.
▶ Standard 5
  ▶ Exhibit (verbally and nonverbally) cooperation, respect, encouragement, and ability to work independently.
▶ Standard 6
  ▶ Seek personally challenging physical activity experiences.

Lesson Objectives

▶ Students will keep their heart rate in their target zone for 20 minutes.
▶ Students will attend to their bodies and adjust their activity level to maintain the ability to talk with a friend during the activity.

Equipment

▶ 6 pinnies
▶ Cones or other items to mark station boundaries
▶ Enough jump ropes for all students at one station (optional)
▶ TV with VCR/DVD player (optional)

▶ Videotape or DVD of aerobic dance, Tae Bo, or kickboxing (optional)

▶ CD player and dance music (optional)

▶ 1 step bench or folded mat for every four students (optional)

Reproducibles

Worksheet 4.2, "Perception of Exertion"

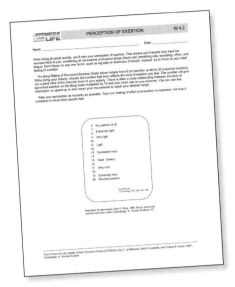

Setup

1. Set up four active aerobics stations, chosen from your favorites or from the following list:

   ▶ Step aerobics station: Create an area with six to eight step benches or folded mats; show an aerobics video or have a student lead the activity.

   ▶ Jump rope station: Create an area with six to eight jump ropes.

   ▶ Tae Bo or kickboxing station: Create some space around a TV with a VCR/DVD cued to an appropriate video.

   ▶ Jogging station: Place one cone about 10 feet (3 meters) in from each corner of the room to create a jogging lane around the perimeter.

   ▶ Calisthenics station: Create a sign that lists the steps in a routine. Example: 10 jumping jacks, 10 half squats, 10 push-ups, 10 lunges, repeat.

   ▶ Dance station: Set up a CD player so that students can play dance music and perform line dances or other dances of their choice (arranged with you ahead of time).

2. Mark each station with a large cone. Tape a sign to each cone to show the station's name and any directions that students will need to do the activity.

3. Make a copy of worksheet 4.2, "Perception of Exertion," for each student.

Delivering the Lesson

Part 1: Instant Activity

Walking Fitness Tag

1. Choose six students (or about one-fourth to one-sixth of the class) to be "It" and give them pinnies to wear.

2. Indicate the boundary of the playing area.

3. Explain that all players must walk, and any student who is "It" must tag gently. When tagged, students go outside the boundary, do 10 jumping jacks, and then reenter. The goal of the students who are "It" is to get all other players outside the boundary at the same time.

4. After one minute, let six different students be "It."

5. Continue the game until all students have been "It." The overall goal is for students to have fun while keeping their heart rates in the target range.

Part 2: Lesson Launcher

1. Review the lesson objectives with students.

2. Teach students how to take their carotid pulse. Review the target heart rate for 11- to 14-year-olds (130 to 180 beats per minute). Explain that they can take their pulse for six seconds and multiply by 10 (13 to 18 beats becomes 130 to 180 beats per minute).

 tech

Heart rate monitors provide immediate feedback to students about their heart rate and keeping it in their target heart rate zone.

Part 3: Lesson Focus

Active Aerobics Circuit

1. Explain that students will do a circuit of active aerobic activities. They will have five minutes at each station. Their goal is to keep active so that their hearts are beating in the target range, but they can still talk with their friends.

2. Give each student a copy of worksheet 4.2, "Perception of Exertion."

 review

Remind students of the importance of strategies discussed in previous lessons: thinking positively, effort, practice, and encouraging each other.

3. Give the signal for students to begin the station activities.

4. After five minutes, give the signal to stop. Students should check their pulse for six seconds and determine if they're in the target zone (13 to 18 beats in six seconds). Based on the answer, students will know whether to work harder, less hard, or the same at the next station.

 check

Ask students to respond to this statement with a thumbs-up (true) or thumbs-down (false): If you can talk with a partner, you're not working hard enough. (Answer: false.)

5. Have students look at the Borg Rating of Perceived Exertion (RPE) scale on their worksheet and circle the number that best corresponds to their level of exertion. Students should share their number with someone else at their station.

6. Give the signal for students to rotate to new stations. Continue until everyone has had a turn at each station.

7. Have students cool down for two minutes by walking around the area talking with a friend.

 observe

Scan for students taking responsibility for adjusting their activity level. When you see good examples of this, provide positive reinforcement.

Part 4: Reflection and Summary

1. Compliment students on working hard, monitoring their heart rate, and adjusting their activity level (self-responsibility).

2. Ask students the following questions:

> ▹ Was it easy for you to stay in the target zone?
>
> ▹ How do you decide whether to work at the top or the bottom of the zone?

3. Have students add worksheet 4.2, "Perception of Exertion," to their *Fitness for Life: Middle School* portfolios.

Take It Home

Encourage students to do cardiovascular activity for 20 minutes every other day at home and to invite someone on their support team to do it with them.

Next Time

▹ Stability and balance

▹ Remind students that worksheet 4.1, "Tuning In," is due next class (recommended).

Assessment

▹ Performance check: Observe students keeping active and adjusting activity levels to keep their heart rate in the target zone for 20 minutes.

▹ Performance check: Observe students attending to their bodies and adjusting their activity level to maintain the ability to talk with a friend during the activity.

In this classroom lesson, students will read and discuss the benefits of active aerobics, learn strategies to increase stability and balance, and recognize when instability helps them get moving quickly.

Performance Outcomes Related to NASPE Standards

▶ Standard 2
  ▶ Demonstrate an understanding of balance and how stability affects movement.
▶ Standard 4
  ▶ Students demonstrate an understanding of the principles of training.
▶ Standard 5
  ▶ Exhibit (verbally and nonverbally) cooperation, respect, encouragement, and ability to work independently.

Lesson Objectives

▶ Students will identify the benefits of active aerobics.
▶ Students will identify three actions they can take to become more stable.
▶ Students will demonstrate how becoming unstable can aid in directing force so they can move quickly.

Equipment

▶ 1 *Fitness for Life: Middle School* student textbook per student
▶ Chalkboard or flip chart
▶ Several sticky notes per student

 tech

Two computer presentation programs (Mount Fitness and Tour de Fitness) are available for reviewing and reinforcing concepts. See page 40 for details.

Reproducibles

▶ Worksheet 4.3, "Stability"

▶ Classroom Quotes

Classroom Quotes

You can print this quote from the CD-ROM and hang it in your room.

▶ "So divinely is the world organized that every one of us, in our place and time, is in balance with everything else."—Johann Wolfgang von Goethe (poet)

Setup

Make a copy of worksheet 4.3, "Stability," for each student.

Delivering the Lesson

Part 1: Gathering Information

1. Ask students whether they know the benefits of active aerobics. Explain that today they'll read about those benefits as well as about balance and how to improve it.

2. Have the students read "Benefits of Active Aerobics," lesson 4.2 in the student textbook (chapter 4, pages 46 to 50), to prepare for a discussion on balance.

3. When students finish the reading, lead a class discussion on the benefits of active aerobics. Have the students generate a list of benefits while you write them on the chalkboard or a flip chart.

Part 2: Lesson Launcher

1. Review the lesson objectives with students.

2. Explain to students that some people call life a balancing act. What does this mean? Is it the same or different in sports and movement? In movement, knowing how to be more stable and how to use instability to move quickly is advantageous.

 tech

Find and show video clips that illustrate stability or balance (for example, skateboarding, surfing, running out of starting blocks at the beginning of a race, or playing defense in basketball). If possible, run the clips in slow motion.

Part 3: Lesson Focus

1. Have students read "Biomechanical Principles: Stability and Balance" (chapter 4, pages 48 to 49) to prepare for a discussion on how we use those principles in activity.

2. Arrange the students in pairs, and hand out worksheet 4.3, "Stability." Pairs can work together, but each student must complete his or her own worksheet.

3. Ask a few students to act out the movements shown on the worksheet. For each movement, have them place sticky notes on their bodies to show the location of their center of gravity.

Part 4: Reflection and Summary

1. Compliment students on communicating quietly with their partners.

2. Ask students the following questions:
   - ▸ What are two differences between lifestyle activity and active aerobics?
   - ▸ What is one health benefit of active aerobics?
   - ▸ Can you describe a situation in which you might want to be very stable?
   - ▸ Can you describe a situation in which you might want to move very quickly? How could you arrange to have your center of gravity in position to move quickly?

3. Have students add completed worksheets 4.1, "Tuning In," and 4.3, "Stability," to their *Fitness for Life: Middle School* portfolios.

Take It Home

Tell students to pay attention to their balance and their center of gravity as they are being active during the next few days. When they want to move quickly, they should think about how they lean in the direction they want to go by bringing their center of gravity over to the edge of their base right before they want to move or change direction.

Next Time

Fitnessgram PACER test to assess cardiovascular fitness

Assessment

▸ Comprehension check: Student responses and discussions serve as a check for understanding of the benefits of active aerobics.

▸ Performance check: Observe students identifying and performing actions they can take to become more stable, and how becoming unstable can aid in directing force so they can move quickly.

▸ Assess completed worksheets 4.1, "Tuning In," and 4.3, "Stability," in students' *Fitness for Life: Middle School* portfolios. Use the worksheet rubric (available on the CD-ROM or on page 34) to assess student work, or modify the rubric to meet your specific objectives.

In this activity lesson, students will assess their level of cardiovascular fitness (cardiorespiratory endurance) using the Fitnessgram PACER test.

Performance Outcomes Related to NASPE Standards

▶ Standard 2
  ▸ Identify proper warm-up and cool-down techniques and reasons for using them.

▶ Standard 4
  ▸ Achieve and maintain a health-related level of physical fitness.

▶ Standard 5
  ▸ Exhibit (verbally and nonverbally) cooperation, respect, encouragement, and ability to work independently.

▶ Standard 6
  ▸ Seek personally challenging physical activity experiences.

Lesson Objectives

▶ Students will learn about and perform the PACER test.

▶ Students will determine where they fall in relation to the healthy zone in the PACER test.

▶ Students will encourage others by providing positive feedback on successful execution of the PACER test.

Equipment

▶ 12 cones

▶ 1 pencil for each pair of students

▶ PACER soundtrack on CD and CD player

Reproducibles

Worksheet 4.4, "PACER Test"

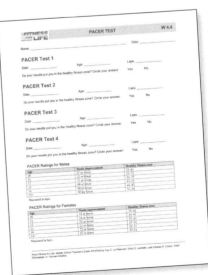

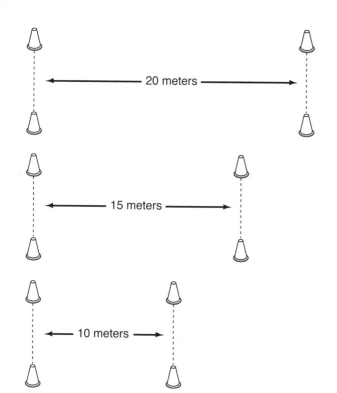

20 meters

15 meters

10 meters

Setup

1. Place the cones for the PACER test as follows (see diagram):

   ▸ Place the starting line cones far enough apart so that each student performing the test is 3 feet (about 1 meter) from the students on either side. Place the ending line cones 20 meters away.

   ▸ Place the second set of cones next to the first set, but only 15 meters apart.

   ▸ Place the third set of cones next to the second set, but only 10 meters apart.

2. Make a copy of worksheet 4.4, "PACER Test," for each student.

Delivering the Lesson

Part 1: Instant Activity

Active Rock, Paper, Scissors

1. Have the students practice doing rock, paper, scissors with a partner.

2. Divide the area into three sections: bronze, silver, and gold. If desired, widen the 10-meter and 15-meter PACER areas to create three equal spaces.

3. At your signal, students play a round of rock, paper, scissors with their partners.

   ▸ The winners of the round move up one section, from bronze to silver or from silver to gold. Winners already in the gold section stay there.

   ▸ The losers of the round move down one section, from gold to silver or from silver to bronze. Students already in the bronze section stay there.

4. Students find a new partner in their section and play again. The goal is to reach the gold section and stay there for as long as possible.

5. If you moved any of the cones for the PACER test, put them back.

Developed by Jim DeLine.

Part 2: Lesson Launcher

1. Review the lesson objectives with students.

2. Remind students that you've been talking about active aerobics and cardiovascular fitness. Today they'll take the PACER test, which requires them to run back and forth between the sets of cones at a speed determined by the CD soundtrack. The test will help students determine if this is an area in which they have enough fitness or if they need to work to improve their fitness for good health.

Part 3: Lesson Focus

Fitnessgram PACER Test

1. Arrange students into pairs using one of the methods described in "Groups and Teams" (see pages 26 to 27). Briefly discuss the need for all students to support their partners and keep health information confidential.

2. Within each pair, students can determine who will take the test first by using rock, paper, scissors or simply by agreeing on the order.

3. Give each student a copy of worksheet 4.4, "PACER Test."

4. Play the CD for several beeps and have a few students practice running back and forth between the lines of cones. Make sure that everyone understands how the test works.

5. Have the first runners line up at the starting line.

6. Play the CD from the beginning. When the first beep sounds, students run to the opposite line of cones, turn, and prepare to run again. When the next beep sounds, they run back to the starting line. Each time, they should try to reach the line before the next beep.

7. After each beep, the runner's partner counts the total number of laps.

8. The beeps will come faster over time. Students continue to run back and forth until they fail to reach the line before the next beep.

   ▸ The first time this happens, the student just turns around and runs back to the other line with everyone else.

   ▸ If a student fails to reach the line a second time, the partner stops counting laps and records the lap number on the worksheet. The runner moves to the next shorter set of cones and continues to practice until the test is completed.

   ▸ If a student fails to reach the 15-meter line before the beep, he or she moves to the 10-meter section. If a student fails to reach the line at the 10-meter distance, he or she just turns around and keeps running.

9. When all the students performing the test have completed it, partners switch roles, and the test begins again.

 check

> **Ask the class the following questions:**
>
> ✳ **Should runners move to a shorter set of cones after the first missed beep or the second missed beep? (Answer: second.)**
>
> ✳ **Should partners count the first time a runner fails to reach the line as a length? (Answer: yes.)**
>
> ✳ **Should partners count the second time a runner fails to reach the line as a length? (Answer: yes; the last attempted length is counted.)**
>
> ✳ **Why might someone not be honest in this activity? Does that make sense when you're trying to assess yourself?**

Part 4: Reflection and Summary

1. Discuss with students the healthy fitness zone guidelines and why girls' zones and boys' zones might be different. (Possible answers: more boys have longer legs than girls do, boys get more practice than girls do, more boys tend to be more active than girls are, and sometimes girls are discouraged from being active.)

2. Ask students the following questions:
   - ▸ Does the difference in standards mean that all boys perform better than all girls?
   - ▸ Do some girls usually score in the healthy zone for boys?
   - ▸ Is it OK for girls to try to meet a higher standard?
   - ▸ What would happen to the standards if many girls become more active?
   - ▸ Has anyone heard of Title IX? How has Title IX affected how active girls are?
   - ▸ Do problems with gender discrimination still exist?
3. Discuss the importance of cooling down after being active.
4. Ask for an example of a student who gave positive feedback to a partner.
5. Ask what students can do to improve their cardiovascular fitness. How would they know if they were getting better?
6. Have students add completed worksheet 4.4, "PACER Test," to their *Fitness for Life: Middle School* portfolios.

Take It Home

Ask students to spend 20 minutes every other night doing an active aerobic activity to build up their endurance.

Next Time

Active aerobic choices

Assessment

- ▸ Assess completed "PACER Test" worksheets in students' *Fitness for Life: Middle School* portfolios.
- ▸ Performance check: Observe students performing the PACER test and supporting each other. Do they meet the class climate goals?
- ▸ Performance check: Observe students independently placing themselves at the shorter distance and recording for each other. Are they able to be accurate and honest?
- ▸ Comprehension check: Responses to the Reflection and Summary questions serve as a check for student understanding of the healthy fitness zone and their understanding of how to improve cardiovascular fitness.

Lesson Plan 4.5 Active Aerobics Choices

In this activity lesson, students will practice effective communication and support techniques as they participate in their choice of active aerobic activities.

Performance Outcomes Related to NASPE Standards

▸ Standard 3
  ▸ Have an increasing awareness of the opportunities for participation in a broad range of activities that may meet their needs and interests.
  ▸ Participate in health-enhancing physical activities both during and outside of school.
▸ Standard 4
  ▸ Achieve and maintain a health-enhancing level of physical fitness.
▸ Standard 5
  ▸ Exhibit (verbally and nonverbally) cooperation, respect, encouragement, and ability to work independently.
▸ Standard 6
  ▸ Recognize the role of physical activity in getting to know and understand others.
  ▸ Recognize physical activity as a positive opportunity for social and group interaction.
  ▸ Identify potential social and health benefits from participation in physical activity.

Lesson Objectives

▸ Students will describe why cardiovascular fitness is important.
▸ Students will attend to their bodies and keep their heart rate in the target zone for at least 20 minutes.
▸ Students will demonstrate effective communication and support techniques.

Equipment

▸ Enough pinnies for one-fourth of the class
▸ Appropriate for the chosen activity stations:
  ▸ Step aerobics: TV, VCR/DVD player, aerobics video

- Step/line dancing: TV, VCR/DVD player, dance video
- Folk dancing: CD player and music; or TV, VCR/DVD player, and video
- Power walking: Cones to designate the area
- Jogging: Cones to designate the area
- Tag: Cones to designate the area
- Jump rope: 8 to 10 jump ropes; cones to designate the area
- Parachute games: Parachute (ask students to lead activities)
- In-line skating: Skates, pads, and helmets for all students

 tech

* Heart rate monitors provide immediate feedback to students about their heart rate and keeping it in their target heart rate zone.

* Pedometers can provide feedback to students about the number of steps accumulated in different physical activities.

Reproducibles

None

Setup

1. Set up activity stations around the area, chosen from this list:
   - Step aerobics
   - Step/line dancing
   - Folk dancing
   - Power walking
   - Jogging
   - Tag
   - Jump rope
   - Parachute games
   - In-line skating

2. Mark each station with a large cone. Tape a sign to each cone to show the station's name and any directions that students will need to do the activity.

Delivering the Lesson

Part 1: Instant Activity

Walking Freeze Tag

1. Designate one-fourth of the students in the class as "It." Students who are "It" should wear pinnies.

2. Students who are "It" try to tag other students. The goal is to get everyone frozen. Those who get tagged are frozen in place until someone who is free stands in front of them and they do five jumping jacks together. Students can't be tagged while doing jumping jacks. Remind everyone to walk—no running.

3. After one minute, let other students have a turn being "It" until everyone in class has been "It."

Part 2: Lesson Launcher

1. Review the lesson objectives with students.

2. Remind students that you've talked a good deal in the last few weeks about how to support each other in physical activity settings and how to work independently. Today they will spend as much of the period as possible participating in active aerobics.

3. Explain that students must stay on task, invite others to work with them, and quickly move to a new task if they tire of the one they're doing.

4. Instruct students to monitor their own activity so that they stay in their target zone, using their heart rate and perceived exertion level as feedback. They should keep their exertion level between "light" and "somewhat hard" on the perceived exertion scale.

 review

> Remind students how to encourage each other, greet each other, and take turns.

Part 3: Lesson Focus

Active Aerobics Choices

1. Give the students a brief tour of the different stations.

2. Explain that because the students have shown that they can take responsibility to choose appropriate activities, monitor themselves, and support others, they can change activities whenever they think it's appropriate. (If a station is too crowded, they should choose a different activity and try again later.)

 observe

> Scan for on-task behavior, sharing, encouraging each other, mixing of groups, level of activity.

3. Give a signal every five minutes to indicate that students should stop what they're doing and prepare to check their heart rate (carotid artery pulse). When you say "Ready—go," they'll check their pulse for six seconds and multiply by 10 to find their beats per minute. Then they can resume their activity or move to a different station.

4. Five minutes before the end of class, give a signal so that students can finish their current activity and clean up before the cool-down.

 check

> ∗ Ask students to identify their target heart rate zone. (Answer: 130 to 180 beats per minute.) How many heartbeats in a six-second period would put them at the top end of this zone? (Answer: 18 beats.) How many heartbeats would put them at the bottom end? (Answer: 13 beats.)
>
> ∗ Ask students to provide good reasons for changing from one activity to another. (Possible answers: they like many activities and want to try them all; they become bored with their current activity; their friend likes a different activity and they want to try it together.)
>
> ∗ Ask students to provide good reasons for not changing activities. (Possible answers: they enjoy what they're doing; a partner or group is counting on them to stay; they think a different activity would be more difficult.)
>
> ∗ Ask students whether they must change activities when you give the signal. (Answer: no, they can remain at their current station.)

Part 4: Reflection and Summary

1. Compliment students on working together and using the communication skills discussed (listening, responding, repeating; asking if they have questions; giving their full attention).
2. Ask students the following questions:
   - Why is cardiovascular fitness important?
   - What stations challenged your cardiovascular fitness the most? How could you tell?
   - Which activities were the most popular?
   - Do you like noncompetitive activities? If so, raise your right hand.
   - Do you like competitive activities? If so, raise your left hand.
   - If you like both noncompetitive and competitive activities, raise both hands.
   - What are the components of skill-related fitness required for the activity at your favorite station? Explain them to the person next to you. (Call on a few students to share the answers they heard from their partner.)

Take It Home

Tell students to do some of these activities at home each day. Ask which stations they would be able to do at home.

Next Time

- Active sports and recreation
- Remind students that worksheet 3.1b, "Making Changes," is due next class (recommended).

Assessment

- Comprehension check: Responses to the Reflection and Summary questions serve as a check for student understanding of the importance of cardiovascular fitness.
- Performance check: Observe students checking their heart rate and adjusting their activities to keep their heart rate in the target zone for at least 20 minutes.
- Note the stations that students chose and their interactions (e.g., inviting each other to participate, problem-solving difficulties).
- Performance check: Observe students demonstrating effective communication and support techniques.

Supplemental Materials

If you choose to use the semester or year scheduling version of *Fitness for Life: Middle School* (see appendix B), there are excellent opportunities to insert activity-based skill units and to review and reinforce the concepts in each chapter using the *Fitness for Life: Middle School* computer programs: Mount Fitness and Tour de Fitness. You will find information about the two computer programs in appendix C. Listed below are suggestions of activity-based skill units that would go well with this chapter and resources that will help you develop great lessons.

As indicated in the "Scheduling" section (pages 13 to 18), integrating activity-based skill units with the *Fitness for Life: Middle School* lesson plans provides a great opportunity for reinforcing key concepts and for developing students' skills in a wide range of physical activities. The activity-based skill unit suggestions provided below were chosen specifically to complement chapter content. In addition, there are selected resources that can provide you with excellent lesson plans and lesson plan ideas. Approaches to teaching activity-based skill units can be found in appendix A.

JUMPING ROPE

- ▶ **Key concepts to reinforce:** Monitoring heart rate, self-esteem, stability and balance, positive thinking, cardiovascular fitness
- ▶ **Resources:**
  - ▸ *Quality Lesson Plans for Secondary Physical Education* (Zakrajsek, Carnes, and Pettigrew, 2003, Human Kinetics)
  - ▸ *Complete Physical Education Plans for Grades 7-12* (Kleinman, 2001, Human Kinetics)

ORIENTEERING

- ▶ **Key concepts to reinforce:** Monitoring heart rate, self-esteem, stability and balance, positive thinking, cardiovascular fitness
- ▶ **Resources:** *Quality Lesson Plans for Secondary Physical Education* (Zakrajsek, Carnes, and Pettigrew, 2003, Human Kinetics)

KICKBOXING, TAE BO, NIA, STEP

Sample one unit each day.

- ▶ **Key concepts to reinforce:** Monitoring heart rate, self-esteem, stability and balance, positive thinking, cardiovascular fitness
- ▶ **Resources:** Invite a professional from the community to provide a class.

BIKING OR MOUNTAIN BIKING

- ▶ **Key concepts to reinforce:** Monitoring heart rate, self-esteem, stability and balance, positive thinking, cardiovascular fitness
- ▶ **Resources:**
  - ▸ *It's Not Just Gym Anymore: Teaching Secondary School Students How to Be Active for Life* (McCracken, 2001, Human Kinetics)
  - ▸ www.bicyclinginfo.org/ee/ed_young.cfm

Active Sports and Recreation

Chapter 5 lesson plans focus on student preferences for active sports and recreation activities, and explores the issues of following rules in sports and games. The concepts of acceleration, deceleration, and velocity are explored and applied to sports and selected physical activities. Additionally, students are required to locate active sports and recreation opportunities in their community that appeal to them.

* 5.1 Active Sports and Recreation: Level 2 of the Physical Activity Pyramid (classroom lesson)
* 5.2 Active Sports and Recreation Circuit With Frisbees (activity lesson)
* 5.3 Benefits of Active Sports and Recreation: Plus Fitness, Velocity, and Acceleration (classroom lesson)
* 5.4 Modifying Ultimate Games (activity lesson)
* 5.5 Modified Ultimate Tournament (activity lesson)

5.1 **Active Sports and Recreation: Level 2 of the Physical Activity Pyramid**

This classroom lesson provides students an opportunity to identify and discuss active sports and active recreation pursuits in a group setting. A discussion of the importance of playing within the rules and accepting decisions by officials will also take place.

Performance Outcomes Related to NASPE Standards

▶ Standard 2
  ▸ Identify skill-related fitness components required for a variety of physical activities.

▶ Standard 5
  ▸ Exhibit (verbally and nonverbally) cooperation, respect, encouragement, and ability to work independently.

▶ Standard 6
  ▸ Analyze selected physical activity experiences for social, emotional, and health benefits.

Lesson Objectives

▶ Students will identify active sports and active recreation activities that they participate in.

▶ Students will communicate their interests in active sports and recreation.

- Students will share their thoughts on following rules in small-group settings.
- Students will actively listen to and encourage others (i.e., use positive feedback), participate, and refrain from interrupting others in small-group settings.

Equipment

- 1 *Fitness for Life: Middle School* student textbook per student
- Chalkboard or flip chart (optional)

 tech

Find and show video clips of several types of active sports and active recreation activities.

Reproducibles

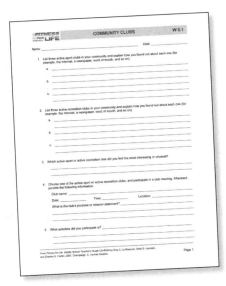

- Worksheet 5.1, "Community Clubs"
- Classroom Quotes

Classroom Quotes

You can print these quotes from the CD-ROM and hang them around your room.

- "Sports do not build character; they reveal it."—John Wooden (basketball coach)
- "People who cannot find time for recreation are obliged sooner or later to find time for illness."—John Wanamaker (businessman)

Setup

1. Write the following instructions on the board for part 3 of the lesson focus:
   - Create two group lists
     - List of active sports and active recreation pursuits that you participate in now
     - "Fantasy" list of active sports and recreation pursuits that you would like to try
   - Report to the class
     - The most popular participation category—active sports or recreation?
     - The most popular fantasy category—active sports or recreation?
     - The most unusual active sport or recreation? Why was that person interested in this activity?
2. Make a copy of worksheet 5.1, "Community Clubs," for each student.

Delivering the Lesson

Part 1: Gathering Information

1. Ask the class if anyone can explain what makes an activity a sport. Do they know the difference between active recreation and recreation? Explain that today they will learn about and discuss active sports and active recreation.

2. Have the students read "Active Sports and Recreation: Level 2 of the Physical Activity Pyramid," lesson 5.1 in the student textbook (chapter 5, pages 53 to 57).

Part 2: Lesson Launcher

1. Review the lesson objectives with students.

2. Ask all students who participate in active sports or active recreation to raise their hands. (Most students should do so.) Explain that for many of them, sports and recreation are just play, and that the movement we get from active playing is an important part of life.

Part 3: Lesson Focus 1

Active Sports and Recreation Preferences

1. Organize students into small groups of three or four using one of the methods in "Groups and Teams" (pages 26 to 27).

2. Within each group, have students identify a leader, a recorder, and a reporter. The leader will guide the group's discussion, the recorder will generate the lists created by the group, and the reporter will present the results to the class. If there are four in a group, the fourth member can be a "brainstormer," or group contributor.

3. Have each group generate two lists.

   ▸ A list of active sports and active recreation pursuits that they participate in now.

   ▸ A "fantasy" list of active sports and recreation pursuits that they would like to try. Students should encourage each other to share their reasons for wanting to participate in the fantasy activities.

4. Give the reporters one minute to share the following information with the class:

   ▸ What was the most popular participation category—active sports or recreation?

   ▸ What was the most popular fantasy category—active sports or recreation?

   ▸ What was the most unusual active sport or recreation? Why was the person interested in this activity?

 review

> Review some of the effective communication skills from last week (such as active listening, not interrupting, sharing the "stage," and respecting opinions).

Part 4: Lesson Focus 2

Following Rules

1. Have the students read "Moving Together: Following Rules" in the student textbook (chapter 5, page 56).

2. In each small group, have leaders, recorders, and reporters exchange roles. The leader will pose the "Moving Together" discussion questions to his or her group, the recorder will write notes about the responses, and the reporter will prepare to share the answers with the class.

3. Bring the class back together and ask the discussion questions to the larger group. After the reporters present their answers, encourage others in the class to contribute answers and generate discussion.

4. Extend the discussion about following rules using your own experiences. Encourage students to do the same.

Part 5: Reflection and Summary

1. Ask students the following questions:
   ▸ Who can explain what makes an activity a sport?
   ▸ What's the difference between active recreation and recreation?
   ▸ What are some important guidelines for following rules?
2. Have students add completed worksheet 3.1b, "Making Changes," to their *Fitness for Life: Middle School* portfolios.

Take It Home

▸ Hand out worksheet 5.1, "Community Clubs." This worksheet requires students to find active recreation clubs and active sport clubs in their community using resources such as newspapers, community guides, recreation center calendars, the Internet, or word of mouth. Students will list several clubs, participate in a club meeting, and write a short reflection about the experience.

▸ Tell students when to return the completed worksheet to class. (Recommended: lesson 6.1.)

Next Time

Active sports and recreation circuit with Frisbees

Assessment

▸ Comprehension check: Class discussions and responses to the Reflection and Summary questions serve as a check for student understanding of activities that are classified as active sports and active recreation activities.

▸ Performance check: Observe students sharing their thoughts on following rules in small-group settings while actively listening to each other.

▸ Assess completed worksheet 3.1b, "Making Changes," in students' *Fitness for Life: Middle School* portfolios. Use the worksheet rubric (available on the CD-ROM or on page 34) to assess student work, or modify the rubric to meet your specific objectives.

Active Sports and Recreation Circuit With Frisbees

This activity lesson will allow students to participate in active sports and recreation activities using Frisbees.

Performance Outcomes Related to NASPE Standards

▶ Standard 1
  ▶ Perform activities that require several components of skill- and health-related fitness.
▶ Standard 5
  ▶ Play within the rules of sports and show self-control by accepting the decisions of teammates and competitors.
  ▶ Exhibit (verbally and nonverbally) cooperation, respect, encouragement, and ability to work independently.
▶ Standard 6
  ▶ Appreciate the aesthetic and creative aspects of skilled performance in others and themselves.

Lesson Objectives

▶ Students will participate in an active sports and recreation circuit designed to challenge components of their skill- and health-related fitness.
▶ Students will demonstrate honesty, fairness, and cooperation by following the rules and working out disputes with competitors.

FITNESS FOR LIFE FRISBEE STATIONS R 5.2

Ultimate

Equipment: 1 Frisbee and 4 cones

• Teams begin the game in their end zones. To start the game, Team A throws the Frisbee to Team B.
• Players from Team B travel toward Team A's end zone while passing the Frisbee back and forth.
• If a player from Team B catches the Frisbee while in the end zone, Team B scores 1 point.
• Once a player has caught the Frisbee, he or she can't take more than two steps.
• Defenders must give the player with the Frisbee two big steps of space.
• If the Frisbee hits the floor during a pass (whether it's dropped or knocked down), the other team gains possession of the Frisbee.

From *Fitness for Life: Middle School Teacher's Guide CD-ROM* by Guy C. Le Masurier, Dolly D. Lambdin, and Charles B. Corbin. 2007. Champaign, IL: Human Kinetics.

Equipment

▶ 20 regulation Frisbees of different sizes, colors, and materials
▶ 6 spinning Frisbees with cone in center for easy spinning on one finger
▶ CD player and beach music
▶ Web resource: www.ultimatehandbook.com/Webpages/Beginner/physics.html

Reproducibles

Resource 5.2, "Frisbee Stations"

Setup

1. Print one set of the "Frisbee Stations" activity cards.

2. Set up the five Frisbee stations described on the cards. Make sure to allow enough space for each activity.

Delivering the Lesson

Part 1: Instant Activity

Have students pair up. Partners should find their own space and throw a Frisbee back and forth under control. Move students closer together if they are having problems making successful throw and catch sequences.

Part 2: Lesson Launcher

1. Review the lesson objectives with students.

2. Tell the class the history of the Frisbie Baking Company (1871-1958) of Bridgeport, Connecticut, which made pies that were sold to many New England colleges. Hungry college students soon discovered that the empty pie tins could be tossed and caught, providing endless hours of recreation and sport.

3. Explain that today, students will do activities with Frisbees. Some of the circuit activities are considered active sports, while others are considered active recreation.

Part 3. Lesson Focus

Active Sports and Recreation Circuit With Frisbees

1. Organize the class into five small groups using one of the methods in "Groups and Teams" (pages 26 to 27).

2. Briefly explain the five Frisbee stations.

3. Send each group to a different station with its own "Frisbee Stations" activity card. Point out that Ultimate is officiated by players at the world championships. Students will be responsible for officiating each other at the Ultimate, bocce, and golf stations.

 review

Ask students to provide some guidelines for following rules.

4. Give the signal for students to begin. After three to five minutes, give the signal for them to switch stations. Continue until all students have tried each station.

 observe

Visit the bocce and Ultimate stations to make sure the students understand the objects and rules of those games.

Part 4: Reflection and Summary

Ask students the following questions:

▸ Who enjoyed the active sports activities more than the active recreation activities? Can someone share why?

▸ Who enjoyed the active recreation activities more than the active sports activities? Can someone share why?

▸ Can someone compliment a classmate on following the rules? How did this make you feel about this person?

Take It Home

Go outside with family or friends this week and throw a Frisbee around.

Next Time

Fitness, velocity, and acceleration in active sports and recreation

Assessment

▸ Performance check: Observe students participating in Ultimate activities and demonstrating honesty, fairness, and cooperation by following the rules and working out disputes with competitors.

▸ Comprehension check: Responses to Reflection and Summary questions serve as a check for student understanding of following the rules.

Lesson Plan **5.3** **Benefits of Active Sports and Recreation: Plus Fitness, Velocity, and Acceleration**

This classroom lesson will provide time for students to discuss the benefits of participation in active sports and recreation, and expose them to the concepts of velocity and acceleration.

Performance Outcomes Related to NASPE Standards

▶ Standard 2
  ▶ Demonstrate an understanding of the health benefits achieved through participation in regular physical activity.
▶ Standard 3
  ▶ Demonstrate an understanding of the concepts of velocity, acceleration, and deceleration in active sports and recreation.

Lesson Objectives

▶ Students will demonstrate an understanding of the important health- and skill-related fitness benefits from participating in their favorite active sports or active recreation pursuits.
▶ Students will demonstrate an understanding of how velocity, acceleration, and deceleration are used in physical activities using examples of their favorite activities.

Equipment

▶ 1 *Fitness for Life: Middle School* student textbook per student
▶ 1 sticky note per student
▶ Chalkboard or flip chart (optional)

tech

  ∗ Find and show video clips of several types of active sports and active recreation activities.
  ∗ Two computer presentation programs (Mount Fitness and Tour de Fitness) are available for reviewing and reinforcing concepts. See page 40 for details.

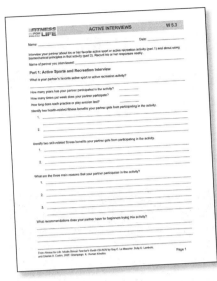

Reproducibles

▶ Worksheet 5.3, "Active Interviews"
▶ Classroom Quotes

Classroom Quotes

You can print these quotes from the CD-ROM and hang them around your room.

▶ "If you can't accept losing, you can't win."—Vince Lombardi (football coach)
▶ "Practice, which some regard as a chore, should be approached as just about the most pleasant recreation ever devised."—Babe Didrikson Zaharias (multisport athlete)

Setup

Make a copy of worksheet 5.3, "Active Interviews," for each student.

Delivering the Lesson

Part 1: Gathering Information

1. Explain to students that active sports and recreation can provide many health-related fitness benefits, such as improving cardiovascular fitness, muscular endurance, and body composition.
2. Have the students read "Benefits of Sports and Recreation," lesson 5.2 in the student textbook (chapter 5, pages 58 to 62), to prepare for discussion. As they read, they should think about the health-related fitness benefits of the active sports or active recreation activities they already participate in.

Part 2: Lesson Launcher

1. Review the lesson objectives with students.
2. Ask students to name the five health-related fitness components and the six skill-related fitness components.
3. Explain that today, students will interview a classmate and discover how that person's active sports or active recreation pursuits improve their health- and skill-related fitness.

Part 3: Lesson Focus 1

Benefits of Active Sports and Active Recreation

1. Organize students in pairs. Give each student one sticky note and a copy of worksheet 5.3, "Active Interviews."
2. Allow four to six minutes for each pair to complete part 1 of the worksheet. This requires them to interview each other about their active sports and recreation choices. Interviewers should record their partner's responses neatly.

review

Remind students that they should be prepared to share their examples with the rest of the class.

3. Have students write their favorite active recreation or active sports activity on their sticky notes.

4. Create a graph of the activities using the sticky notes. Identify the most popular activities, the most popular category (active sports or active recreation), and some of the more unusual activities.

Part 4: Lesson Focus 2

Velocity, Acceleration, and Deceleration in Active Sports and Active Recreation

Ask the class if anyone can explain the terms *acceleration, velocity,* and *deceleration.* Explain that many active sports require rapid changes in direction, bursts of speed, and constant changes in speed.

1. Have the students read "Biomechanical Principles: Velocity, Acceleration, and Deceleration" (chapter 5, pages 60 to 61 of the student textbook).

2. Allow four to six minutes for each pair to complete part 2 of the worksheet. This requires them to interview each other about how acceleration, deceleration, and velocity are used in one of the active sports or active recreation activities they named in part 1 of the worksheet. Interviewers should record their partner's responses neatly.

review

Remind students that they should be prepared to share their examples with the rest of the class.

3. Bring the class together and ask selected students to share examples from part 1 or part 2 of their worksheets. Facilitate the discussion by relating their examples to game strategy, tactics, or successful completion of a skill.

Part 5: Reflection and Summary

1. Ask students the following questions:

   ▸ Why do you think active sports and recreation are placed with active aerobics at level 2 of the Physical Activity Pyramid?

   ▸ Who can explain the term *velocity?*

   ▸ Who can explain the terms *acceleration* and *deceleration?*

2. Have students add completed worksheet 5.3, "Active Interviews," to their *Fitness for Life: Middle School* portfolios.

Take It Home

Seek out activities in your neighborhood or community. After participating, share your knowledge of how acceleration, deceleration, and velocity are used in that activity.

Next Time

Students will play Ultimate.

Assessment

▶ Comprehension check: Student discussions during the Lesson Focus and responses to the Reflection and Summary questions serve as a check for student understanding of the important health- and skill-related fitness benefits from participating in their favorite active sports or active recreation pursuits, and an understanding of the concepts of velocity, acceleration, and deceleration.

▶ Assess completed worksheet 5.3, "Active Interviews," in students' *Fitness for Life: Middle School* portfolios. Use the worksheet rubric (available on the CD-ROM or on page 34) to assess student work, or modify the rubric to meet your specific objectives.

5.4 Modifying Ultimate Games

In this activity lesson, students will play Ultimate games and create rules to promote full inclusion.

Performance Outcomes Related to NASPE Standards

▶ Standard 3
  ▶ Participate in health-enhancing physical activities both during and outside of school.
▶ Standard 5
  ▶ Modify and participate in physical activities that allow all to participate.
▶ Standard 6
  ▶ Use physical activity as a positive opportunity for social and group interaction.

Lesson Objectives

▶ Students will participate in an active sport that improves their health-related fitness.
▶ Students will demonstrate honesty, fairness, and cooperation by following the rules and working out disputes with competitors.

Equipment

▶ 8 regulation Frisbees
▶ 6 foam Frisbees
▶ 6 spinning Frisbees
▶ 12 cones
▶ Pinnies for half the class

Reproducibles

None

Setup

1. Place Frisbees so that they're easily accessible for the instant activity.
2. Create three small-sided Ultimate fields in your activity area. Use four cones to mark each field; if desired, use more cones to specify the depth of each end zone.

Delivering the Lesson

Part 1: Instant Activity

As students enter the playing area, have them jog with a partner while throwing a Frisbee of their choice back and forth. Challenge students to see if they can jog one lap around all three Ultimate fields without dropping the Frisbee.

Part 2: Lesson Launcher

1. Review the lesson objectives with students.
2. Ask all students who had to accelerate and decelerate during their warm-up to raise their hands. Explain that whether they play with a disc for recreation or for sport, they need to make constant adjustments in their position by accelerating and decelerating. Ask students how acceleration and deceleration can help them in Ultimate. (Possible answers: getting away from defense; moving toward the Frisbee.)
3. Explain that today, they will play games of Ultimate, focusing on officiating their own games and following the rules. They'll also modify the rules to encourage participation and make the game more fun.

Part 3: Lesson Focus

Playing and Modifying Ultimate

1. Organize the class into six teams of four or five students each using one of the methods in "Groups and Teams" (pages 26 to 27).
2. Briefly explain the object and basic rules of Ultimate:
   ▸ Teams begin the game in their end zones. To start the game, Team A throws the Frisbee to Team B.
   ▸ Players from Team B travel toward Team A's end zone while passing the Frisbee back and forth. If a player from Team B catches the Frisbee while in the end zone, Team B scores 1 point.
   ▸ When a player catches the Frisbee, he or she can't take more than two steps.
   ▸ Defenders must give the player with the Frisbee two big steps of space.
   ▸ If the Frisbee hits the floor during a pass (whether it's dropped or knocked down), the other team gains possession of the Frisbee.
3. Give pinnies to three of the teams. Arrange the teams so that on each field, a team with pinnies plays against a team without pinnies.
4. Give the signal for the teams to start playing. All three games will be played simultaneously.

5. After five minutes of play, give the signal for all teams to stop.

 observe

Scan the games for cooperation, following the rules, and encouragement of others. Stop a game if you hear arguing and negative talk, and explain to students your expectations for appropriate game play and classroom interactions.

6. On each field, ask the two teams to brainstorm one rule modification that would make the game more fun for everyone. Examples:

▸ Players can take three steps instead of two after catching a pass.

▸ Defenders can't come within one giant step of the player with the Frisbee.

▸ All players on a team must touch the Frisbee at least once before the team can try to score.

 observe

Scan the groups for cooperation during the brainstorming sessions.

7. After two minutes, have one person from each field present their rule modification to the entire class.

8. Adapt one of the three new rule modifications by taking a class vote or simply choosing it yourself. Switch teams around so that each faces a new team, and begin new games of Ultimate that include the new modification.

9. After five minutes, stop the games, have the teams brainstorm more rule modifications, and select one for the next round of games. (Optional: Instead of brainstorming new modifications, choose one that was suggested previously.)

10. Continue playing games and trying rule modifications as time permits.

Part 4: Reflection and Summary

Ask students to share the following:

▸ Compliments about players who followed the rules or encouraged others

▸ Examples of how they used acceleration and deceleration to their advantage during the games

▸ Components of health- or skill-related fitness they used during the games

▸ How the rule changes encouraged participation

Take It Home

Consider changing the rules of a game you play with friends and family members to make it more fun for everybody involved. If you find something that works well, share it with the class.

Next Time

Modified Ultimate tournament

Assessment

▶ Performance check: Observe students participating in Ultimate and demonstrating honesty, fairness, and cooperation by following the rules and working out disputes with competitors.

▶ Comprehension check: Responses to the Reflection and Summary questions serve as a check for student understanding of health- and skill-related fitness concepts.

Lesson Plan 5.5 Modified Ultimate Tournament

In this activity lesson, students will play an Ultimate tournament that incorporates rules created by students to promote participation and increase enjoyment.

Performance Outcomes Related to NASPE Standards

- Standard 3
  - Participate in health-enhancing physical activities both during and outside of school.
- Standard 5
  - Modify and participate in physical activities that allow all to participate.
  - Exhibit (verbally and nonverbally) cooperation, respect, encouragement, and ability to work independently.
- Standard 6
  - Use physical activity as a positive opportunity for social and group interaction.

Lesson Objectives

- Students will participate in an active sport that benefits their health-related fitness.
- Students will demonstrate honesty, fairness, and cooperation by following the rules and working out disputes with competitors.

Equipment

- 8 regulation Frisbees
- 6 foam Frisbees
- 6 spinning Frisbees
- 12 cones
- Pinnies for half the class

- ▶ 1 trophy for the team with the best sporting behavior
- ▶ 1 trophy for the winning team

Reproducibles

None

Setup

1. Place Frisbees so that they're easily accessible for the instant activity.
2. Create three small-sided Ultimate fields in your activity area. Use four cones to mark each field; if desired, use more cones to specify the depth of each end zone.
3. Create one trophy for the team that exhibits the best sporting behavior, and create another for the team that wins the tournament.

Delivering the Lesson

Part 1: Instant Activity

Have students pair up. Partners should find their own space and throw a disc back and forth under control. Move students closer together if they are having problems making successful throw and catch sequences.

Part 2: Lesson Launcher

1. Review the lesson objectives with students.
2. Remind the students that during the last class they came up with rule modifications as a team to make Ultimate more fun and to encourage participation. Today, they'll use some of those rules in a mini Ultimate tournament.

Part 3: Lesson Focus

Modified Ultimate Tournament

1. Organize the class into six teams of four or five students each using one of the methods in "Groups and Teams" (pages 26 to 27).
2. Remind students of the basic rules of Ultimate (see page 154), and explain the rule modifications that will be used in the tournament.
3. Give pinnies to three of the teams. Arrange the teams so that on each field, a team with pinnies plays against a team without pinnies.
4. Number the fields 1, 2, and 3.
5. Give the signal for the teams to start playing. All three games will be played simultaneously.
6. After five to eight minutes of play, give the signal for all teams to stop. Have the winning teams move up one field and have losing teams move down one field. If the team on field 1 won its game, the team remains on field 1.

7. Continue playing games and rotating teams as time permits. The team that wins the final game played on field 1 is the champ.

 observe

Scan the games for the team that best demonstrates cooperation, following the rules, and encouragement of others.

8. Award the trophies. Place more emphasis on the trophy for good sporting behavior and less emphasis on the trophy for winning the tournament.

Part 4: Reflection and Summary

Ask students the following questions:

▶ What is your favorite rule modification? Why?

▶ What are some examples of good sporting behavior?

Take It Home

Gather some friends and family together and get a modified game of Ultimate going in your neighborhood.

Next Time

▶ Learn about the benefits of flexibility.

▶ Remind students that worksheet 5.1, "Community Clubs," is due next class (recommended).

Assessment

▶ Performance check: Observe students participating in Ultimate activities and demonstrating honesty, fairness, and cooperation by following the rules and working out disputes with competitors.

▶ Comprehension check: Responses to Reflection and Summary questions serve as a check for student understanding of following the rules.

Supplemental Materials

If you choose to use the semester or year scheduling version of *Fitness for Life: Middle School* (see appendix B), there are excellent opportunities to insert activity-based skill units and to review and reinforce the concepts in each chapter using the *Fitness for Life: Middle School* computer programs: Mount Fitness and Tour de Fitness. You will find information about the two computer programs in appendix C. Listed below are suggestions of activity-based skill units that would go well with this chapter and resources that will help you develop great lessons.

As indicated in the "Scheduling" section (pages 13 to 18), integrating activity-based skill units with the *Fitness for Life: Middle School* lesson plans provides a great opportunity for reinforcing key concepts and for developing students' skills in a wide range of physical activities. The activity-based skill unit suggestions provided below were chosen specifically to complement chapter content. In addition, there are selected resources that can provide you with excellent lesson plans and lesson plan ideas. Approaches to teaching activity-based skill units can be found in appendix A.

BADMINTON, BASKETBALL, FLAG FOOTBALL, SOCCER, VOLLEYBALL, OR TOUCH RUGBY

- ▶ **Key concepts to reinforce:** Fair play, acceleration and velocity, inclusion, choosing competition or recreation, strategy and tactics
- ▶ **Resources:**
  - ▶ *Complete Physical Education Plans for Grades 7-12* (Kleinman, 2001, Human Kinetics)
  - ▶ *Quality Lesson Plans for Secondary Physical Education* (Zakrajsek, Carnes, and Pettigrew, 2003, Human Kinetics)
  - ▶ *Complete Guide to Sport Education Model* (Siedentop, Hastie, and van der Mars, 2004, Human Kinetics)

VOLLEYBALL

- ▶ **Key concepts to reinforce:** Safety, warm-ups and cool-downs, friction, rules, changing physical activity behavior
- ▶ **Resources:**
  - ▶ *Teaching Sport Concepts and Skills: A Tactical Games Approach* (Mitchell, Olsen, and Griffin, 2006, Human Kinetics)
  - ▶ *It's Not Just Gym Anymore: Teaching Secondary School Students How to Be Active for Life* (McCracken, 2001, Human Kinetics)
  - ▶ *Quality Lesson Plans for Secondary Physical Education* (Zakrajsek, Carnes, and Pettigrew, 2003, Human Kinetics)
  - ▶ *Complete Physical Education Plans for Grades 7-12* (Kleinman, 2001, Human Kinetics)

ULTIMATE

- ▶ **Key concepts to reinforce:** Fair play, acceleration and velocity, inclusion, choosing competition or recreation, strategy and tactics
- ▶ **Resources:** *Quality Lesson Plans for Secondary Physical Education* (Zakrajsek, Carnes, and Pettigrew, 2003, Human Kinetics)

RUGBY OR LACROSSE

▸ **Key concepts to reinforce:** Fair play, acceleration and velocity, inclusion, choosing competition or recreation, strategy and tactics

▸ **Resources:** *Teaching Sport Concepts and Skills: A Tactical Games Approach* (Mitchell, Olsen, and Griffin, 2006, Human Kinetics)

Flexibility Exercises

Chapter 6 lesson plans focus on flexibility, the concept of range of motion, and feeling comfortable in physical activity settings. Students engage in flexibility self-assessments, an introduction to yoga postures, and an assignment on teamwork. This is an excellent chapter to bring in an expert from the community to do a unit on yoga. Inform the biology teacher about this unit so the teacher can reinforce the concept of bones, muscles, and ligaments surrounding the body parts addressed in the Fitnessgram self-assessments.

* 6.1 Flexibility Exercises: Level 3 of the Physical Activity Pyramid (classroom lesson)
* 6.2 Yoga Stations (activity lesson)
* 6.3 Benefits of Flexibility (classroom lesson)
* 6.4 Back-Saver Sit-and-Reach Test (activity lesson)
* 6.5 Teamwork Challenges (activity lesson)

Lesson Plan 6.1 Flexibility Exercises: Level 3 of the Physical Activity Pyramid

This classroom lesson provides students with an understanding of the range of motion at a joint and an introduction to the benefits of flexibility.

Performance Outcomes Related to NASPE Standards

▶ Standard 4
  ▸ Achieve and maintain a health-enhancing level of physical fitness.
▶ Standard 5
  ▸ Exhibit (verbally and nonverbally) cooperation, respect, encouragement, and ability to work independently.
▶ Standard 6
  ▸ Identify personally enjoyable physical activity experiences.

Lesson Objectives

▶ Students will know a variety of appropriate ways to stretch their muscles.
▶ Students will describe guidelines for increasing teamwork.
▶ Students will identify ways to help each other be comfortable in physical activity.

Equipment

▶ 1 *Fitness for Life: Middle School* student textbook per student
▶ Chalkboard or flip chart (optional)

tech

Find and show video clips of gymnasts with good flexibility and football players stretching.

Reproducibles

▶ Worksheet 6.1, "Teamwork"
▶ Classroom Quotes

Classroom Quotes

You can print this quote from the CD-ROM and hang it in your room.

▶ "Prepare yourself for the world, as the athletes used to do for their exercise; oil your mind and your manners, to give them the necessary suppleness and flexibility; strength alone will not do it."—Earl of Chesterfield (author)

Setup

1. Create a small area where students can act out the "Moving Together" scenario.
2. Create areas for groups of students to work on flexibility exercises.
3. Make a copy of worksheet 6.1, "Teamwork," for each student.

Delivering the Lesson

Part 1: Gathering Information

1. Ask the students if they consider themselves flexible. If so, is it because they believe they're easygoing and don't mind changing plans, or because they can touch their toes? Explain that flexibility has two related but very different meanings, and that you'll talk about them both today.
2. Have the students read "Flexibility Exercises: Level 3 of the Physical Activity Pyramid," lesson 6.1 in the student textbook (chapter 6, pages 65 to 70).

Part 2: Lesson Launcher

1. Review the lesson objectives with students.
2. Have students read the opening section of "Moving Together: Feeling Comfortable in Physical Activity" in the student textbook (chapter 6, page 68).
3. Tell the students to look over the discussion questions briefly, and then to read the "Guidelines for Feeling Comfortable in Physical Activity." Students should use the guidelines to come up with answers to the discussion questions.
4. Pose the discussion questions to the class.
5. Ask four students to serve as "acting coaches" and four students to role-play the "Moving Together" scenario involving Tenzin, Sam, José, and Jasmine. The coaches help the actors with what to say and do as they role-play. Sometimes just acting out what someone else has suggested makes role-playing easier for the performer.

⟳ review

Review the importance of supporting each other and communicating.

Part 3: Lesson Focus

Flexibility

1. Review the definition of flexibility (range of motion at a joint).

2. Arrange the students in groups of three using one of the methods described in "Groups and Teams" (pages 26 to 27).

3. Provide each group with a different joint (such as toe, ankle, knee, hip, spine, fingers, wrist, elbow, shoulder, neck, or jaw) to determine the range of motion at that joint. Have each group do the following:

   ▸ Determine the type of joint it is (gliding, hinge, or ball and socket/rotation)

   ▸ Determine the direction of the range of motion (none, one plane, or more than one plane)

   ▸ Practice taking the joint through the full range of motion

4. Discuss which joints and directions of motion are most important in daily living.

 check

> ✳ Ask the students to show you what their faces should look like when they're stretching properly. (Response: students should look focused, not anguished.)
>
> ✳ Ask them what they should always do before stretching. (Answer: warm up.)

 observe

> Scan the class to make sure students are moving safely (not hyperextending or hyperflexing joints) when checking flexibility.

Part 4: Reflection and Summary

1. Compliment students for on-task work in their groups and individuals for their acting and coaching.

2. Review the types of stretching discussed in chapter 6 of the student textbook—static (slow and steady) and PNF (contract the muscle first).

3. Indicate that in addition to physical flexibility there is also mental/social flexibility, the ability to adapt to different situations. Ask students what makes physical activity settings comfortable for them. List their answers on the chalk/white board or flip chart.

4. Have students add completed worksheet 5.1, "Community Clubs," to their *Fitness for Life: Middle School* portfolios.

Take It Home

▸ Hand out worksheet 6.1, "Teamwork." This worksheet asks students to set a goal with members of their support team to be active. Everyone will play a specific role in contributing to the success of the team's effort.

▸ Tell students when to return the completed worksheet to class. (Recommended: lesson 6.5.)

Next Time

Yoga circuit focused on flexibility and relaxation

Assessment

▶ Comprehension check: Student discussion and responses to the Reflection and Summary questions serve as a check for student understanding of different types of joints in the body, range of motion, and appropriate stretching procedures.

▶ Comprehension check: Student discussion serves as an opportunity to check for student understanding of the guidelines for increasing teamwork and strategies to help others be comfortable in physical activity.

▶ Assess completed worksheet 5.1, "Community Clubs," in students' *Fitness for Life: Middle School* portfolios. Use the worksheet rubic (available on the CD-ROM or on page 34) to assess student work, or modify the rubric to meet your specific objectives.

In this activity lesson, students will engage in an introduction to yoga.

Performance Outcomes Related to NASPE Standards

▶ Standard 1
  ▶ Perform aerobic activities that require balance and flexibility.
▶ Standard 3
  ▶ Have an increasing awareness of opportunities for participation in a wide range of activities that meet their needs and interests.
  ▶ Participate in health-enhancing physical activities both during and outside of school.
▶ Standard 5
  ▶ Exhibit (verbally and nonverbally) cooperation, respect, encouragement, and ability to work independently.
▶ Standard 6
  ▶ Seek personally challenging physical activity experiences.
  ▶ Appreciate the aesthetic and creative aspects of skilled performance in others and themselves.

Lesson Objectives

▶ Students will be introduced to and practice a variety of yoga positions.
▶ Students will experience a flexibility activity that can reduce stress and increase relaxation.

Equipment

▶ Soft, relaxing music
▶ Enough mats to accommodate class size

Reproducibles

Resource 6.2, "Yoga Poses"

Setup

1. Familiarize yourself with the poses shown on the "Yoga Poses" cards.

2. Collect pictures from magazines or Web sites of strong-looking people doing yoga to post on the wall or bulletin board.

3. Set up five yoga stations throughout the activity area. At each station, place two of the "Yoga Poses" cards and enough mats so there is a place for each student. (For large classes with more than 40 students, make an extra set of cards and create 10 stations so there are fewer students at each station. Have students only rotate to half the stations, doing each set of poses once.)

4. As the students enter, dim the lights, then play relaxing music.

Delivering the Lesson

Part 1: Instant Activity

Have students take off their shoes if they like and walk around the area for three minutes. Encourage them to tune in to their bodies, to feel the bottoms of their feet touch the floor, their arms swing, and so on.

Part 2: Lesson Launcher

1. Review the lesson objectives with students.

2. Remind the class that you've been talking about flexibility and range of motion at joints. Yoga is a popular activity that involves attention to strength, flexibility, relaxation, and breathing.

   ▸ Strength and flexibility are improved through practicing different poses.

   ▸ Specific breath techniques are practiced by attending to various aspects of each inhalation and exhalation.

   ▸ Relaxation is enhanced in many ways including guided visualization.

3. Explain that today, students will try several poses. Instruct them to pay close attention to the position of the feet and arms on the pictures on the cards.

4. Explain that for many of them, this lesson is about trying something that might be different from their normal types of activity. You will know they have developed the ability to work independently and the ability to help everyone have a good experience if they can focus on trying each activity and refrain from making it hard for others through comments or facial expressions. Today will be a great test of the social and personal skills they have been working on all semester.

 tech

> Use heart rate monitors for biofeedback. See if students can reduce their heart rate by breathing and relaxing.

Part 3: Lesson Focus

Introduction to Yoga

1. Start by demonstrating and having everyone do the mountain pose together. Encourage students to look carefully at the position and then attempt the pose.

2. Explain that the value in yoga comes from holding each pose in a position that is comfortable for them (they should adjust how far they stretch or lift a limb to make it appropriate for their body) and learning to attend to their body and breathing while they hold the pose. At each station, they will look at the card showing the pose, try to balance in that pose and breathe slowly, and focus on their body until you signal that it's time to change stations.

3. Divide the students among the stations.

4. Turn the music down after about two minutes to signal a station change.

 review

Bring the students back together. Have them sit comfortably with backs straight and eyes looking straight ahead. Remind them to respect those around them who will be trying to concentrate also.

Review breathing: Invite students to close their eyes in preparation to practice intentional breathing. Tell them to breathe in slowly, filling their abdomens to a slow count of 2 (one one thousand, two one thousand), holding it for a count of 2, releasing it to a count of 2, and holding for a count of 2; repeat 10 times.

Provide affirmations for students to say to themselves on the third, sixth, and ninth breaths. Ask them to repeat to themselves each thought you provide. Say slowly:

* "In two, hold two, out two, hold two."
* "In two, hold two, out two, hold two."
* "I am a strong and capable individual."
* "In two . . ."
* "In two . . ."
* "I have the power to make good choices in my life."
* "In two . . ."
* "In two . . ."
* "I can choose to take care of my body and also help others to do so."
* "In two . . ."

Part 4: Reflection and Summary

Ask students to answer the following questions in a quiet tone.

▶ How did the yoga stations make you feel? Were any of the poses difficult? What did you do to help you hold the poses?

▶ Who can define range of motion?

▶ Who can define flexibility?

▶ Who can name some of the benefits of good flexibility?

Take It Home

Encourage students to do yoga at home three times a week or to look for a yoga class near their home. Encourage students to invite their parents to a yoga class with them.

Next Time

Benefits of flexibility

Assessment

► Comprehension check: Observe students during the yoga stations and determine their ability to interpret the poses.

► Performance check: Observe students during the yoga stations for their willingness to focus and try the activities, practice a variety of yoga positions, and tune in to their bodies.

In this classroom lesson, students will learn the benefits of flexibility and how to determine whether they have enough flexibility at various joints.

Performance Outcomes Related to NASPE Standards

▶ Standard 4
  ▶ Achieve and maintain a health-enhancing level of fitness.
▶ Standard 5
  ▶ Exhibit (verbally and nonverbally) cooperation, respect, encouragement, and ability to work independently.

Lesson Objectives

▶ Students will list three benefits of flexibility.
▶ Students will be able to measure their own flexibility.

Equipment

▶ 1 *Fitness for Life: Middle School* student textbook per student
▶ Chalkboard or flip chart
▶ 1 ruler for every three students

 tech

  * Two computer presentation programs (Mount Fitness and Tour de Fitness) are available for reviewing and reinforcing concepts. See page 40 for more information.
  * Find and show video clips of a diver in pike position, a skateboarder reaching back to grab his or her board, a rock climber, or something similar.

Reproducibles

Classroom Quotes

Classroom Quotes

You can print this quote from the CD-ROM and hang it in your room.

  ▶ "Stay committed to your decisions, but stay flexible in your approach."—Tom Robbins (author)

Setup

1. Print out and post the Classroom Quote at the front of the room.
2. Have *Fitness for Life: Middle School* texts, rulers, paper, and pencils ready to hand out to each group.

Delivering the Lesson

Part 1: Gathering Information

1. Remind students that you've talked about flexibility and range of motion in their bodies as well as flexibility in their approach to different situations. Do they know the benefits provided by physical flexibility? Tell them that today they'll read about those benefits.
2. Have the students read "Benefits of Flexibility," lesson 6.2 in the student text-book (chapter 6, pages 71 to 75).
3. When they're finished reading, lead the class in a discussion of ways to measure and improve flexibility.

Part 2: Lesson Launcher

1. Review the lesson objectives with students.
2. Explain that being flexible allows students to "go with the flow," but it also enables them to reach back and high when they serve a tennis ball. Flexibility has many advantages in daily life, and these advantages increase over time. More and more people are turning to activities such as yoga to increase their range of motion through specific stretching poses.

Part 3: Lesson Focus

Exploring Range of Motion

1. Explain to students that flexibility is specific to each joint. They may have great range of motion in one joint and poor range of motion in the same joint on the opposite side of the body.
2. Demonstrate the Fitnessgram shoulder stretch: Try to have the fingertips of your two hands touch or overlap behind your back by reaching one hand over your shoulder and the other up from behind your back. If they do not touch, use the ruler to measure the distance between the fingertips of the two hands.
3. Hand out paper and pencils so that students can record their flexibility scores.
4. Have students perform the shoulder stretch on their right and left arms and record the number of inches between fingertips on a piece of paper. Ask them why they think many people have more flexibility or strength on one side of their body than the other.
5. Put students into groups of two or three and assign each group a joint (spine, hip, ankle, shoulders). In a class of 24, you will have eight groups of three students, with two groups assigned to each of the four joints. Give each group a ruler.
6. Have each group do the following:
   ▸ Identify what type of joint it is (gliding, hinge, or ball and socket/rotation)

- Experiment with how to measure the range of motion of that joint
- Using the shoulder stretch as an example, create a way of measuring the range of motion of that joint

7. After they have worked on the problem for five to eight minutes, put the groups working on the same joints together. Have each group report its responses to the other group(s) and choose the best method from among the groups.

8. Gather all the groups together and have each large joint group report on their best assessment.

Part 4: Reflection and Summary

1. Compliment students on reading well. Focus on how they have achieved one of the self-responsibility goals by assessing themselves.

2. Have students add their piece of paper with their flexibility scores to their *Fitness for Life: Middle School* portfolios.

3. Ask students the following questions:
   - Why might you be more flexible on one side of your body than on the other? (Answer: Your dominant side is often more flexible because it's used for more movement, which expands the range of motion, compared to the nondominant side.)
   - What is the FIT formula for flexibility exercises? Could you practice flexibility exercises with someone from your support team at least three times a week?

Take It Home

Tell students to pay attention to their physical and social/emotional flexibility in the next couple of days. As they are going through their daily lives, they should identify situations where having good flexibility is helpful (such as watching people drive and noting how often they try to look over their shoulder to see if it's clear to back up, or when they want to have cereal instead of toast for breakfast, but their sibling just drank the last of the milk). Ask them to bring examples so you can collect a great list.

Next Time

Back-saver sit-and-reach test

Assessment

- Comprehension check: Responses to the Reflection and Summary questions serve as a check for student understanding of the benefits of flexibility.
- Performance check: Observe students correctly performing the flexibility self-assessments and working well with their group (cooperation, respect, and encouragement).

6.4 Back-Saver Sit-and-Reach Test

Students will assess their level of hip flexibility using the Fitnessgram back-saver sit-and-reach test.

Performance Outcomes Related to NASPE Standards

▶ Standard 4
  ▶ Self-assess hip flexibility as part of health-related fitness.
  ▶ Meet age- and gender-specific health-related fitness standards as defined by Fitnessgram.
▶ Standard 5
  ▶ Exhibit (verbally and nonverbally) cooperation, respect, encouragement, and ability to work independently.
▶ Standard 6
  ▶ See learning new activities and skills as challenging.

Lesson Objectives

▶ Students will learn about and perform the back-saver sit-and-reach test.
▶ Students will determine where they fall in relation to the healthy zone in the back-saver sit-and-reach test.

Equipment

▶ 8 cones
▶ CD player and upbeat music

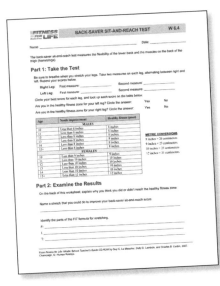

▸ 1 pencil for each student

▸ 4 pinnies

▸ 4 back-saver sit-and-reach measuring stations

▸ Curl-up or push-up CD of three-second counts to guide curl-ups and push-ups (comes with Fitnessgram, but consider making your own three-second interval with a count included [up, 1, 2, down, 1, 2, up, 2, 2, down, 2, 2, up 3, 2, down, 3, 2, up, 4, 2, down, 4, 2, up, 5, 2, etc.])

Reproducibles

Worksheet 6.4, "Back-Saver Sit-and-Reach Test"

Setup

1. To create the back-saver sit-and-reach measuring stations, you can attach a ruler to an old milk crate, box, or folded mat so that the 9-inch mark is at the edge of the box or mat and the 1-inch mark is in open air toward the person being tested. (Instructions for building a formal box are available in the Fitnessgram manual and involve building a plywood box that is about 12 inches square with a top that extends out 9 inches on one side. This piece is marked in 1-inch increments from 0 at the free end to 9 at the edge of the box and from 9 inches to 12 inches on top of the box.)

2. Place the four sit-and-reach stations on the edge of the area where they won't interfere with a tag game.

3. Place cones around the playing area to provide a buffer between the game play area and the walls or other equipment.

4. Make a copy of worksheet 6.4, "Back-Saver Sit-and-Reach Test," for each student.

5. At each station, place one-fourth of the pencils and worksheets.

Delivering the Lesson

Part 1: Instant Activity

Fitness Tag

1. Choose three or four students to be "It" and have them put on pinnies. Their job is to tag as many students as possible.

2. Students who are tagged must go outside the boundary and do 10 reps of an exercise in an area in which they need practice (such as crunches, push-ups, or cardio jumping jacks). When they're finished, they return to the game.

3. After each minute, change the students who are "It" until everyone has had a chance to be "It."

Part 2: Lesson Launcher

1. Review the lesson objectives with students.

2. Remind students that you've been talking about flexibility. Today, they will use the back-saver sit-and-reach test to see whether they have enough flexibility to be in the healthy zone.

Part 3: Lesson Focus

Back-Saver Sit-and-Reach Test

1. Arrange students into pairs using one of the methods described in "Groups and Teams" (pages 26 to 27).

2. Point out the pencils and worksheets that are at each assessment station. When students go to a station, each one should write his or her name on a worksheet. Partners will record the sit-and-reach scores for each other.

 review

Remind students about supporting their partners and keeping information confidential.

3. Explain and demonstrate the Fitnessgram instructions for performing the back-saver sit-and-reach test.

 ▸ Straighten one leg in front of you. Bend your other leg, placing that foot on the floor next to the knee of your straight leg.

 ▸ Have your partner place one hand on the knee of the straight leg so she can let you know if you begin to bend the knee.

 ▸ Place the foot of your straight leg against the measuring box so that the 1-inch mark on the ruler is closest to your waist.

 ▸ Lean your upper body forward over the straight leg, making sure it stays straight. Use both hands to reach along the ruler toward your toes. Keep one hand directly on top of the other, with your fingers lined up. Reach out slowly along the ruler, giving your muscles a chance to relax and stretch.

 ▸ Reach out a second time, and then relax again.

 ▸ Reach out a third time, and hold the reach along the ruler while your partner reads the number on the ruler. If one hand is farther back than the other, the measurement is taken from the tip of the back hand.

 ▸ Switch which leg is bent and which is straight and repeat the assessment.

 ▸ Check if you can reach to your shin, ankle, or toes. Toes generally constitute the healthy zone.

 check

Ask students to suggest factors that might cause people to record incorrect information on their worksheet. (Answers: bending the knee of the straight leg; measuring from the forward hand if the hands are not together; placing the ruler incorrectly; mixing up the scores for the two legs; or recording the number you wish rather than the number you measure.)

4. Send one pair of students to each of the four stations. Each pair will test each other, record their scores, and then switch places with another pair that is waiting "on deck" to take the test.

5. Students who are not at a station will stay warm by playing an active tag game or doing an active sports or recreation activity. Choose any of the warm-up activities used in previous lessons, and change taggers every three minutes.

► *Freeze tag:* Taggers try to freeze the others. Students who are not frozen can rescue those who are frozen by stopping in front of a frozen student and doing five jumping jacks together.

► *Olympic rock, paper, scissors:* The playing is divided lengthwise into three sections with cones—sections are named gold, silver, and bronze. Students find someone to do rock, paper, scissors with. The winner goes up a section (or stays if in gold) and the loser goes down a section (or stays if in bronze), and then they find another person to play with.

► *Fitness tag:* Choose three or four students to be "It." Their goal is to get all other students off the floor at the same time. Students who are tagged must go outside the boundary and do 10 reps of an exercise in an area in which they need practice (such as crunches, push-ups, or cardio jumping jacks). When they're finished, they return to the game.

6. When everyone has completed the back-saver sit-and-reach, have students walk two laps to cool down and then give them a few minutes to complete worksheet 6.4, "Back-Saver Sit-and-Reach Test." Tell them that the healthy zone for the back-saver sit-and-reach for boys is between 8 and 12 inches (20 and 31 centimeters) and for girls between 10 and 12 inches (25 and 31 centimeters).

Part 4: Reflection and Summary

1. Ask students the following questions:

► Why might someone record false information on their worksheet? Does that make sense when you're trying to assess yourself?

► Why might healthy fitness zone scores for girls and boys be different? (Answer: Girls typically have better flexibility scores than boys, just as boys tend to have higher fitness scores than girls in some areas. Hereditary differences in joints, muscles, and bones are thought to be the reason. This is why there are different standards for boys and girls in some of the fitness self-assessments.) What should a boy do if his score is in the healthy fitness zone for boys, but it falls short of the healthy fitness zone for girls?

► Who can provide an example of a partner who gave positive feedback or helped them get an accurate score?

► If you wanted to improve your flexibility, what might you do? (Answer: warm up and stretch on a regular basis, following the FIT guidelines.) How would you know whether you were getting better? (Answer: notice that you can reach farther; retest yourself.)

2. Have students add worksheet 6.4, "Back-Saver Sit-and-Reach Test," to their *Fitness for Life: Middle School* portfolios.

Take It Home

Instruct students to spend 20 minutes every other night doing an active aerobics activity to build up their cardiovascular fitness and follow it with a stretch to improve their flexibility.

Next Time

▶ Teamwork

▶ Remind students that worksheet 6.1, "Teamwork," is due next class (recommended).

Assessment

▶ Performance check: Observe students performing the back-saver sit-and-reach test correctly and supporting each other.

▶ Comprehension check: Responses to the Reflection and Summary questions serve as a check for student understanding of the healthy fitness zone and how flexibility can be improved.

▶ Assess completed worksheet 6.4, "Back-Saver Sit-and-Reach Test," in students' *Fitness for Life: Middle School* portfolios, and determine the percentage of students in class who are in the healthy zone for flexibility. Use the worksheet rubric (available on the CD-ROM or on page 34) to assess student work, or modify the rubric to meet your specific objectives.

In this activity lesson, students will participate in innovative challenges that require teamwork.

Performance Outcomes Related to NASPE Standards

▸ Standard 5
  ▹ Exhibit (verbally and nonverbally) cooperation, respect, encouragement, and ability to work independently.

▸ Standard 6
  ▹ Recognize the role of physical activity in getting to know and understand others.
  ▹ Recognize physical activity as a positive opportunity for social and group interaction.
  ▹ Identify potential social and health benefits from participation in physical activity.

Lesson Objectives

▸ Students will use brainstorming, compromise, and good communication to solve teamwork challenges.
▸ Students will demonstrate effective communication and support techniques.

Equipment

  ▸ 1 soft ball (such as a foam ball, a volleyball, or a playground ball) for every two students; balls should be of different sizes
  ▸ 5 pinnies
  ▸ 5 hula hoops
  ▸ 8 bandannas or scarves

Reproducibles

None

Setup

Have one bin of bandannas or scarves and another bin of balls in locations that will make it easy for students to access the equipment during the lesson activities.

Delivering the Lesson

Part 1: Instant Activity

See Ya Later Tag

1. Choose four or five students to be "It," and have them wear pinnies.

2. When two students link arms, they can't be tagged. If a third student links onto one end of a pair, the student on the other end must break off and leave. (Optional: Instead, lay hula hoops on the ground to form safe zones; only one student may be in a hoop at a time. If a new person comes in to the hoop, the first student must leave.)

3. If a person is tagged, the tagger gives him or her the pinny, and the person tagged becomes "It."

Part 2: Lesson Launcher

1. Review the lesson objectives with students.

2. Remind students that you've been talking about how to communicate and how to support each other's learning. This week you have talked specifically about teamwork and how it requires flexibility by all members of the team. Tell them that today they'll participate in several challenges that will take teamwork, communication, and supportive behaviors.

 review

> Remind students how to listen to everyone in the group, take turns, and encourage each other.

Part 3: Lesson Focus 1

Teamwork Challenge: Untying Knots (see page 22)

1. Arrange students into groups of six to eight using one of the methods in "Groups and Teams" (pages 26 to 27).

2. Give each student a bandanna or scarf. Have each group find its own space and make a tight circle with everyone facing in.

3. Have each group member reach into the center with his or her bandanna in one hand and grab someone else's bandanna with the other hand. Students can't grab the bandanna of someone on either side of them, and they can't grab the bandanna of someone who has grabbed their own bandanna. This will create a "knot" of arms with everyone connected by the bandannas. (Optional: Students can hold hands instead, but the bandannas give them more room to move and eliminate problems with holding hands and twisting arms as they untangle.)

4. Explain that each group must work together to untie the knot without breaking the links between people. The group may come out in a circle, a figure eight, two circles interlocked, or two separate circles.

check

Ask students what health-related fitness component that you talked about this week will be used in this activity. (Answer: flexibility.) What other health-related fitness components might they use? (Answer: muscular endurance to hold positions as you untangle.)

observe

Scan for joints in awkward positions and students listening to each other, taking turns, and suggesting ideas.

Part 4: Lesson Focus 2

Teamwork Challenge: Group Juggling (see lesson 2.4 on page 82)

1. Arrange students into groups of six to eight using one of the methods in "Groups and Teams" (pages 26 to 27). Have each group form a circle.

2. Without using any balls yet, have the students in each group practice a pattern for throwing a ball back and forth. Start by asking one student to call the name of the person that he or she will throw the ball to, and then ask that student to name another person, and so on. Remind students that everyone must toss and catch the ball at least once, and that the group's success will depend on having a good pattern for throwing.

3. Ask the students to raise their hands when their group has established its pattern. Give one ball to each group. Tell them they are going to continue to use the same pattern. Remind everyone to
   - call the name of the person they are throwing to each time,
   - make eye contact before throwing the ball, and
   - practice their good manners by saying thank you when someone throws them the ball.

4. Have each group begin its pattern. If a ball is dropped before it goes through the whole sequence and returns to the starting person, the group starts over again, beginning with the next student in the pattern. Students should count how many times it takes their group to complete the pattern without dropping the ball.
   - Challenge the groups to see how many times they can go through the pattern without dropping the ball. Go through the sequence as above, starting with a different person each time; a group earns 1 point each time the ball goes all the way around.
   - Challenge the groups to see how many times the ball can go through the pattern in 30 seconds (or until the music stops) without being dropped.

5. Add a second ball to each group. The first person in the pattern throws the first ball. Once the ball has been caught and thrown by the second person, the first person starts the second ball.

6. Add a third ball, starting all three balls with the first person in the pathway.

7. Have each group try to move. Have the students move randomly around their group's section of the playing area. Keep throwing the ball in the same sequence as before. Start with one ball and build to three. It becomes even more important now to call out names and make eye contact before throwing the ball.

8. Have a student in each group take one ball at a time out of circulation and return them to the ball bags/carts.

9. Interesting variations include the following:

- ▸ Provide students with a variety of balls and objects to make the tasks easier or harder.

- ▸ Provide cooperative groups with a crazy ball (one with knobs that make it bounce in crazy ways). Have them stand in a circle and take turns trying to bounce the ball to a teammate. See how many catches in a row the team can make.

- ▸ Encourage students who have "mastered" the tasks to provide tips and encouragement to students who have not mastered them.

 observe

> Review what it would look like if everyone did great work—making eye contact before throwing, using names, making throws that others can catch, supporting each other when mistakes are made, encouraging others when they are successful, and so on.

Part 5: Reflection and Summary

1. Ask students the following questions:

- ▸ What did their group do well?

- ▸ What was the most important factor in achieving success in the Untying Knots challenge?

- ▸ What was the most important factor in achieving success in the Group Juggling challenge?

- ▸ Who can name an aspect of fitness that was part of one of the challenges?

2. Have students add completed worksheet 6.1, "Teamwork," to their *Fitness for Life: Middle School* portfolios.

Take It Home

Encourage students to teach one of the challenges they learned today to a group at home.

Next Time

Muscle fitness

Assessment

- ▸ Comprehension check: Responses to the Reflection and Summary questions serve as a check for student understanding of effective communication and support techniques.

- ▸ Performance check: Observe the class climate behaviors (such as including each other, complimenting each other, and listening to each other).

- ▸ Assess completed worksheet 6.1, "Teamwork," in students' *Fitness for Life: Middle School* portfolios. Use the worksheet rubric (available on the CD-ROM or on page 34) to assess student work, or modify the rubric to meet your specific objectives.

Supplemental Materials

If you choose to use the semester or year scheduling version of *Fitness for Life: Middle School* (see appendix B), there are excellent opportunities to insert activity-based skill units and to review and reinforce the concepts in each chapter using the *Fitness for Life: Middle School* computer programs: Mount Fitness and Tour de Fitness. You will find information about the two computer programs in appendix C. Listed below are suggestions of activity-based skill units that would go well with this chapter and resources that will help you develop great lessons.

As indicated in the "Scheduling" section (pages 13 to 18), integrating activity-based skill units with the *Fitness for Life: Middle School* lesson plans provides a great opportunity for reinforcing key concepts and for developing students' skills in a wide range of physical activities. The activity-based skill unit suggestions provided below were chosen specifically to complement chapter content. In addition, there are selected resources that can provide you with excellent lesson plans and lesson plan ideas. Approaches to teaching activity-based skill units can be found in appendix A.

SELF-DEFENSE

- ▶ **Key concepts to reinforce:** Flexibility, inclusion, teamwork, range of motion
- ▶ **Resources:**
  - ▶ *Teaching Martial Arts for Fitness and Fun: A Noncontact Approach for Young People* (Winkle, 2001, Human Kinetics)
  - ▶ Find an expert in your community.

YOGA

- ▶ **Key concepts to reinforce:** Flexibility, inclusion, teamwork, range of motion
- ▶ **Resources:**
  - ▶ Find an expert in your community with a yoga teaching certification who has experience working with youth.
  - ▶ *Yoga for Inflexible People*—Bodywise Interactive Yoga Series #6307326050, Baker & Taylor Inc. 800-755-1800
  - ▶ *Power Yoga for Flexibility*—Rodney Yee #1592504418, Baker & Taylor Inc. 800-775-1800
  - ▶ *Yoga for Beginners*—Gaiam, Patricia Walden #1930814828, Baker & Taylor Inc. 800-755-1800

TAI CHI

- ▶ **Key concepts to reinforce:** Flexibility, inclusion, teamwork, range of motion
- ▶ **Resources:** Find an expert in your community who has experience working with youth.

Muscle Fitness Exercises

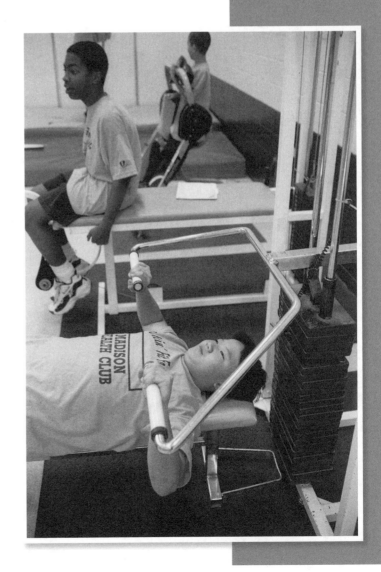

Chapter 7 lesson plans expose students to the training principles of overload and progression for building strength and muscular endurance. Students self-assess their muscular fitness and identify muscle fitness exercises that would increase muscular fitness for their preferred physical activities. Student discussions about bullying precede an assignment on exploring strength of character. The biomechanical principle of resistance is discussed and students apply the principle to physical activity settings.

* 7.1 Muscle Fitness Exercises: Level 3 of the Physical Activity Pyramid (classroom lesson)
* 7.2 Strength and Muscular Endurance Circuit (activity lesson)
* 7.3 Benefits of Muscle Fitness Exercises (classroom lesson)
* 7.4 Muscular Endurance Self-Assessments (activity lesson)
* 7.5 Muscular Endurance Exercise Circuit (activity lesson)

7.1 Muscle Fitness Exercises: Level 3 of the Physical Activity Pyramid

This classroom lesson provides students with an opportunity to learn about muscle fitness and the principle of specificity. Additionally, students will have an opportunity to discuss the problem of bullying and strategies for preventing bullying.

Performance Outcomes Related to NASPE Standards

▶ Standard 3
  ▶ Describe the FIT formula for strength and muscular endurance exercises.
  ▶ Demonstrate an understanding of the principle of specificity as it relates to muscle fitness.
▶ Standard 5
  ▶ Demonstrate respect for others by preventing bullying.

Lesson Objectives

▶ Students will demonstrate an understanding of the difference between strength and muscular endurance.

▶ Students will demonstrate different muscle fitness exercises and explain the correct FIT formula for building strength and muscular endurance.

▶ Students will demonstrate an understanding of the principle of specificity, isotonic resistance exercises, and isometric resistance exercises by providing muscle fitness examples relevant to their interests.

▶ Students will demonstrate an understanding of the guidelines for preventing bullying through class discussions.

Equipment

▶ 1 *Fitness for Life: Middle School* student textbook per student
▶ Chalkboard or flip chart (optional)

 tech

Find and show video clips of male and female athletes performing muscle fitness exercises.

Reproducibles

▶ Worksheet 7.1a, "Respect and Protect Oath"

▶ Worksheet 7.1b, "Strength of Character"

▶ Classroom Quotes

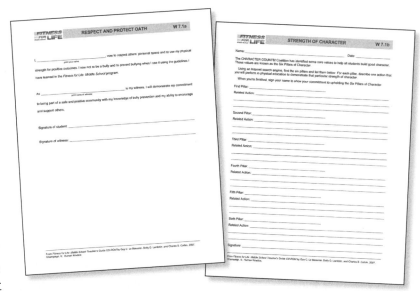

Classroom Quotes

You can print these quotes from the CD-ROM and hang them around your room.

▶ "O, it is excellent to have a giant's strength, but it is tyrannous to use it like a giant."—William Shakespeare (playwright and poet)

▶ "What is strength without a double share of wisdom?"—John Milton (poet)

Setup

1. Write the following instructions on the chalkboard or flip chart:

   ▶ Create two muscular endurance exercises (one isotonic, one isometric) and two strength exercises (one isotonic, one isometric) that are specific for activities that some group members participate in.

   ▶ Identify the muscles involved in these exercises.

   ▶ What is the FIT formula for strength and muscular endurance exercises?

2. Make a copy of worksheets 7.1a, "Respect and Protect Oath," and 7.1b, "Strength of Character," for each student.

Delivering the Lesson

Part 1: Gathering Information

1. Explain to the class that muscle fitness exercises are on level 3 of the Physical Activity Pyramid. Muscle fitness exercises can be done to develop strength and muscular endurance. Ask if anyone can explain the difference between strength and endurance. Tell them that today you'll be discussing muscle fitness and how to build it.

2. Have the students read "Muscle Fitness Exercises: Level 3 of the Physical Activity Pyramid," lesson 7.1 in the student textbook (chapter 7, pages 79 to 84).

Part 2: Lesson Launcher

1. Review the lesson objectives with students.

2. Ask students to share examples of activities that require strength. Where on the Physical Activity Pyramid would they put those activities?

3. Ask students to share examples of activities that require muscular endurance. Where on the Physical Activity Pyramid would they put those activities?

Part 3: Lesson Focus 1

Isotonic and Isometric Exercise for Strength and Endurance

1. Arrange students in groups of three or four using one of the methods described in "Groups and Teams" (see pages 26 to 27).

2. Have each group quickly identify a leader, a recorder, and a reporter. The group leader will guide the discussion, the recorder will generate the list created by the group, and the reporter will report the results to the class. In a group of four, the fourth member could be a "brainstormer," or group contributor.

3. Provide expectations for each of the roles in the group so that all members contribute. Provide an example of how this might sound, such as:

▸ In order to get things started, the leader might say, "So let's look at question #1: I'll read it out loud. . . . What does everybody think?"

▸ The recorder should make a list of phrases or ideas provided by group members. The recorder doesn't need to write down every word spoken—just the key words that convey the idea.

▸ The reporter doesn't have to share all of the ideas—just the main ideas brought up by the group. For example, "Our group came up with two examples of strength exercises, which are. . . ."

↻ **review**

Remind students that they will know they are doing good work as individuals if they fulfill the responsibilities of their roles in the group. They will know they are doing great work as a group if they help and encourage each other to work productively together.

4. Have each group create two muscular endurance exercises and two strength exercises that would be specific for activities that some members participate in. For the strength and muscular endurance exercises, one must be an isotonic exercise (e.g., leg extension for soccer players) and one must be an isometric exercise (e.g., bent-arm hang for rock climbers). Have students identify the muscle(s) that are involved in the exercises and describe the FIT formula for strength and muscular endurance exercises.

? **check**

Ask students to show you how many total exercises each group will create by holding up the correct number of fingers. (Answer: four.) How many of those will be isometric exercises? (Answer: two.) How many of those will be isotonic exercises? (Answer: two.)

5. Give students five to eight minutes to come up with their exercises.

6. Ask selected group reporters to present their examples to the class. Demonstrations can be performed by other group members while the reporter explains.

↻ **review**

Review some of the effective communication skills discussed in recent lessons (such as active listening, not interrupting, sharing the "stage," respecting opinions).

Part 4: Lesson Focus 2

Bullying

1. Have students read the opening section of "Moving Together: Bullying" in the student textbook (chapter 7, page 83).

2. Tell the students to look over the discussion questions briefly, and then to read the "Guidelines for Preventing Bullying." Students should use the guidelines to come up with answers to the discussion questions.

3. In each group, all students should change roles so that different students become the new leader, recorder, and reporter. The leader will pose the discussion questions, the recorder will record the theme of the responses, and the reporter will be prepared to share an answer with the larger group.

4. Bring the class together and ask the discussion questions to the larger group. Have the reporters and others contribute answers and generate discussion.

5. Extend the discussion about bullying using your own personal experiences or those of students. Explain that cyberbullying, such as threatening others via e-mail or text messaging, is becoming a real problem. (For more information on cyberbullying, see Web Topic 7.4 on the *Fitness for Life: Middle School* Web site.)

6. Hand out worksheet 7.1a, the "Respect and Protect Oath." Each student should read and sign their sheet, and then have another group member sign as their witness. (Optional: Have students take the worksheet home and have a parent or guardian sign as their witness.)

Part 5: Reflection and Summary

1. Ask students the following questions:
   - What's the difference between muscular strength and muscular endurance?
   - What is the FIT formula for strength?
   - What is the FIT formula for muscular endurance?

2. If the students completed worksheet 7.1a, "Respect and Protect Oath," during class, have them add it to their *Fitness for Life: Middle School* portfolios.

Take It Home

- Hand out worksheet 7.1b, "Strength of Character," to each student. Instruct them to complete the worksheets at home by looking up the Six Pillars of Character on the Internet and describing how they'll demonstrate those pillars in physical education.

- Tell students when to return the completed worksheets to class. (Recommended: lesson 7.2 for worksheet 7.1a, if they're taking it home; lesson 7.3 for worksheet 7.1b.) Some students might not have Internet access at home, so you may want to extend the due date for worksheet 7.1b to accommodate them.

Next Time

▶ Strength and muscular endurance circuit

▶ If students take worksheet 7.1a, "Respect and Protect Oath," home, remind them that it is due next class.

Assessment

▶ Performance check: Observe students working effectively in groups.

▶ Comprehension check: Class discussions and responses to the Reflection and Summary questions serve as a check for students' understanding of the difference between strength and muscular endurance, principle of specificity, isotonic and isometric resistance exercises, and the FIT formula for building strength and muscular endurance.

▶ Comprehension check: Class discussions will serve as a check for understanding of the guidelines for preventing bullying.

▶ Assess completed worksheet 7.1a, "Respect and Protect Oath," in students' *Fitness for Life: Middle School* portfolio if students completed it in class. Use the worksheet rubric (available on the CD-ROM or on page 34) to assess student work, or modify the rubric to meet your specific objectives.

7.2 Strength and Muscular Endurance Circuit

This activity lesson provides students with the opportunity to try several muscular strength and endurance exercises.

Performance Outcomes Related to NASPE Standards

▶ Standard 1
  ▶ Perform muscle fitness activities that require strength and endurance.
▶ Standard 3
  ▶ Participate in health-enhancing physical activities both during and outside of school.
▶ Standard 5
  ▶ Exhibit (verbally and nonverbally) cooperation, respect, encouragement, and ability to work independently.
▶ Standard 6
  ▶ Seek personally challenging physical activity experiences.

Lesson Objectives

▶ Students will participate in a circuit designed to challenge their muscular fitness.
▶ Students will demonstrate an understanding of the FIT formula for strength and muscular endurance exercises, the difference between strength and muscular endurance exercise, and the principle of specificity.
▶ Students will communicate and cooperate effectively during the muscle fitness circuit.

Equipment

- 3 pinnies or scarves
- 8 cones
- 6 exercise mats
- 2 stable benches
- 4 movable benches
- CD player and music (optional)

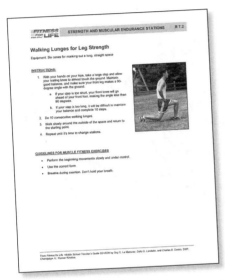

Reproducibles

Resource 7.2, "Strength and Muscular Endurance Stations"

Setup

1. Make one set of "Strength and Muscular Endurance Stations" cards.
2. Set up six stations to match the cards:
   - *Walking lunges for leg strength:* 6 cones (3 pairs lined up 20 to 40 feet [6 to 12 meters] apart)
   - *Push-up variations:* 3 exercise mats for knee push-ups
   - *Abdominal variations:* 3 exercise mats
   - *Calf raises:* 2 cones to mark an area along the wall
   - *Bench dip variations:* 2 stable benches (or 2 rows of the first level of bleachers)
   - *Bench pulls for shoulders and back:* 4 movable benches (2 rows of 2 each placed end to end)
3. Hang each card with its corresponding station.

Delivering the Lesson

Part 1: Instant Activity

Freeze Tag

1. Designate three students in the class as "It." Students who are "It" should wear pinnies or scarves.
2. Students who are "It" try to tag other students. The goal is to get everyone frozen. Those who get tagged are frozen in place until someone who is free does a crab walk around them. (Optional: Periodically, change what students must do to unfreeze each other.)
3. After one minute, let other students have a turn being "It" until everyone in class has been "It."

Part 2: Lesson Launcher

1. Review the lesson objectives with students.

2. Ask the class to name a sport that requires muscular strength and an active recreation activity that requires muscular endurance. Ask if anyone has heard of, and can explain, circuit training. Explain that today, they'll go through a strength and muscular endurance circuit.

3. Advise students that when performing muscle fitness exercises and tests, there's always the potential for injury. Discuss three important guidelines to remember (which also appear on each "Strength and Muscular Endurance Stations" card):

   ▸ Perform the beginning movements slowly and under control.

   ▸ Use correct form.

   ▸ Breathe during exertion. Don't hold your breath.

Part 3: Lesson Focus

Strength and Muscular Endurance Circuit

1. Divide the class into groups of six using one of the methods described in "Groups and Teams" (see pages 26 to 27).

2. Assign one group to each station. Have the students become "experts" at their assigned station. To do this, students will read the "Strength and Muscular Endurance Stations" card, perform the activity, and come up with technique cues for performing it successfully.

3. Rearrange the groups so that one student from each station is in each group. Possible method: Have students in each group line up in order according to the dates of their birthdays (e.g., 1, 4, 17, 23, 25, and 31). The first person in each line goes to station 1, the second person goes to station 2, and so on.

   ▸ If you have more than six students per station, assign two experts to share the duty of explaining the station.

   ▸ If you have fewer than six students per station, some groups will be without an expert at some stations. Have students in these groups work cooperatively at stations without experts.

4. Have groups rotate through the activities. At each station, the designated expert for that station will lead the group.

 observe

Ask the class to name the three important guidelines for muscle fitness exercises.

Part 4: Reflection and Summary

1. Ask students the following questions:

   ▸ Could a muscle fitness exercise be a strength exercise for one person and an endurance exercise for another? (Answer: yes. An exercise that challenges strength for one person [6 reps] might challenge muscular endurance for a stronger person who can lift that weight 20 reps.)

   ▸ How do you know whether an exercise is a muscular strength or a muscular endurance exercise for you? (Answer: If you can do 15 to 20 repetitions, it's a muscular endurance exercise.)

   ▸ What active sports or active recreation activities would benefit from one of the exercises in the circuit? (Possible answers: walking lunge—volleyball, hiking; push-ups—basketball, mountain biking; abdominal exercises—boxing, skateboarding; calf raises—gymnastics, beach volleyball; bench dips—football, karate; bench pulls—swimming, rock climbing.)

2. Have students add completed worksheet 7.1a, "Respect and Protect Oath," to their *Fitness for Life: Middle School* portfolios if they didn't complete it in the last class.

Take It Home

Ask students to try some of these exercises with members of their support team. For each team member, students should decide whether the exercises are muscular strength or muscular endurance exercises. Base the decision on the number of reps the person is able to do and on the FIT formula.

Next Time

▶ Benefits of muscle fitness

▶ Remind students that worksheet 7.1b, "Strength of Character," is due next class (recommended).

Assessment

▶ Performance check: Observe students performing the exercises using correct form and working effectively in groups (such as communicating, cooperating, and encouraging each other).

▶ Comprehension check: Responses to the Reflection and Summary questions serve as a check for student understanding of the FIT formula for strength and muscular endurance exercises, the difference between strength and muscular endurance exercise, and the principle of specificity.

▶ Assess completed worksheet 7.1a, "Respect and Protect Oath," in students' *Fitness for Life: Middle School* portfolio if students didn't complete it in the last class. Use the worksheet rubric (available on the CD-ROM or on page 34) to assess student work, or modify the rubric to meet your specific objectives.

Lesson Plan 7.3 Benefits of Muscle Fitness Exercises

In this classroom lesson, students will have the opportunity to explore how strength and muscular endurance benefit humans and other animals. In addition, students will be introduced to the concept of resistance.

Performance Outcomes Related to NASPE Standards

▶ Standard 2
  ▶ Demonstrate an understanding of muscle fitness and how it is used by various populations.
▶ Standard 3
  ▶ Demonstrate an understanding of the concept of resistance and how it affects human movement in a variety of physical activities.
▶ Standard 5
  ▶ Exhibit (verbally and nonverbally) cooperation, respect, encouragement, and ability to work independently.

Lesson Objectives

▶ Students will demonstrate, using specific examples, an understanding of how various populations use strength and muscular endurance to their benefit.
▶ Students will be able to describe how resistance affects human movements in a variety of physical activities.

Equipment

▶ 1 *Fitness for Life: Middle School* student textbook per student
▶ Chalkboard or flip chart (optional)

 tech

  * Two computer presentation programs (Mount Fitness and Tour de Fitness) are available for reviewing and reinforcing concepts. See page 40 for more information.
  * Find and show video clips of several types of active sports and active recreation activities.

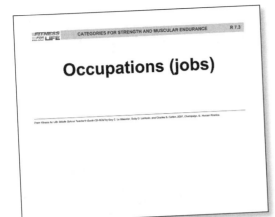

Reproducibles

▶ Resource 7.3, "Categories for Strength and Muscular Endurance"
▶ Classroom Quotes

Classroom Quotes

You can print these quotes from the CD-ROM and hang them around your room.

▶ "Strength does not come from winning. Your struggles develop your strengths. When you go through hardships and decide not to surrender, that is strength."—Arnold Schwarzenegger (actor, politician)
▶ "Strength is the ability to break a chocolate bar into four pieces with your bare hands—and then eat just one of those pieces."—Judith Viorst (author)

Setup

1. Write the following instructions on the board: Provide two examples of muscular strength and two examples of muscular endurance for your category.
2. Make one set of "Categories for Strength and Muscular Endurance" cards. Add more categories of your own if you choose.

Delivering the Lesson

Part 1: Gathering Information

1. Have the students read "Benefits of Muscle Fitness Exercises," lesson 7.2 in the student textbook (chapter 7, pages 85 to 90).
2. Instruct students to pay particular attention to the principle of specificity as they read.

Part 2: Lesson Launcher

1. Review the lesson objectives with students.
2. Remind students that in the last classroom session, they determined the difference between muscular strength and muscular endurance, and they learned about the FIT formula for muscle fitness exercises. Tell them that today, they'll explore the importance of muscle fitness for humans and other living creatures.

Part 3: Lesson Focus 1

Muscle Fitness in Action

1. Organize students into groups of three or four using one of the methods described in "Groups and Teams" (see pages 26 to 27).

2. Have each group identify a leader, a recorder, and a reporter. Encourage students to take on a different group role than the one they played in the last classroom session. In each group, the leader will guide the discussion, the recorder will generate the list created by the group, and the reporter will report results to the class. If a group has four students, the fourth member can be a "brainstormer", or group contributor.

3. Have each group choose a "Categories for Strength and Muscular Endurance" card at random, and ask students to brainstorm examples of how living beings in that category use strength and muscular endurance. Have each member of the group contribute two examples for muscular strength and two examples for muscular endurance for the category. Categories include occupations (such as mail carriers, wildlife photographers, and fishermen), athletes (such as gymnasts, soccer players, racecar drivers, and golfers), and living creatures (such as reptiles, birds, fish, and insects).

 observe

Ask students how many examples they will contribute to their group. (Answer: two examples from each student.)

4. Ask selected group reporters to present their examples to the class. Each reporter should present two examples of muscular strength and two examples of muscular endurance from their category. Demonstrations can be performed by other group members while the reporter explains.

5. Ask the class the following questions about muscle fitness:

- Who can explain the principle of specificity for building muscle fitness using an example generated by your group?
- Who can provide an example of how humans use the principle of specificity to build muscle fitness? (Answer: leg strength exercises for soccer, football, and hockey players.)
- Who can provide an example of a test that humans could do to determine their level of muscular endurance? (Answer: push-ups or sit-ups.)
- Who can provide an example of a test that humans could do to determine their level of strength? (Answer: maximum bench press or maximum squat.)

6. Explain that in the next class, students will learn about Fitnessgram tests of strength and muscular endurance.

Part 4: Lesson Focus 2

Resistance

1. Have students read "Biomechanical Principles: Resistance" in the student textbook (chapter 7, page 89).

2. In each group, all students should change roles so that different students become the new leader, recorder, and reporter. The leader will pose a question to the group, the recorder will record the theme of the responses, and the reporter will be prepared to share answers with the larger group. Have the students answer the question on page 89: For each of the following activities, describe how resistance will make the activity harder or easier:

- Mowing the lawn
- Playing tug-of-war

- ▸ Doing push-ups
- ▸ Doing biceps curls
- ▸ Wrestling
- ▸ Playing softball
- ▸ Running with and against the wind
- ▸ Swimming

3. Ask students to provide a unique example from their category of how resistance is used to make performing an activity easier or harder.

4. Bring the class together and ask the question to the larger group. Have the reporters and others contribute answers and generate discussion.

Part 5: Reflection and Summary

1. Ask the class the following questions:
   - ▸ What are some things that affect your ability to build muscle fitness? (Answers: heredity, diet [nutrition], and sleep.)
   - ▸ Who can explain why the principle of specificity is important for muscle fitness training? (Possible answers: You want to increase strength in the muscles you use for your activity. Also, when you increase strength you often increase your weight. You might not want to carry extra weight around for some sports. For example, you wouldn't want too much upper-body strength for soccer, cycling, and figure skating, and you might not want too much lower-body strength for rock climbing and swimming.)
   - ▸ Who can explain resistance?

2. Have students add completed worksheet 7.1b, "Strength of Character," to their *Fitness for Life: Middle School* portfolios.

Take It Home

Talk to members of your support team about the muscle fitness training they do, or have done, for activities. See if they are following the principle of specificity.

Next Time

Muscular endurance self-assessments

Assessment

- ▸ Performance check: Observe students working effectively in groups.
- ▸ Comprehension check: Student discussion and responses to the Reflection and Summary questions serve as a check for student understanding of how various populations use strength and muscular endurance to their benefit, and how resistance affects human movements in a variety of physical activities.
- ▸ Assess completed worksheet 7.1b, "Strength of Character," in students' *Fitness for Life: Middle School* portfolios. Use the worksheet rubric (available on the CD-ROM or on page 34) to assess student work, or modify the rubric to meet your specific objectives.

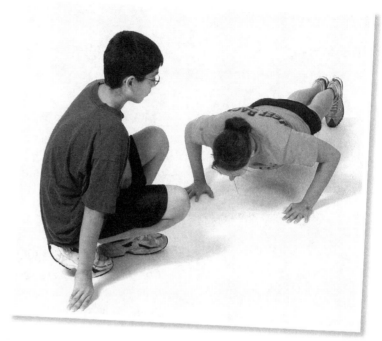

Lesson Plan 7.4 Muscular Endurance Self-Assessments

This activity lesson will provide students with the opportunity to self-assess their muscular endurance.

Performance Outcomes Related to NASPE Standards

- ▶ Standard 4
  - ▶ Self-assess muscular endurance as part of health-related fitness.
  - ▶ Meet age- and gender-specific health-related fitness standards as defined by Fitnessgram.
- ▶ Standard 5
  - ▶ Exhibit (verbally and nonverbally) cooperation, respect, encouragement, and ability to work independently.
- ▶ Standard 6
  - ▶ See learning new activities and skills as challenging.

Lesson Objectives

- ▶ Students will learn about and perform several assessments of their muscular endurance.
- ▶ Students will determine whether they meet the healthy fitness zone for muscular endurance.

Equipment

- ▶ Items for the instant activity: basketballs, jump ropes, hacky sacks, volleyballs, juggling scarves
- ▶ 6 cones
- ▶ 3 rulers
- ▶ 3 strips of cardboard (4 1/2 inches [11.5 centimeters])
- ▶ 3 padded benches
- ▶ Chinning bar or monkey bars

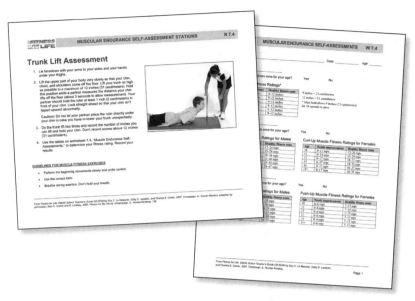

▸ Stopwatch

▸ 12 exercise mats

Reproducibles

▸ Resource 7.4, "Muscular Endurance Self-Assessment Stations"

▸ Worksheet 7.4, "Muscle Endurance Self-Assessments"

Setup

1. Place basketballs, jump ropes, hacky sacks, volleyballs, and juggling scarves throughout the activity area so students can access them as they enter the gym. (Optional: Use cones to designate areas for the different activities.)

2. Create five stations and hang one "Muscular Endurance Self-Assessment Stations" card at each station. Stations and equipment include:

   ▸ *Trunk lift*: 3 exercise mats and 3 rulers (36 inches [91 centimeters])

   ▸ *Curl-up*: 3 to 6 exercise mats, 3 strips of cardboard taped down across the mat

   ▸ *Push-up*: 3 exercise mats (optional)

   ▸ *Bent-arm hang*: Chinning bar or monkey bars

   ▸ *Leg change*: Stopwatch

3. Make a copy of worksheet 7.4, "Muscle Endurance Self-Assessments," for each student. Place eight copies at each station so they'll be available for the first group of students to use the station.

Delivering the Lesson

Part 1: Instant Activity

Offer students a choice of activities using the basketballs, jump ropes, hacky sacks, volleyballs, and juggling scarves. On your signal, have students put away equipment and get into their squads.

Part 2: Lesson Launcher

1. Review the lesson objectives with students.

2. Explain to students that adults in the United States spend millions of dollars each year paying certified strength and conditioning instructors to assess their muscular strength and muscular endurance. With a little knowledge, practice, and experience, everyone is capable of assessing his or her own strength and muscular endurance.

3. Explain that in today's lesson, students will have a chance to gather the knowledge, engage in practice, and gain some experience assessing their own muscular fitness.

Part 3: Lesson Focus

Muscle Fitness Self-Assessments

1. Divide the class into groups of six to eight using a method described in "Groups and Teams" (see pages 26 to 27).

2. Assign one group to each station. Have the students become "experts" at their assigned station. To do this, students will read the "Muscular Endurance Self-Assessment Stations" card, perform the self-assessment, and come up with technique cues for performing it successfully.

3. Have one member from each group briefly demonstrate their station while the other groups watch. The presenter should name the assessment, explain what component(s) of health-related fitness it assesses, explain how to do the assessment, and explain any other technical or safety guidelines that should be followed. Each presentation should last about one minute.

 review

Remind students of the potential for injury when performing muscle fitness exercises and tests. Ask them to name the three important guidelines:

* Perform the beginning movements slowly and under control.
* Use correct form.
* Breathe during exertion. Don't hold your breath.

4. On your signal, have the groups rotate through the muscle fitness self-assessment circuit. Give students time to record their scores before moving to the next station.

Part 4: Reflection and Summary

1. Have the students answer the reflection questions on worksheet 7.4, "Muscular Endurance Self-Assessments."

2. Have students add completed worksheet 7.4, "Muscular Endurance Self-Assessments," to their *Fitness for Life: Middle School* portfolios.

Take It Home

Invite a member of your support team to try one of these self-assessments, and explain to them the healthy fitness zone.

Next Time

Muscular endurance exercise circuit

Assessment

▶ Performance check: Observe students performing assessments of their muscular endurance.

▶ Assess completed worksheet 7.4, "Muscular Endurance Self-Assessments," in students' *Fitness for Life: Middle School* portfolios to determine whether students have identified the correct healthy fitness zone for their muscular endurance self-assessments. Use the worksheet rubric (available on the CD-ROM or on page 34) to assess student work, or modify the rubric to meet your specific objectives.

In this activity lesson, students will participate in a muscular endurance exercise circuit.

Performance Outcomes Related to NASPE Standards

▶ Standard 1
  ▸ Perform exercises that require muscular endurance.
▶ Standard 3
  ▸ Participate in health-enhancing physical activities both during and outside of school.
▶ Standard 5
  ▸ Exhibit (verbally and nonverbally) cooperation, respect, encouragement, and ability to work independently.

Lesson Objectives

▶ Students will perform several muscular endurance exercises with correct form, tempo, and breathing.
▶ Students will work effectively in groups, using good communication, cooperation, and encouragement.

Equipment

▶ 9 cones
▶ 18 exercise mats for comfort at some stations
▶ Stopwatch

Reproducibles

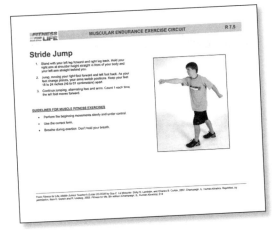

Resource 7.5, "Muscular Endurance Exercise Circuit"

Setup

1. Set up nine stations for the muscular endurance circuit:
   - ▸ *Stride jump:* No equipment needed
   - ▸ *Side leg raise:* 3 exercise mats for comfort (optional)
   - ▸ *Trunk lift:* 3 exercise mats for comfort (optional)
   - ▸ *Bridging:* 3 exercise mats for comfort (optional)
   - ▸ *90-degree push-up:* No equipment needed
   - ▸ *Knee push-up:* 3 exercise mats for comfort (optional)
   - ▸ *Curl-up with twist:* 3 exercise mats for comfort (optional)
   - ▸ *High knee jog:* No equipment needed
   - ▸ *Prone arm lift:* 3 exercise mats for comfort (optional)

2. Place a cone to mark each station, and hang the corresponding "Muscular Endurance Exercise Circuit" card to provide instructions for the students.

Delivering the Lesson

Part 1: Instant Activity

Amoeba Tag

1. Choose one student to be "It."
2. When "It" tags another student, both students must remain connected as they move around the area trying to tag others. Continue until numerous students have been tagged and "It" has become a big group.
3. Restart the game several times to prevent very large amoebas and to give everyone a chance to be "It."
4. Finish by having students stretch their upper- and lower-body muscles.

Part 2: Lesson Launcher

1. Review the lesson objectives with students.
2. Ask different students to name activities that require muscular endurance. Explain that, as the range of answers shows, muscular endurance is required for a wide variety of activities, including activities of daily living, specific occupations, and active sports and active recreation pursuits.
3. Remind students that in the last class, they performed self-assessments of their muscular endurance. Today, they will participate in an exercise circuit that focuses on muscular endurance.

Part 3: Lesson Focus

Muscular Endurance Circuit

1. Organize the class into nine groups of three or four students each using one of the methods described in "Groups and Teams" (see pages 26 to 27). Assign one group to each station.

2. Give students one minute to read the "Muscular Endurance Exercise Circuit" card at their station. Point out that students at the trunk lift station and the prone arm lift station should be careful not to hyperextend their backs.

 observe

> Ask groups if anyone has a question about their station.

3. On your signal, the students at each station will engage in their muscular endurance activity for one minute. Tell students that they should *not* try to do the exercises as quickly as possible. They should accumulate approximately 20 reps in one minute.

4. Have students change stations on your signal. Continue until all students have had a turn at each station.

 check

> Remind students of the potential for injury when performing muscle fitness exercises and tests. Ask them to name the three important guidelines:
>
> * Perform the beginning movements slowly and under control.
> * Use correct form.
> * Breathe during exertion. Don't hold your breath.

 observe

> Scan the area and look for examples of good posture to point out to other students. Visit stations to make sure that students are performing the exercises correctly.

Part 4: Reflection and Summary

Ask students the following questions:

▶ Who can give an example of an activity that would benefit from a specific muscular endurance exercise that we performed today?

▶ What principle are we following when we train using exercises that directly benefit a muscle used in an activity or improve movements that we perform in an activity? (Answer: principle of specificity.)

▶ Who can give an example of a muscular endurance exercise that would directly benefit their favorite activity?

Take It Home

The muscular endurance stations don't require much equipment. Ask students to do one or more stations (or create a new circuit of their own) with a member of their support team.

Next Time

Body composition

Assessment

▶ Performance check: Observe students working well in their groups (for example, communicating, cooperating, and encouraging each other), participating in the exercise circuit, and performing the exercises correctly (staying under control, using proper technique, and breathing during exertion).

▶ Comprehension check: Responses to the Reflection and Summary questions serve as a check for student understanding of muscular endurance and the principle of specificity.

Supplemental Materials

If you choose to use the semester or year scheduling version of *Fitness for Life: Middle School* (see appendix B), there are excellent opportunities to insert activity-based skill units and to review and reinforce the concepts in each chapter using the *Fitness for Life: Middle School* computer programs: Mount Fitness and Tour de Fitness. You will find information about the two computer programs in appendix C. Listed below are suggestions of activity-based skill units that would go well with this chapter and resources that will help you develop great lessons.

As indicated in the "Scheduling" section (pages 13 to 18), integrating activity-based skill units with the *Fitness for Life: Middle School* lesson plans provides a great opportunity for reinforcing key concepts and for developing students' skills in a wide range of physical activities. The activity-based skill unit suggestions provided below were chosen specifically to complement chapter content. In addition, there are selected resources that can provide you with excellent lesson plans and lesson plan ideas. Approaches to teaching activity-based skill units can be found in appendix A.

WEIGHT TRAINING

▶ **Key concepts to reinforce:** Strength of character, principle of specificity, principle of overload, principle of progression, preventing bullying, resistance

▶ **Resources:**
  ▶ *Complete Physical Education Plans for Grades 7-12* (Kleinman, 2001, Human Kinetics)
  ▶ *It's Not Just Gym Anymore: Teaching Secondary School Students How to Be Active for Life* (McCracken, 2001, Human Kinetics)
  ▶ *Quality Lesson Plans for Secondary Physical Education* (Zakrajsek, Carnes, and Pettigrew, 2003, Human Kinetics)

ROCK CLIMBING

▶ **Key concepts to reinforce:** Strength of character, principle of specificity, principle of overload, principle of progression, preventing bullying, resistance

▶ **Resources:**
  ▶ *Rock Climbing* (Watts, 1996, Human Kinetics)
  ▶ Variety of climbing resources: www.traversewall.com

Body Composition, Physical Activity, and Nutrition

Chapter 8 lesson plans focus on the concepts of body composition, energy balance, and efficiency. Students engage in self-assessments of body mass index and an assignment in energy balance that requires basic mathematics. Additionally, students are provided with an opportunity to discuss peer pressure issues and examine television advertising.

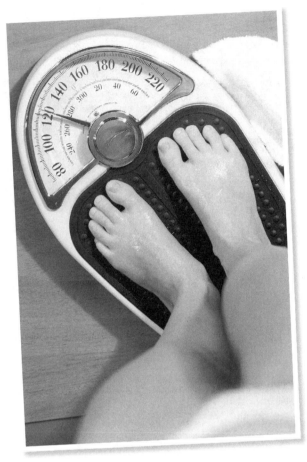

In this classroom lesson, students will have the opportunity to discuss the concept of body composition and the factors that affect body composition, as well as self-assess their body mass index.

Performance Outcomes Related to NASPE Standards

▶ Standard 3
  ▶ Describe the concept of body composition and the factors that affect it.

▶ Standard 4
  ▶ Calculate body mass index and identify the body mass index necessary to be in the healthy fitness zone.

▶ Standard 5
  ▶ Demonstrate respect for the privacy of others during self-assessments.

Lesson Objectives

▶ Students will identify the components of body composition and the factors that affect body composition.

▶ Students will self-assess their body mass index and determine whether they are in the healthy fitness zone.

▶ Students will demonstrate respect for the privacy of others' personal health information.

Equipment

▶ 1 *Fitness for Life: Middle School* student textbook per student

▶ Chalkboard or flip chart (optional)

▶ 1 calculator for every two students

▶ 1 pencil per student

▶ 1 roll of white athletic tape

▶ Weight scales (as many as you can get)

▶ Measuring tape

▶ Rolling blackboards or ping-pong tables for screens at the weight stations

Reproducibles

▶ Worksheet 8.1a, "Body Mass Index (BMI)"

▶ Worksheet 8.1b, "Give Me a Commercial Break"

▶ Classroom Quotes

Classroom Quotes

You can print these quotes from the CD-ROM and hang them around your room.

▶ "What fools indeed we mortals are / To lavish care upon a car, / With ne'er a bit of time to see / About our own machinery!"—John Kendrick Bangs (author)

▶ "I finally realized that being grateful to my body was key to giving more love to myself."—Oprah Winfrey (TV personality)

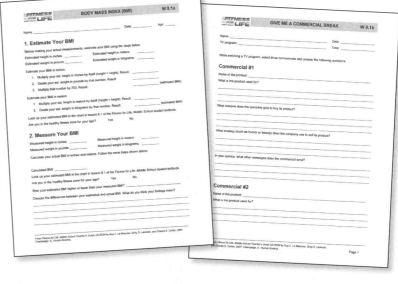

Setup

1. Create five height stations using the measuring tape and the white athletic tape. Place a strip of white tape vertically on the wall so that it spans about 2-1/2 feet (.75 meters) between the measurements of 4 feet 5 inches and 6 feet 5 inches (135 and 196 centimeters), or use the heights of the shortest and tallest students in class. Mark the strip of tape in 1-inch (2.5 centimeter) increments.

2. If you have several scales, place them between the height stations. If you have ping-pong tables or rolling blackboards, make screens to ensure privacy for the weight stations.

3. Make a copy of worksheets 8.1a, "Body Mass Index (BMI)," and 8.1b, "Give Me a Commercial Break," for each student.

Delivering the Lesson

Part 1: Gathering Information

Have the students read "Body Composition," lesson 8.1 in the student textbook (chapter 8, pages 93 to 98).

Part 2: Lesson Launcher

1. Review the lesson objectives with students.

2. Inform the class that the majority of adults in the United States and Canada are either overweight or obese. Ask if anyone can explain the reason. Can anyone explain how we determine whether a person is overweight or obese?

3. Explain that chapter 8 of the student textbook focuses on body composition. In today's lesson, students will learn what body composition is and how it can be measured, and they will examine their own body composition.

Part 3: Lesson Focus 1

Body Composition and Body Mass Index

1. Ask students the following questions:
   - ▸ People often focus on body fat when they talk about body composition, but what are some other components of your body that make up your body composition? (Answers: muscle, bone.)
   - ▸ What factors affect a person's body composition? (Answers: heredity, diet, exercise, occupation.)
   - ▸ Which factors do you have control over when maintaining a healthy body composition? (Answers: diet, exercise, occupation.)

2. Explain to the class that body composition can be determined in a number of ways. A commonly used method to determine body fatness is the skinfold technique, which requires special equipment (skinfold calipers) and a trained exercise professional. Measurements of the thickness of the skin and the fat below the skin's surface are taken at various sites on the body to estimate body fatness. The accuracy of this technique depends on the equipment and the person taking the measurements.

3. Explain that because you don't have skinfold calipers, students will use another method to determine whether they're overweight or underweight. They will examine their body mass index (BMI), which is an estimation of body composition based on measurements of height and weight. Basically, the BMI tells them if they are the right weight for their height, too light for their height, or too heavy for their height.

 review

> Remind students that the information they'll record on their worksheet is personal and confidential. If they are working alone, they don't have to share their information. If they are working with a partner, they should respect their partner's privacy and keep his or her personal information confidential.

4. Have students work alone or with a partner who is a friend that they trust.

5. Give each student a copy of worksheet 8.1a, "Body Mass Index (BMI)." Have the students determine their body mass index using their own estimates of their height and weight.

6. Ask students to answer the questions on worksheet 8.1a, "Body Mass Index (BMI)."

Part 4: Lesson Focus 2

Peer Pressure

1. Have students read "Moving Together: Peer Pressure" in the student textbook (chapter 7, page 97).

2. Arrange students in groups of three or four using one of the methods described in "Groups and Teams" (see pages 26 to 27).

3. Have each group quickly identify a leader, a recorder, and a reporter. The group leader will pose the discussion questions from "Moving Together: Peer Pressure," the recorder will write down the theme of the responses, and the reporter will prepare to share the results with the class. In a group with four students, the fourth member can be a "brainstormer," or group contributor.

4. Bring the class together and ask the discussion questions to the larger group. Have the reporters and others contribute answers and generate discussion.

5. Extend the discussion about peer pressure using your personal experiences or those of students. One example could be students pressuring others to share their BMI results.

Part 5: Reflection and Summary

1. Ask students the following questions:

   ▶ Did your measured BMI score differ from your estimated BMI score? (No response required; ask students to think about the answer.)

   ▶ Was your measured BMI score higher than your estimated BMI score? (No response required; ask students to think about the answer.)

   ▶ What are some reasons why measured BMI scores are often higher than estimated BMI scores among United States adults? (Answer: underestimating weight.)

   ▶ Who can explain what essential fat is? (Answer: fat necessary for transporting nutrients, providing cushion, and providing insulation.)

   ▶ Who can identify a disease that is the result of having too little fat? (Answer: anorexia nervosa.)

   ▶ If you have a high BMI, you are at higher risk for some diseases. What are some of these diseases? (Answers: diabetes, high blood pressure, cardiovascular [heart] disease.)

2. Have students add completed worksheet 8.1a, "Body Mass Index (BMI)," to their *Fitness for Life: Middle School* portfolios.

Take It Home

▶ Explain to students that we are bombarded by advertising on billboards, clothing, magazines, and especially television. Ask them if they've ever taken the time to analyze what commercials are really trying to sell.

▶ Give each student a copy of worksheet 8.1b, "Give Me a Commercial Break." To complete the sheet, students will analyze three commercials related to food, exercise, fitness, or health during their favorite TV program.

▶ Tell students when to return the completed worksheet to class. (Recommended: lesson 8.3.)

Next Time

Calorie-counting activity circuit

Assessment

▶ Comprehension check: Class discussions serve as a check for student understanding of the different components that make up body composition and factors that affect body composition.

▶ Performance check: Observe students respecting each other's privacy during the body composition self-assessments.

▶ Comprehension check: Assess student worksheet 8.1a, "Body Mass Index (BMI)," to determine whether students have calculated body mass index correctly and have identified the correct healthy fitness zone score for their body mass index self-assessment. Use the worksheet rubric (available on the CD-ROM or on page 34) or modify the rubric to meet your specific objectives.

Lesson Plan 8.2 Calorie-Counting Activity Circuit

In this activity lesson, students will participate in an exercise circuit that incorporates activities of various intensities. Students are required to rate the intensity of each activity and complete a calorie-counting worksheet for homework.

Performance Outcomes Related to NASPE Standards

▶ Standard 3
  ▶ Participate in health-enhancing physical activities both during and outside of school.
▶ Standard 4
  ▶ Self-assess heart rate before, during, and after physical activity.
▶ Standard 6
  ▶ Seek personally challenging physical activity experiences.

Lesson Objectives

▶ Students will participate in a variety of physical activities.
▶ Students will attend to their bodies and adjust their activity levels to maintain activity for the duration of each station.

Equipment

▶ 6 basketballs
▶ 3 hoops
▶ Variety of hacky sack objects (such as balloons, hacky sacks, beach balls, and soccer balls)
▶ 2 or 3 short nets for foot volleying
▶ 4 cones
▶ 3 sets each of a variety of objects (such as scarves, beanbags, and balls)
▶ 4 long ropes and 6 short ropes
▶ 30 to 40 pencils
▶ CD player and upbeat music

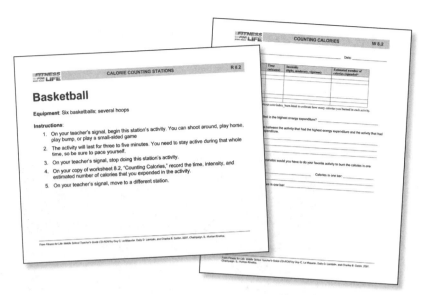

Reproducibles

▶ Resource 8.2, "Calorie Counting Stations"

▶ Worksheet 8.2, "Counting Calories"

Setup

1. Create the activity stations shown below, or create five stations of your own. Each station should take about the same amount of time to complete because the student worksheet has questions that compare the calories expended in each activity.

   ▶ Basketball station: 6 basketballs and 2 or 3 hoops

   ▶ Hacky sack station: A variety of balls (such as balloons, hacky sacks, beach balls, and soccer balls), and short nets for foot volleying

   ▶ Walking, jogging, or running station: 4 cones to mark the area

   ▶ Juggling station: A variety of juggling implements (such as scarves, beanbags, and balls)

   ▶ Rope jumping station: 4 long ropes (for double dutch jumping) and 6 short ropes

2. Make a copy of worksheet 8.2, "Counting Calories," for each student.

3. At each station, place five to eight worksheets and pencils.

4. Hang the "Calorie Counting Stations" cards at the stations.

Delivering the Lesson

Part 1: Instant Activity

Walk and Talk

1. Give students 15 seconds to find someone who walks at the same pace that they walk (someone who seems to have legs of the same length).

2. Partners will walk around the outside of the gym while carrying on a conversation. Each student must find out something new that's happening with his or her partner.

3. After about two minutes, give the signal to change partners. All students stop walking and say good-bye to their current partners. Then each partner on the right moves up one pair so that all students now have new partners.

4. Give the signal to start walking again. Have students walk and switch partners until the class is warmed up.

Part 2: Lesson Launcher

1. Review the lesson objectives with students.

2. Remind students that during classroom lesson 8.1 you talked about having control over two things when trying to maintain a health body composition. Ask if anyone can tell you what these two things are. (Answer: physical activity and diet.)

3. Explain that today, students will participate in an activity circuit and estimate the number of calories they expend during the activities. Understanding how to calculate energy expenditure is a necessary step in understanding energy balance.

Part 3: Lesson Focus

Calorie Counting Circuit

1. Organize the class into five groups of four to six students each, using one of the methods described in "Groups and Teams" (see pages 26 to 27).

2. Briefly explain the five stations, and assign one group to each station.

3. Have the students do their station activity for three to five minutes. Make sure that all stations take about the same amount of time to complete because the student worksheet has questions that compare the calories expended in each activity.

4. On your signal, students will pick up a copy of worksheet 8.2, "Counting Calories," and record the time, intensity, and estimated calories expended in the activity they just finished. Explain the intensity categories as follows:

   ▸ Light: Little change in breathing and temperature

   ▸ Moderate: Heavier breathing, change in body temperature, not sweating

   ▸ Vigorous: Heavy breathing, hot, possibly sweating

 review

  ∗ You can have students take a six-second pulse immediately following each station so that they have a more objective reference for estimating physical activity intensity.

  ∗ Explain to students that they need to be active for the full duration of the station (three to five minutes), so they should pace themselves at each station.

Part 4: Reflection and Summary

Provide time for students to complete the information on worksheet 8.2, "Counting Calories."

Take It Home

▸ Instruct students to complete the last column of worksheet 8.2, "Counting Calories," and questions 1 through 5 using the Internet.

▸ Tell students when to return the completed worksheets to class. (Recommended: lesson 8.4.)

Next Time

▸ Energy balance, nutrients, and efficiency

▸ Remind students that worksheet 8.1b, "Give Me a Commercial Break," is due next class (recommended).

Assessment

Performance check: Observe students participating in the stations and attending to their bodies (such as adjusting their activity levels to maintain activity for the duration of each station).

In this classroom lesson, students will discuss the concept of energy balance and identify the three macronutrients (carbohydrates, fat, and protein). In addition, students will discuss the concept of efficiency.

Performance Outcomes Related to NASPE Standards

▶ Standard 3
  ▶ Describe the meaning of energy balance.
  ▶ Demonstrate an understanding of efficiency using physical activity examples.
  ▶ Demonstrate an understanding of nutrients using self-generated examples.

▶ Standard 5
  ▶ Exhibit (verbally and nonverbally) cooperation, respect, encouragement, and the ability to work independently.

Lesson Objectives

▶ Students will be able to describe the concept of energy balance.
▶ Students will be able to identify the three macronutrients.
▶ Students will demonstrate an understanding of the concept of efficiency by describing strategies for increasing efficiency in a variety of physical activities.

Equipment

▶ 1 *Fitness for Life: Middle School* student textbook per student
▶ Sticky notes
▶ Chalkboard or flip chart (optional)

 tech

  ✳ Two computer presentation programs (**Mount Fitness** and **Tour de Fitness**) are available for reviewing and reinforcing concepts. See page 40 for more information.
  ✳ Find and show video clips or a presentation showing nutrition labels on a variety of foods.

Reproducibles

Classroom Quotes

Classroom Quotes

You can print this quote from the CD-ROM and hang it in your room.

> ▶ "Thank you for calling the Weight Loss Hotline. If you'd like to lose a half pound right now, press '1' 18,000 times."—Randy Glasbergen (cartoonist)

Setup

Write a list of activities on the chalkboard or flip chart (e.g., basketball, hacky sack, walking, jogging, running, juggling, and rope jumping, or create some of your own).

Delivering the Lesson

Part 1: Gathering Information

Have the students silently read "Energy Balance: Physical Activity and Nutrition," lesson 8.2 in the student textbook (chapter 8, pages 99 to 102).

Part 2: Lesson Launcher

1. Review the lesson objectives with students.
2. Explain that American adults spend billions of dollars on weight loss products, diet books, and diet foods. Yet, most U.S. adults are overweight or obese. Ask students why this might be. Suggest that the reason might be that people focus too much on diet and not enough on physical activity. To maintain a healthy weight, people need to understand the concept of energy balance.
3. Ask if anyone can explain what energy balance means. Explain that energy balance is the balancing of calories consumed (energy intake) in the diet with calories expended (energy expended) through activities of daily living. Tell the class that today you will discuss energy balance, nutrients, and efficiency in movement related to energy expenditure.

Part 3: Lesson Focus 1

Energy Expenditure and MyPyramid

1. Have students select the activity that they think expends the most energy in five minutes. Use activities from lesson 8.2 (basketball, hacky sack, walking, jogging, running, juggling, and rope jumping) or create some of your own.
2. Have students write the activity on a sticky note.
3. Have students make a bar graph by placing the sticky notes on the wall. Similar activities are placed one above the other.
4. Have students discuss the graph.

5. Arrange students in groups of three or four using one of the methods described in "Groups and Teams" (see pages 26 to 27).

6. Have each group quickly identify a leader, a recorder, and a reporter. The group leader will guide the discussion, the recorder will generate the list created by the group, and the reporter will present the results to the class. In a group of four, the fourth member can be a "brainstormer," or group contributor.

7. Have each group make a list of three foods that they eat from each stripe of MyPyramid (page 99 of the student textbook) and identify one food that contains items from each stripe of the pyramid (for example, lasagna, pizza, or burritos).

8. Ask a reporter from each group to share their answers with the whole class. Also ask students the following questions:

   ▸ Is each food a carbohydrate, a fat, or a protein?

   ▸ What does *basal metabolism* mean? (Answer: energy expended at rest.)

   ▸ Is your metabolism currently high or low?

Part 4: Lesson Focus 2

Efficiency in Movement

1. Have students read "Biomechanical Principles: Efficiency" in the student textbook (chapter 8, page 101).

2. In each group, students should change roles so that different students become the new leader, recorder, and reporter. The leader will direct the group in discussion, the recorder will record the theme of the responses, and the reporter will be prepared to share answers with the larger group.

3. Ask each group to follow the directions given in "Applying the Principle." The directions instruct students to describe how they can improve efficiency (conserve energy) when performing the activities listed below, and to describe which activities would be best for helping someone maintain a healthy body weight by expending calories.

   ▸ Swimming

   ▸ Running

   ▸ Walking

   ▸ Resistance exercises

   ▸ Soccer

   ▸ Digging in a garden

   ▸ Watching TV

 review

Remind students of the class agreements for working in groups (include everyone, listen to the person who is talking, give helpful feedback to improve performance, participate, and contribute).

4. Bring the class together. Have the reporters and others contribute their groups' answers and generate discussion.

Part 5: Reflection and Summary

1. Ask students the following questions:
   ▶ What are the two important components of energy balance? (Answer: diet and exercise.)
   ▶ Why are progressive resistance exercises for muscle fitness effective for weight maintenance? (Answer: Progressive resistance exercises build muscles, and muscles are the engines of the body that burn fuel, so building muscles builds your body's engine and allows you to burn more fuel.)
   ▶ What are the three main types of nutrients? (Answer: carbohydrates, fats, and protein.)
2. Have students add completed worksheet 8.1b, "Give Me a Commercial Break," to their *Fitness for Life: Middle School* portfolios.

Take It Home

When you eat a meal in the next day or so, do a rough calculation of the calories consumed by looking at the nutritional information on the packaging of the foods. Think about the exercises done in class, and determine how long you'd have to do one of the exercises to expend the calories from your meal.

Next Time

▶ Physical activity pyramid circuit with pedometers
▶ Remind students that worksheet 8.2, "Counting Calories," is due next class (recommended).

Assessment

▶ Comprehension check: Class discussions and responses to the Reflection and Summary questions serve as a check for student understanding of the concept of energy balance, efficiency, and the three macronutrients.
▶ Assess completed worksheet 8.1b, "Give Me a Commercial Break," in students' *Fitness for Life: Middle School* portfolios. Use the worksheet rubric (available on the CD-ROM or on page 34) to assess student work, or modify the rubric to meet your specific objectives.

Lesson Plan 8.4 Pyramid Pedometer Circuit

In this activity lesson, students will participate in physical activities from all levels of the Physical Activity Pyramid. Students will also wear pedometers and participate in a game in which they try to predict the number of steps they will take during the circuit.

Performance Outcomes Related to NASPE Standards

► Standard 1
  ► Perform physical activities that require a variety of skill- and health-related fitness components.
► Standard 3
  ► Participate in health-enhancing physical activities both during and outside of school.
► Standard 4
  ► Demonstrate an understanding of the relative contribution that selected physical activities make toward energy expenditure.
► Standard 5
  ► Exhibit (verbally and nonverbally) cooperation, respect, encouragement, and the ability to work independently.
► Standard 6
  ► Seek personally challenging physical activity experiences.

Lesson Objectives

► Students will participate in activities from all levels of the Physical Activity Pyramid.

▶ Students will calculate the difference between predicted and actual steps taken.

▶ Students will demonstrate an understanding of energy expenditure.

Equipment

▶ 1 pedometer for each student

▶ 1 pencil per student

▶ 4 cones to mark out a walking area

▶ 2 benches or 2 rows of bleachers for step aerobics

▶ CD player with upbeat music (100 to 120 bpm)

▶ Door frame for chest stretch

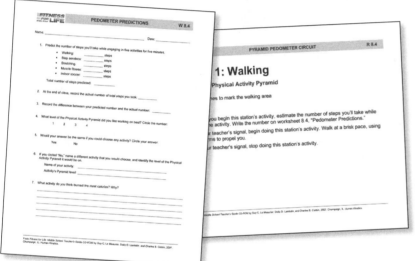

▶ 4 to 10 exercise mats and yoga bands (optional)

▶ 2 to 4 exercise balls (optional)

▶ 2 floor hockey nets (or 4 cones)

▶ 1 indoor soccer ball

▶ 3 to 5 pinnies

Reproducibles

▶ Worksheet 8.4, "Pedometer Predictions"

▶ Resource 8.4, "Pyramid Pedometer Circuit"

Setup

1. Make a copy of worksheet 8.4, "Pedometer Predictions," for each student.

2. Make one copy of resource 8.4, "Pyramid Pedometer Circuit" cards.

3. Set up the following stations, spaced far enough apart for safety:

▶ *Walking station*: 4 cones to mark out a walking area (such as the perimeter of the activity area)

▶ *Step aerobics station*: 2 benches or 2 rows of bleachers (first level); CD player with upbeat music (100 to 120 bpm)

▶ *Stretching station*: A door frame for chest stretch; 4 exercise mats and yoga bands (optional)

▶ *Muscle fitness station*: 4 exercise mats; 2 to 4 exercise balls (optional)

▶ *Indoor soccer station*: 2 floor hockey nets or 4 cones; 1 indoor soccer ball; 3 to 5 pinnies

4. Depending on the size of your class, place up to 8 pencils and 8 copies of worksheet 8.4, "Pedometer Predictions," at each station.

Delivering the Lesson

Part 1: Instant Activity

As students enter the gym, have them pick up a pedometer and walk and talk with a partner. Instruct students to review the four levels and six categories of the Physical Activity Pyramid.

Part 2: Lesson Launcher

1. Review the lesson objectives with students.
2. Ask students to identify the six categories of the Physical Activity Pyramid. Remind them that physical activity from all levels except level 4 (sedentary activities) are effective at burning calories.
3. Explain that today, they will split into groups and explore activities from the first three levels of the pyramid in an activity circuit. In addition, they will predict how many steps they will take at each station. Each team's goal is to have the most accurate prediction.

Part 3: Lesson Focus

Physical Activity Pyramid Circuit

1. Organize the class into five groups using one of the methods described in "Groups and Teams" (see pages 26 to 27).
2. Briefly explain the five stations, and assign one group to each station.
3. Before beginning the station activity, each student should pick up a copy of worksheet 8.4, "Pedometer Predictions," and complete part 1 to predict how many steps they'll take at each station.

Ask the students how many stations they will be doing today. (Answer: five.) Ask them how long they will spend at each station. (Answer: five minutes.) Ask them how many numbers they will write down for their pedometer predictions. (Answer: six—one number for each station, plus one number for the overall total.)

4. Have students set their pedometers to zero.

Remind students of the "you shake it, I take it" rule regarding the pedometers. Tell them that the only time they will be able to look at the number of steps recorded on their pedometers is between stations.

5. On your signal, students do their station activity for five minutes.
6. On your signal, students stop, check their pedometers to see how many steps they took, and record their actual number of steps on their worksheet.
7. Have groups switch stations, and repeat steps 5 through 7 until all students have had a turn at each station.
8. Ask the students to answer question 3 on their worksheet. This requires them to calculate the difference between their predicted steps and their actual steps. (Record a negative number for underpredictions.)

Part 4: Reflection and Summary

1. Have the students complete their worksheets (answering questions 5 through 7) and add them to their *Fitness for Life: Middle School* portfolios.
2. Have the students add completed worksheet 8.2, "Counting Calories," to their *Fitness for Life: Middle School* portfolios.

Take It Home

Organize a walk with a member of your support team. Have each member predict how long the walk will take before you go. Create a reward for the person who makes the most accurate prediction.

Next Time

Activity choices for energy expenditure

Assessment

▶ Performance check: Observe students participating in all circuit stations and working effectively with their group members (communicating, cooperating, encouraging, and following rules).

▶ Comprehension check: Responses to the questions on worksheet 8.4, "Pedometer Predictions," serve as a check for student understanding of energy expenditure.

▶ Assess student worksheets 8.2, "Counting Calories," and 8.4, "Pedometer Predictions," in students' *Fitness for Life: Middle School* portfolios. Use the worksheet rubric (available on the CD-ROM or on page 34) to assess student work, or modify the rubric to meet your specific objectives.

Lesson Plan 8.5 Activity Choices for Energy Expenditure

In this activity lesson, students will make physical activity choices based on their physical activity preferences.

Performance Outcomes Related to NASPE Standards

▶ Standard 1
  ▶ Participate in physical activities that have skill- and health-related fitness benefits.
▶ Standard 4
  ▶ Describe how physical activities contribute to health- and skill-related fitness.
▶ Standard 5
  ▶ Exhibit (verbally and nonverbally) cooperation, respect, encouragement, and the ability to work independently.
▶ Standard 6
  ▶ Use physical activity as a positive opportunity for social and group interactions.

Lesson Objectives

▶ Students will participate in physical activity for more than half of class time.
▶ Students will create positive movement settings through communication, cooperation, and fair play.

Equipment

Because this lesson plan focuses on student choice, depends on your class location (indoor/outdoor), and is affected by space availability, we cannot provide equipment and activity specifics. Instead, look over student responses to questions 5 through 7 on worksheet 8.4, "Pedometer Predictions," to decide on activities. Try to have a variety of active aerobics, sports, and recreational activities.

Possible outdoor choices:

▶ *Ultimate:* 4 cones per Ultimate field, 1 disc per field

▶ *Fitness walking:* 4 cones to mark walking perimeter, or use athletic field boundaries

▶ *Soccer:* 10 cones to mark each field (4 for end lines, 4 for goals, and 2 for midfield), 1 ball per field

Possible indoor choices:

▶ *Active aerobics:* Aerobics (or kickboxing) video and a television with DVD/VCR

▶ *Basketball:* 1 or 2 courts, depending on class interest; 1 or 2 basketballs

▶ *Indoor soccer:* 2 floor hockey nets (or 4 cones), 1 soccer ball, 2 different colored sets of 4 or 5 pinnies

 tech

    ✳ Heart rate monitors provide students feedback on whether they are in their target heart rate zones.

    ✳ Pedometers allow students to see how many steps they accumulate in different activities.

Reproducibles

None

Setup

1. Create three or four areas for activity, depending on your location (indoor or outdoor), the amount of space you have, and student responses to questions 5 through 7 on worksheet 8.4, "Pedometer Predictions."

2. Set up three or four cones, depending on the number of stations you have, and space them about 4 feet (1.2 meters) apart. Put the cones in a location where you want to organize students.

Delivering the Lesson

Part 1: Instant Activity

Team Follow-the-Leader

1. Organize students into groups of six, using one of the methods in "Groups and Teams" (see pages 26 to 27). Have each group line up. Explain that all groups will walk around the gym in a line, following the path of the leader—the first student in the line.

2. Instruct leaders to move at a pace that is appropriate for the whole group.

3. Each time the signal sounds, the leader steps aside and the line moves past with a new leader. The former leader goes to the end of the line. Each time there's a new leader, call out a new, progressively more active locomotor skill (for example, power walk, skip, gallop, change lead foot, slide, change lead side, or jog).

Part 2: Lesson Launcher

1. Review the lesson objectives with students.

2. Remind the class that in the past few lessons, they have been counting calories and steps. Both are indicators of energy expenditure. However, they shouldn't choose activities for the sole purpose of expending calories. Ask students if they know why. (Possible answer: Those activities might not be fun, so they might lose interest and stop participating.) Explain that, in fact, few U.S. and Canadian adults are regular exercisers. People who are regularly physically active probably do it because they love the activity.

3. Explain that you set up activity stations based on student responses to worksheet 8.4, "Pedometer Predictions." You couldn't include all of their favorite activities, but you included several that were requested.

Part 3: Lesson Focus

Activity Choices for Energy Expenditure

1. Describe the activity stations that you created.

2. Ask students to line up behind cone 1 for the first activity, cone 2 for the second activity, and so on.

3. Instruct students interested in individual physical activities to go to their station and begin the activity.

4. Create teams for active sports activities and send the students out to play. Remind them to follow rules, communicate, and cooperate.

5. After 5 to 10 minutes, signal the students to stop. Let them decide whether to remain at their current station or switch to a new station. Explain that you'll stop them again in another 5 to 10 minutes for the next choice.

 review

Ask students to list participation guidelines to follow to have an enjoyable experience at their station, such as:

* Cooperation: taking turns with the equipment
* Communication: calling "ball" and asking someone else for help if a ball rolls away
* Following rules: calling a foul on yourself and respecting each other (such as giving each other personal space and avoiding put-downs)

Part 4: Reflection and Summary

Ask students the following questions:

▶ Who was able to remain active for the entire class period?

▶ Do your feelings about participation in physical activity change when you have a choice? Explain.

- What are some of the health- or skill-related fitness benefits of the activity you participated in?
- Which of the activity choices offered today burns the most calories? (Help them understand that the answer depends on the participant, effort, efficiency, and resistance—each factor plays a part.)

Take It Home

Ask the students to think about the choices they have for activity after school or at home. Which ones do they most like? Which ones do people on their support teams most like? Ask them to invite someone to do a favorite activity together this week.

Next Time

Planning for a lifetime of physical activity

Assessment

Performance check: Observe students for examples of cooperation, respect, encouragement, following rules, and the ability to work independently in the activities.

Supplemental Materials

If you choose to use the semester or year scheduling version of *Fitness for Life: Middle School* (see appendix B), there are excellent opportunities to insert activity-based skill units and to review and reinforce the concepts in each chapter using the *Fitness for Life: Middle School* computer programs: Mount Fitness and Tour de Fitness. You will find information about the two computer programs in appendix C. Listed below are suggestions of activity-based skill units that would go well with this chapter and resources that will help you develop great lessons.

As indicated in the "Scheduling" section (pages 13 to 18), integrating activity-based skill units with the *Fitness for Life: Middle School* lesson plans provides a great opportunity for reinforcing key concepts and for developing students' skills in a wide range of physical activities. The activity-based skill unit suggestions provided below were chosen specifically to complement chapter content. In addition, there are selected resources that can provide you with excellent lesson plans and lesson plan ideas. Approaches to teaching activity-based skill units can be found in appendix A.

CROSS-TRAINING AND CIRCUITS

▶ **Key concepts to reinforce:** Body composition, energy balance, peer pressure, efficiency, nutrition, media influence
▶ **Resources:**
  ▶ *Complete Physical Education Plans for Grades 7-12* (Kleinman, 2001, Human Kinetics)
  ▶ *It's Not Just Gym Anymore: Teaching Secondary School Students How to Be Active for Life* (McCracken, 2001, Human Kinetics)
  ▶ *Quality Lesson Plans for Secondary Physical Education* (Zakrajsek, Carnes, and Pettigrew, 2003, Human Kinetics)

FITNESS WALKING (PEDOMETERS)

▶ **Key concepts to reinforce:** Body composition, energy balance, peer pressure, efficiency, nutrition, media influence
▶ **Resources:**
  ▶ *Pedometer Power* (Pangrazi, Beighle, and Sidman, 2003, Human Kinetics)
  ▶ *Walking Games and Activities* (Decker and Mize, 2002, Human Kinetics)

ACTIVE SPORTS AND RECREATION UNITS

▶ **Key concepts to reinforce:** Communication, building a community, energy and force, physical activity, and health-related fitness
▶ **Resources:** See activity-based skill unit suggestions at the end of chapter 5.

Planning for Physical Activity

Chapter 9 focuses on integrating all of the elements of *Fitness for Life: Middle School.* The lesson plans engage students in self-assessment, goal setting, and self-monitoring activities. Students compile a physical fitness summary based on Fitnessgram tests, and class discussions and homework assignments set the stage for students to begin planning for physical activity based on their fitness needs and physical activity preferences. While the *Fitness for Life: Middle School* program is completed following these lessons, physical educators are urged to continue monitoring student physical activity logs, periodically have students self-assess their fitness, recognize students for their commitment to physical activity, and allow students to reward themselves for meeting their goals.

* 9.1 Assessing Fitness and Physical Activity Levels (classroom lesson)
* 9.2 Physical Activity Choices (activity lesson)
* 9.3 Creating a Physical Activity Plan (classroom lesson)
* 9.4 Executing Your Physical Activity Plan (activity lesson)
* 9.5 Executing Your Physical Activity Plan (activity lesson)

9.1 Assessing Fitness and Physical Activity Levels

In this classroom lesson, students will perform a self-assessment of their current fitness level and physical activity patterns and identify areas of fitness and physical activity they are interested in improving.

Performance Outcomes Related to NASPE Standards

▶ Standard 4
  ▸ Learn to assess physical fitness and physical activity.
  ▸ Identify physical activities that will build components of fitness.

Lesson Objectives

▶ Students will create a fitness summary based on their self-assessments.

▶ Students will create a physical activity summary based on their self-assessments.

▶ Students will identify areas of strength and weakness based on their fitness summary.

Equipment

▶ 1 *Fitness for Life: Middle School* student textbook per student

▶ *Fitness for Life: Middle School* portfolios for all students

▶ Chalkboard or flip chart (optional)

Reproducibles

- ▶ Worksheet 9.1a, "Fitness and Physical Activity Summary"
- ▶ Worksheet 9.1b, "Support Team Physical Activity Summary"
- ▶ Classroom Quotes

Classroom Quotes

You can print these quotes from the CD-ROM and hang them around your room.

- ▶ "He who fails to plan, plans to fail."—proverb
- ▶ "To be prepared is half the victory."—Miguel de Cervantes Saavedra (author)
- ▶ "A good plan is like a road map: it shows the final destination and usually the best way to get there."—H. Stanley Judd (author)

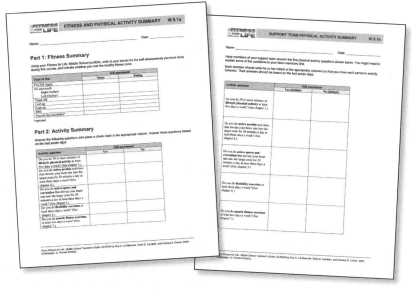

Setup

1. Make a copy of worksheets 9.1a, "Fitness and Physical Activity Summary," and 9.1b, "Support Team Physical Activity Summary," for each student.
2. Write the following discussion questions on the chalkboard or flip chart:
   - ▶ What parts of your physical fitness do you want to improve? Why?
   - ▶ What activities can you do to improve your fitness?
   - ▶ Would you do those activities for competition or for fun?
   - ▶ Will you do the activities alone, with friends, with family, on a team, or in some combination of these?
   - ▶ Will you do the activities outdoors, indoors, or both?

Delivering the Lesson

Part 1: Gathering Information

Have the students read "Self-Assessing Fitness and Physical Activity Needs," lesson 9.1 in the student textbook (chapter 9, pages 105 to 109).

Part 2: Lesson Launcher

1. Review the lesson objectives with students.
2. Explain that some people are active for a lifetime because they find activities that they love. Others, though, have to make a plan to be physically active for their health. To make a physical activity plan, students must know how fit they are and how fit they want to be, and they must make a plan to participate in activities that improve their fitness. Even those who have found activities they

love must periodically determine if they are maintaining healthy levels of fitness in all areas.

3. Remind students that they have done several fitness assessments as part of the *Fitness for Life: Middle School* program. Today, they will create a fitness summary, which will help them develop a physical activity plan.

Part 3: Lesson Focus 1

Building Physical Fitness and Physical Activity Summaries

1. Have students get out their *Fitness for Life: Middle School* portfolios.

2. Give each student a copy of worksheet 9.1a, "Fitness and Physical Activity Summary."

3. Lead a discussion of Keisha's fitness summary (see table 9.1 on page 105 of the student textbook).

4. Ask students to fill in the "Self-Assessment" columns in part 1 of the worksheet by retrieving information from the following items in their portfolios:

   ▸ worksheet 4.4, "PACER Test,"

   ▸ worksheet 6.4, "Back-Saver Sit-and-Reach Test,"

   ▸ worksheet 7.4, "Muscular Endurance Self-Assessments," and

   ▸ worksheet 8.1a, "Body Mass Index (BMI)."

   For each test, students should record their self-assessment score and indicate whether that score puts them in the healthy fitness zone.

 review

> Remind students that these results are personal and confidential. They don't have to share their results and should respect the privacy of others.

5. Have students complete part 2 of their "Fitness and Physical Activity Summary" worksheets by making checkmarks under "Yes" or "No" to answer the five questions.

Part 4: Lesson Focus 2

Getting Fit and Active

1. Have students read the opening section of "Moving Together: Getting Active and Fit" in the student textbook (chapter 9, page 108), look over the discussion questions briefly, and read the "Guidelines for Getting Active and Fit."

2. Organize students into small groups using one of the methods described in "Groups and Teams" (see pages 26 to 27), and have them use the guidelines to come up with answers to the discussion questions.

3. Within each group, have students share their thoughts about getting fit and active by addressing the following questions:

   ▸ What parts of your physical fitness do you want to improve? Why?

   ▸ What activities can you do to improve your fitness?

   ▸ Would you do those activities for competition or for fun?

   ▸ Will you do the activities alone, with friends, with family, on a team, or in some combination of these?

   ▸ Will you do the activities outdoors, indoors, or both?

4. Bring the class together and discuss the "Moving Together" questions with the larger group. As time permits, have students share their small group's answers to the questions posed in step 3. Make some notes of student responses to help you plan activity choices for students in lessons 9.2, 9.4, and 9.5.

5. Extend the discussions by using your own personal experiences or those of students.

Part 5: Reflection and Summary

Have students add completed worksheet 9.1a, "Fitness and Physical Activity Summary," to their *Fitness for Life: Middle School* portfolios.

Take It Home

▶ Explain to the class that as physically educated people, they know the benefits of regular physical activity. Not only can they become more physically active, but they can also help members of their support team do the same. Because students see those teammates daily, planning shared physical activity is a great way to ensure regular participation.

▶ Give each student a copy of worksheet 9.1b, "Support Team Physical Activity Summary," to complete at home.

▶ Tell students when to return the completed worksheets to class. (Recommended: lesson 9.3.)

Next Time

Physical activity choices

Assessment

▶ Comprehension check: Class discussions serve as a check for student understanding of health-related fitness strengths and weaknesses based on their fitness summary.

▶ Assess completed worksheet 9.1a, "Fitness and Physical Activity Summary," in students' *Fitness for Life: Middle School* portfolios. Use the worksheet rubric (available on the CD-ROM or on page 34) to assess student work, or modify the rubric to meet your specific objectives.

In this activity lesson, students will make physical activity choices based on their physical activity preferences.

Performance Outcomes Related to NASPE Standards

▸ Standard 1
  ▸ Participate in physical activities that have skill- and health-related fitness benefits.
▸ Standard 4
  ▸ Describe how physical activities contribute to health- and skill-related fitness.
▸ Standard 5
  ▸ Exhibit (verbally and nonverbally) cooperation, respect, encouragement, and the ability to work independently.
▸ Standard 6
  ▸ Use physical activity as a positive opportunity for social and group interactions.

Lesson Objectives

▸ Students will participate in physical activity for at least 50 percent of the class period.
▸ Students will create positive movement settings through communication, cooperation, and fair play.

Equipment

Because this lesson plan focuses on student choice, depends on your class location (indoor/outdoor), and is affected by space availability, we cannot provide equipment and activity specifics. Instead, consider student responses to questions from lesson 9.1 (Part 4: Lesson Focus 2, steps 3 and 4) and questions 5 through 7 on worksheet 8.4, "Pedometer Predictions," to decide on activities. Try to have a variety of active aerobics, sports, and recreational activities.

Possible outdoor choices:

▶ *Ultimate:* 4 cones per Ultimate field, 1 disc per field

▶ *Fitness walking:* 4 cones to mark walking perimeter, or use athletic field boundaries

▶ *Soccer:* 10 cones to mark each field (4 for end lines, 4 for goals, and 2 for midfield), 1 ball per field

Possible indoor choices:

▶ *Active aerobics:* Aerobics (or kickboxing) video and a television with DVD/VCR

▶ *Basketball:* 1 or 2 courts, depending on class interest; 1 or 2 basketballs

▶ *Indoor soccer:* 2 floor hockey nets (or 4 cones), 1 soccer ball, 2 different colored sets of 4 or 5 pinnies

 tech

* Heart rate monitors provide students feedback on whether they are in their target heart rate zones.
* Pedometers allow students to see how many steps they accumulate in different activities.

Reproducibles

None

Setup

1. Create three or four areas for activity, depending on your location (indoor or outdoor), the amount of space you have, and student responses to questions from lesson 9.1 (Part 4: Lesson Focus 2, steps 3 and 4) and questions 5 through 7 on worksheet 8.4, "Pedometer Predictions."

2. Set up three or four cones, depending on the number of stations you have, and space them about 4 feet (1.2 meters) apart. Put the cones in a location where you want to organize students.

Delivering the Lesson

Part 1: Instant Activity

Team Follow-the-Leader

1. Organize students into groups of six, using one of the methods in "Groups and Teams" (see pages 26 to 27). Have each group line up. Explain that all groups will walk around the gym in a line, following the path of the leader—the first student in the line.

2. Instruct leaders to move at a pace that is appropriate for the whole group.

3. Each time the signal sounds, the leader steps aside and the line moves past with a new leader. The former leader goes to the end of the line. Each time there's a new leader, call out a new, progressively more active locomotor skill (for example, power walk, skip, gallop, change lead foot, slide, change lead side, or jog).

Part 2: Lesson Launcher

1. Review the lesson objectives with students.

2. Remind the class that they determined their physical activity and fitness needs last class. Today's class is an opportunity for them to choose activities that help them meet those needs. Choice also allows them to pick activities that they like.

3. Explain that you set up activity stations based on discussions from last class (9.1) and their responses to worksheet 8.4, "Pedometer Predictions." You couldn't include all of their favorite activities, but you included several that were requested.

Part 3: Lesson Focus

Physical Activity Choices

1. Describe the activity stations that you created.

2. Ask students to line up behind cone 1 for the first activity, cone 2 for the second activity, and so on.

3. Instruct students interested in individual physical activities to go to their station and begin the activity.

4. Create teams for active sports activities and send the students out to play. Remind them to follow rules, communicate, and cooperate.

5. After 5 to 10 minutes, signal the students to stop. Let them decide whether to remain at their current station or switch to a new station. Explain that you'll stop them again in another 5 to 10 minutes for the next choice.

 review

Ask students to list participation guidelines to follow to have an enjoyable experience at their station, such as:

* Cooperation: taking turns with the equipment
* Communication: calling "ball" and asking someone else for help if a ball rolls away
* Following rules: calling a foul on yourself and respecting each other (such as giving each other personal space and avoiding put-downs)

Part 4: Reflection and Summary

Ask students the following questions:

▶ Who was able to remain active for the entire class period?

▶ Do your feelings about participation in physical activity change when you have a choice? Explain.

▶ What are some of the health- or skill-related fitness benefits of the activity you participated in?

▶ Which of the activity choices offered today burns the most calories? (Help them understand that the answer depends on the participant, effort, efficiency, and resistance—each factor plays a part.)

Take It Home

Ask the students to think about the choices they have for activity after school or at home. Which ones do they most like? Which ones do people on their support teams most like? Ask them to invite someone to do a favorite activity together this week.

Next Time

- Creating a physical activity plan
- Remind students that worksheet 9.1b, "Support Team Physical Activity Summary," is due next class (recommended).

Assessment

- Performance check: Observe students for examples of cooperation, respect, encouragement, following rules, and the ability to work independently in the activities.
- Performance check: Observe students participating in the activities for the full class period and creating a positive movement setting through communication, cooperation, and fair play.

Lesson Plan 9.3 Creating a Physical Activity Plan

This classroom lesson will allow students to explore and determine what their physical activity needs and goals are, and how to make a physical activity plan to address and meet their needs and goals.

Performance Outcomes Related to NASPE Standards

▶ Standard 1
  ▶ Perform physical activity using knowledge and the appropriate skills.

▶ Standard 3
▶ Demonstrate an understanding of the concept of integration of biomechanical principles using selected physical activity examples.

▶ Standard 4
  ▶ Establish realistic goals for physical activity and fitness.
  ▶ Describe how physical activity contributes to health- and skill-related fitness.

▶ Standard 5
  ▶ Exhibit the ability to work independently.

Lesson Objectives

▶ Students will be able to identify their fitness and activity needs based on their self-assessments.

▶ Students will be able to identify their short-term activity goals based on personal preferences.

▶ Students will demonstrate an understanding of SMART goals by creating a short-term physical activity plan.

▶ Students will demonstrate an understanding of the integration of biomechanical principles (i.e., how several biomechanical principles are involved in selected physical activities).

Equipment

- ▶ 1 *Fitness for Life: Middle School* student textbook per student
- ▶ Each student's *Fitness for Life: Middle School* portfolio
- ▶ Chalkboard or flip chart (optional)

 tech

> Two computer programs (Mount Fitness and Tour de Fitness) are available for reviewing and reinforcing concepts. See page 40 for more information.

Reproducibles

- ▶ Worksheet 9.1a, "Fitness and Physical Activity Summary" (retrieved from the student portfolios)
- ▶ Worksheet 9.3a, "Personal Physical Activity Plan"
- ▶ Worksheet 9.3b, "Support Team Physical Activity Plan"
- ▶ Classroom Quotes

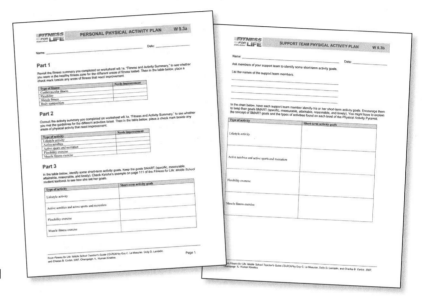

Classroom Quotes

You can print these quotes from the CD-ROM and hang them around your room.

- ▶ "A goal properly set is halfway reached."—Abraham Lincoln (U.S. president)
- ▶ "You have to set goals that are almost out of reach. If you set a goal that is attainable without much work or thought, you are stuck with something below your true talent and potential."—Steve Garvey (baseball player)

Setup

1. Make a copy of worksheet 9.3a, "Personal Physical Activity Plan," and 9.3b, "Support Team Physical Activity Plan," for each student.
2. Write the following on the chalkboard or a flip chart: Describe how tennis, golf, baseball, and walking require the integration of several biomechanical principles.

Delivering the Lesson

Part 1: Gathering Information

Have the students read "Creating a Physical Activity Plan," lesson 9.2 in the student textbook (chapter 9, pages 110 to 114).

Part 2: Lesson Launcher

1. Review the lesson objectives with students.

2. Ask students if they have heard the saying, "He can talk the talk, but he can't walk the walk." Explain that it's one thing to talk about being physically active, but it's another thing to actually do it. Many people need to plan for physical activity to help them do it successfully.

Part 3: Lesson Focus 1

Physical Activity Goal Setting

1. Have students retrieve their worksheet 9.1a, "Fitness and Physical Activity Summary," from their *Fitness for Life: Middle School* portfolios.

2. Ask students how they might identify their physical activity needs based on their "Fitness and Physical Activity Summary."

3. Give each student a copy of worksheet 9.3a, "Personal Physical Activity Plan." Have them complete parts 1 and 2 by using the information they recorded on worksheet 9.1a, "Fitness and Physical Activity Summary." Students will not have scores for their muscular endurance reassessments; instruct them to use their self-assessment scores instead.

4. Ask students to explain how "needs" can differ from "goals." Explain that today they will identify some of their goals related to physical activity and fitness using the SMART approach. Ask if anyone knows what SMART stands for.

5. Write out the SMART acronym on the chalkboard or flip chart:
   - S stands for specific
   - M stands for measurable
   - A stands for attainable
   - R stands for reasonable
   - T stands for timely

   Talk about why each concept in the acronym is important.

6. Have students establish some short-term activity goals and record them in part 3 of worksheet 9.3a, "Personal Physical Activity Plan."

7. While the students work on their goals, visit individual students and discuss their goals and the goal-setting process.

Part 4: Lesson Focus 2

Integration in Physical Activity

1. Have students read "Biomechanical Principles: Integration" (chapter 9, page 113).

2. Organize students into groups of three to five students each using one of the methods described in "Groups and Teams" (see pages 26 to 27).

3. Have students identify a group leader, a recorder, and a reporter in their group. Encourage students to take on a different role from the one(s) they played before. The group leader will guide the discussion, the recorder will generate the list created by the group, and the reporter will report the results to the class. Any others in the group will actively contribute ideas.

4. Have each group explore the concept of integration by answering the question posed at the end of the "Applying the Principle" section. The question asks students to describe how tennis, golf, baseball, and walking require the integration of several biomechanical principles.

Remind students of the class agreements for working in groups (for example, include everyone, listen to the person who is talking, give helpful feedback to improve performance, and participate and contribute).

5. Bring the class together. Have the reporters and others contribute their group's answers and generate discussion.

Part 5: Reflection and Summary

Have students add completed worksheets 9.1b, "Support Team Physical Activity Summary," and 9.3a, "Personal Physical Activity Plan," to their *Fitness for Life: Middle School* portfolios.

Take It Home

▶ Explain that planning for physical activity with your support team is a great way to become a healthy and connected family.

▶ Give each student a copy of worksheet 9.3b, "Support Team Physical Activity Plan," to complete at home.

▶ Tell students when to return the completed worksheets to class. (Recommended: lesson 9.5.)

Next Time

Executing your physical activity plan

Assessment

▶ Performance check: Assess the completed worksheets 9.1b, "Support Team Physical Activity Summary," and 9.3a, "Personal Physical Activity Plan," in students' *Fitness for Life: Middle School* portfolios to see if students were able to identify their fitness and activity needs based on their self-assessments and establish short-term activity goals. Use the worksheet rubric (available on the CD-ROM or on page 34) to assess student work, or modify the rubric to meet your specific objectives.

▶ Comprehension check: Class discussions serve as a check for student understanding of how several biomechanical principles are involved in selected physical activities.

In the next two activity lessons, students will be given an opportunity to participate in activities that relate to their short-term physical activity goals. Specifically, activities from all levels of the Physical Activity Pyramid should be available for students.

Performance Outcomes Related to NASPE Standards

▸ Standard 1
  ▸ Participate in physical activities that have skill- and health-related fitness benefits.
▸ Standard 4
  ▸ Describe how physical activities contribute to health- and skill-related fitness.
▸ Standard 5
  ▸ Exhibit (verbally and nonverbally) cooperation, respect, encouragement, and the ability to work independently.

Lesson Objectives

▸ Students will participate in physical activity for at least 50 percent of the class period.
▸ Students will create positive movement settings through communication, cooperation, and fair play.

Equipment

▸ 1 pencil per student

▶ Because this lesson plan focuses on student choice, depends on your class location (indoor/outdoor), and is affected by space availability, we cannot provide equipment and activity specifics. Instead, look over students' short-term activity goals in part 3 of worksheet 9.3a, "Personal Physical Activity Plan," to decide on a selection of activities.

 tech

* Heart rate monitors provide students feedback on whether they are in their target heart rate zones.
* Pedometers allow students to see how many steps they accumulate in different activities.

Reproducibles

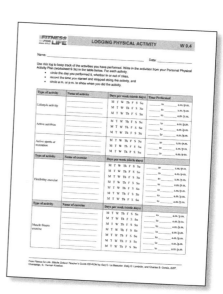

▶ Worksheet 9.3a, "Personal Physical Activity Plan" (retrieved from portfolios)
▶ Worksheet 9.4, "Logging Physical Activity"

Setup

1. Create five activity stations that relate to each of the activity categories of the Physical Activity Pyramid. Look over students' short-term activity goals in part 3 of worksheet 9.3a, "Personal Physical Activity Plan," to decide on a selection of activities. Try to include activities from the first three levels of the Physical Activity Pyramid.

2. Make a copy of worksheet 9.4, "Logging Physical Activity," for each student.

Delivering the Lesson

Part 1: Instant Activity

1. Have students retrieve worksheet 9.3a, "Personal Physical Activity Plan," from their *Fitness for Life: Middle School* portfolios.

2. Have students partner up and discuss their plans with their partner.

3. Once all students have arrived in the area, organize the class into squads or teams using one of the methods described in "Groups and Teams" (see pages 26 to 27).

Part 2: Lesson Launcher

1. Review the lesson objectives with students.

2. Remind students that they established short-term physical activity goals in worksheet 9.3a, "Personal Physical Activity Plan." Today they will start meeting those goals.

3. Explain that you created activity stations from each activity category of the Physical Activity Pyramid based on students' short-term physical activity goals.

Part 3: Lesson Focus

Activity Choices for Physical Fitness and Fitness Planning

1. Briefly explain the five activity stations.

2. Have students quickly and quietly go to a station of their choice. Remind them that the station they choose should reflect the physical activity goals they established.

 review

> Ask students to list behaviors related to the class participation guidelines they should exhibit to help everyone have an enjoyable experience at their station (such as cooperation, communication, following rules, and respecting each other).

3. Give the signal for students to begin doing their chosen activity.

4. After 10 to 15 minutes, give the signal to stop. Let the students decide whether to remain at the same station or switch to a new one.

5. Once all students have chosen a station, give the signal for them to start doing their activity.

Part 4: Reflection and Summary

1. Discuss how logging physical activity is the best way for students to determine if they are meeting their physical activity goals.

2. Give each student a copy of worksheet 9.4, "Logging Physical Activity," and explain how to complete the worksheet. Tell them approximately how long they participated in activity today.

3. Have the students make their first entry on the worksheet. Move around the room to make sure everyone understands how to record the information.

4. Have students return worksheets 9.3a, "Personal Physical Activity Plan," and 9.4, "Logging Physical Activity," to their *Fitness for Life: Middle School* portfolios.

Take It Home

Tell students that if they have made physical activity goals with their support team and want to keep track of their progress, you can give them extra copies of worksheet 9.4, "Logging Physical Activity."

Next Time

▶ Working on your physical activity plan

▶ Remind students that worksheet 9.3b, "Support Team Physical Activity Plan," is due next class (recommended).

Assessment

▶ Performance check: Observe students participating in the activities for the full class period and creating a positive movement setting through communication, cooperation, and fair play.

▶ Comprehension check: Check to make sure students are logging physical activity correctly on worksheet 9.4, "Logging Physical Activity."

9.5 Executing Your Physical Activity Plan

In this activity lesson, students will be given an opportunity to participate in activities that relate to their short-term physical activity goals. Specifically, activities from all levels of the Physical Activity Pyramid should be available for students.

Performance Outcomes Related to NASPE Standards

▶ Standard 1
  ▶ Participate in physical activities that have skill- and health-related fitness benefits.
▶ Standard 4
  ▶ Describe how physical activities contribute to health- and skill-related fitness.
▶ Standard 5
  ▶ Exhibit (verbally and nonverbally) cooperation, respect, encouragement, and the ability to work independently.
▶ Standard 6
  ▶ Use physical activity as a positive opportunity for social and group interactions.

Lesson Objectives

▶ Students will participate in physical activity for at least 50 percent of the class period.
▶ Students will create positive movement settings through communication, cooperation, and fair play.

Equipment

▶ 1 pencil per student
▶ Equipment for activities: Because this lesson plan focuses on student choice, depends on your class location (indoor/outdoor), and is affected by space availability, we cannot provide equipment and activity specifics. If the stations in lesson 9.4 worked well, use them again. If you plan to change the stations, consult students' short-term physical activity goals from worksheet 9.3a.

tech

* Heart rate monitors provide students feedback on whether they are in their target heart rate zones.
* Pedometers allow students to see how many steps they accumulate in different activities.

Reproducibles

Worksheet 9.4, "Logging Physical Activity" (retrieved from portfolios)

Setup

1. Create five activity stations that relate to each of the activity categories of the Physical Activity Pyramid. Use the stations from lesson 9.4, or look over students' short-term activity goals in part 3 of worksheet 9.3a to decide on a new selection of activities. Try to include activities from the first three levels of the Physical Activity Pyramid.
2. Make sure students brought worksheet 9.4, "Logging Physical Activity," back to class. Make extra copies in case some students didn't.

Delivering the Lesson

Part 1: Instant Activity

1. As students enter the activity area, have them partner up and walk around the area.
2. Once all students have arrived in the area, organize the class into their squads or teams using one of the methods described in "Groups and Teams" (see pages 26 to 27).

Part 2: Lesson Launcher

1. Review the lesson objectives with students.
2. Remind students that they established short-term physical activity goals in worksheet 9.3a, "Personal Physical Activity Plan". Today, they will continue working on these goals.
3. Explain that you created activity stations from each activity category of the Physical Activity Pyramid based on the preferences the students expressed in previous lessons.

Part 3: Lesson Focus

Activity Choices for Physical Fitness and Fitness Planning

1. Briefly explain the five activity stations.
2. Have students quickly and quietly go to a station of their choice. Remind them that the station they choose should reflect the physical activity goals they established. Encourage students to focus on a different short-term physical activity goal today.

3. Give the signal for students to begin doing their chosen activity.

4. After 10 to 15 minutes, give the signal to stop. Let the students decide whether to remain at the same station or switch to a new station.

5. Once all students have chosen a station, give the signal for them to start doing their activity.

Part 4: Reflection and Summary

1. Discuss how logging physical activity is the best way for students to determine if they are meeting their physical activity goals.

2. Have each student get out their copy of worksheet 9.4, "Logging Physical Activity," and remind them how to complete the worksheet. Tell them approximately how long they participated in activity today.

3. Have the students make their first entry on the worksheet. Move around the room to make sure everyone understands how to record the information.

4. Have students add completed worksheet 9.3b, "Support Team Physical Activity Plan," to their *Fitness for Life: Middle School* portfolios.

Take It Home

Tell students that if they have made physical activity goals with their support team and want to keep track of their progress, you can give them extra copies of worksheet 9.4.

Next Time

▶ Consider having students keep their copies of worksheet 9.4, "Logging Physical Activity," for the rest of the semester so they can determine whether they've met their physical activity goals.

▶ Consider having students add other assignments related to physical education to their *Fitness for Life: Middle School* portfolios. This serves as a good check of their progress throughout the semester and can be used to show parents what has been happening in class.

▶ Consider partnering up with classroom teachers on topics that can be integrated into physical education. Students can add projects completed for those teachers to their *Fitness for Life: Middle School* portfolios.

▶ If you plan to continue working on students' physical activity plans, consider giving students the following instructions: "We'll be working on physical activity units until the end of the semester, and you will be turning in your activity log after one month and then hopefully continuing it for the rest of the semester."

Assessment

▶ Performance check: Observe students participating in the activities for the full class period and creating a positive movement setting through communication, cooperation, and fair play.

▶ Assess completed worksheet 9.3b, "Support Team Physical Activity Plan," in students' *Fitness for Life: Middle School* portfolios. Use the worksheet rubric (available on the CD-ROM or on page 34) to assess student work, or modify the rubric to meet your specific objectives.

▶ Using the provided rubric or your own rubric, assess each student's completed *Fitness for Life: Middle School* portfolio.

Supplemental Materials

If you choose to use the semester or year scheduling version of *Fitness for Life: Middle School* (see appendix B), there are excellent opportunities to insert activity-based skill units and to review and reinforce the concepts in each chapter using the *Fitness for Life: Middle School* computer programs: Mount Fitness and Tour de Fitness. You will find information about the two computer programs in appendix C. Listed below are suggestions of activity-based skill units that would go well with this chapter and resources that will help you develop great lessons.

As indicated in the "Scheduling" section (pages 13 to 18), integrating activity-based skill units with the *Fitness for Life: Middle School* lesson plans provides a great opportunity for reinforcing key concepts and for developing students' skills in a wide range of physical activities. The activity-based skill unit suggestions provided below were chosen specifically to complement chapter content. In addition, there are selected resources that can provide you with excellent lesson plans and lesson plan ideas. Approaches to teaching activity-based skill units can be found in appendix A.

UNIT WITH CONSTRAINED CHOICE

Students can select from a variety of activities.

▶ **Key concepts to reinforce:** Planning for physical activity, setting goals, logging physical activity, integrating biomechanical principles

▶ **Resources:** See resources for activity-based skill units at the ends of chapters 1 through 8.

Appendix A: Activity-Based Skill Units

As noted previously in the *Teacher's Guide,* integration of skill-learning units (activity-based skill units) is encouraged. Several plans for scheduling integrated units were described in "Scheduling" (pages 13 to 18). Additional information is provided here:

▶ Resources for developing skill units
▶ A format for delivering skill units

Resources

There are several lesson plan books that are appropriate resources to use in conjunction with *Fitness for Life: Middle School.* Units in these books contain 5 to 20 lessons and offer a wide variety of activities. In this *Teacher's Guide,* the "Supplemental Materials" pages that follow each group of lesson plans offer suggestions for using specific activities from these books. The suggestions were made based on how the activities would complement the key chapter concepts from *Fitness for Life: Middle School.* A reference list for some of these excellent resource books with a brief description of each is contained below:

▶ *Teaching Sport Concepts and Skills: A Tactical Games Approach* (Mitchell, Olsen and Griffin, 2006, Human Kinetics). These authors use the Teaching Games for Understanding approach, which means that their lessons deal with learning how to appropriately apply different strategies and tactics in games. Each of their lessons presents a strategic problem to be solved and leads the students to an understanding of how that strategy is used in the activity being played. They provide lesson plans for seven team sports and four individual sports. For each sport they provide lessons for several different levels of skill and experience. For each level of skill they provide five or more specific lesson plans. In the *Fitness for Life: Middle School* program, students are introduced to biomechanical principles that they are required to apply in practice. In addition to discussing tactics and strategy, students could explore how to move most efficiently when executing game strategies and tactics.

▶ *It's Not Just Gym Anymore: Teaching Secondary School Students How to Be Active for Life* (McCracken, 2001, Human Kinetics). This resource takes a lifetime activity approach, encouraging students to learn and practice skills and also to learn more about how and where they can participate in their community. *It's Not Just Gym Anymore* includes units in basketball, volleyball, tennis, golf, outdoor adventure, downhill skiing, mountain biking, bow hunting and fly fishing, personal fitness, and conditioning and weight training. Most units include 10 lessons, making it perfect for two-week interspersed units.

▶ *Quality Lesson Plans for Secondary Physical Education* (Zakrajsek, Carnes, and Pettigrew, 2003, Human Kinetics). This lesson plan book provides lesson units for a host of activities at a variety of lengths. They include major units of instruction for 10 lessons, minor units of instruction for 5 lessons, and single-day lessons in a large variety of nontraditional activities. This text provides several options for integrating skill units with various *Fitness for Life: Middle School* schedules.

▶ *Complete Physical Education Plans for Grades 7-12* (Kleinman, 2001, Human Kinetics). This lesson plan book includes plans for beginning, intermediate, and advanced levels of six team sports and six individual activities, including dance. Most units include 15 lessons at each level and could be used when integrating the *Fitness for Life: Middle School* program with three-week skill units.

Finally, you may want to plan your own one- to three-week skill units that complement the *Fitness for Life: Middle School* program. The grid teaching method (see below) or the Sport Education format (see page 259) provide excellent formats for organizing lessons. Being consistent in format from one unit to the next supports student responsibility because once students are familiar with the general format they can help set up and organize the lessons. It also saves a tremendous amount of time not having to explain how the unit or class is structured. However, using the same format for every unit might also lead to boredom, so it would be best to use at least two formats over the course of the year and alternate them as you see fit.

Formats for Delivering Activity-Based Skill Units

Whichever activity-based skill units you choose to implement, don't forget to apply and highlight the content learned in the *Fitness for Life: Middle School* lessons. Each activity will fall into one or more of the categories found in the Physical Activity Pyramid. The FIT principles for each category can easily be applied. The "Moving Together" concepts will be applicable in the social interactions that are part of each activity. The "Biomechanics Principles" will often be important to successful importance. Finally, providing large quantities of appropriate practice will be important to successful learning and performance.

Grid teaching as explained in the next section provides a simple organizational format for activity units where students get many opportunities to play in small aside games and integrate the learning of strategies and tactics into skill learning.

Grid Teaching

In grid teaching, the unit is planned on the basis of progressively increasing activity spaces and numbers of students on teams. A grid is laid out on the field or court so that there is a square for each student in the class. Initial activities might involve individual or partner practice. Then two pairs might be put together to play with or against another pair, and then those four may be merged to play with or against another four. A weeklong format might look like this:

▶ Day 1: Individual or pair work and 1-on-1 and 2-on-2 games

▶ Day 2: Individual or pair work and 1-on-1 and 2-on-1 games

▶ Day 3: 3-on-3 and 4-on-3 with coach

- Day 4: Strategy session, practice, and 3-on-3
- Day 5: Strategy session, practice, and 3-on-3

If the unit is to be two weeks long, each day might be repeated to allow for greater practice. During the first two days you can set up the grid assignments so that the student skill levels are mixed, and students are asked to coach each other. Sometimes it's a good idea to give students the choice of playing in a competitive game or a recreational game during the larger aside games (3-on-3, 4-on-4, etc.).

Following is a basic example of a basketball unit done in this format. It can easily be transformed to a soccer, Ultimate, team handball, speedball, or any other invasion sport unit by changing the skills. Here are a few protocols to reinforce with students:

- Each time the size of the area being played in changes, have the players walk their boundaries until you are sure they are aware of them and will not run into other games.
- Require players to stop at the edge of their own square if the ball goes out and call "ball please" rather than run into another playing square.
- Make sure that all players display good body control before allowing games to be played next to each other. Start all games at a walk speed and gradually allow faster movement after good body control is shown.

DAY 1

1. Assign each student a square in the grid (see figure A.1).
2. Have students practice dribbling around personal squares (review dribbling cues).
3. Put two squares together, give each player a scarf or flag, and have the two players dribble in their area and try to get each other's scarves away (match by skill or have stronger players use their weaker hand). Once a player has grabbed an opponent's scarf, the scarfless one says "good job," the victor returns the scarf, and play continues.

   - Encourage students to coach each other where needed.
   - Have students change partners often by rotating one player from each pair one square clockwise (the tallest, the one with the most siblings, rock/paper/scissors).

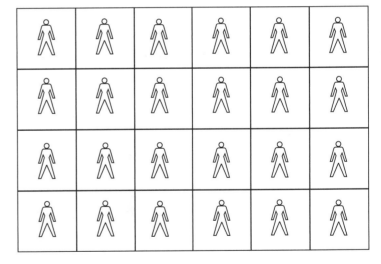

Figure A.1 The grid format with each student assigned to a box.

4. Have students practice their shooting form, with one partner shooting in a high arc to the other partner, who passes it back.

5. Put four boxes together, and have students play the scarf dribbling game. Players who lose scarves have to go outside the boundary to put it back on, dribble five times with their weak hand for some extra practice, and then return to the game. Again, rotate players periodically.

DAY 2

1. Review or redo all activities from day 1 using short time periods.
2. With four boxes together, have one player be the coach and the others play 2-on-1 keep-away, practicing passing, pivoting, and dribbling.
   - ▸ Recreation format: Just play, switching off positions every minute or two
   - ▸ Competitive format: 1 point for each completed pass, play for one minute with each combination of players, each passing pair keeps own score
3. Give a short clinic (short lesson) on how to get free and how to pass to a space.
4. Rotate pairs to play with others.

DAY 3

1. Review 2-on-1 game. Ask students to supply cues for passing to space.
2. Put six squares together and have groups play 3-on-2 keep-away with one student playing coach.
3. Give a short clinic on 1-on-1 guarding and looking for the open player to pass.
4. If you have four baskets, have each set of six practice shooting at one basket, first from a stationary position and then with a guard coming out from under the basket toward the shooter.

DAY 4

1. Have students play 3-on-3 at each basket.
2. Stop periodically for a coaching clinic (getting free, 1-on-1 guarding).

DAY 5

1. Have students play a 3-on-3 round robin. Allow students to decide whether they want to play a competitive or recreational game.

If the class has 24 students, create a 4 × 6 grid (see figure A.1). If possible, maintain small-sided games (less than or equal to 4-on-4). For larger classes you can make the grid 6 × 6 (36). For class sizes that do not have obvious multiples or even numbers, add an extra person to each set of six squares and instead of 2-on-1 make it 3-on-2 with no coach.

When the activity area is outdoors (or where there is sufficient space), grids are best made with buffer zones (see figure A.2). These buffers can be added into the game squares when appropriate (e.g., 4-on-4 activities).

Outside games can go to 5-on-5 (with two officials) and be played across the grid with goals made at each sideline. Games of 2-on-2 can require trapping or catching the ball on the sideline.

Grids work nicely with squad lines to provide space for individual activity and to enable grouping of students quickly into pairs, threes, fours, sixes, and so on.

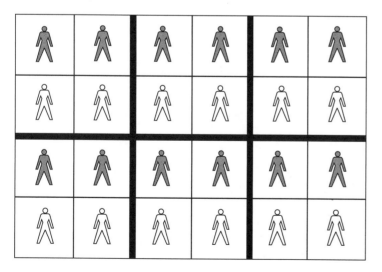

Figure A.2 Two-on-two games with buffer zones between games.

Sport Education Model

Daryl Siedentop's Sport Education model is another option for organizing activity-based skill units. It has several strengths that are worth noting. First, students are given much of the responsibility of running the class, and students learn the roles common to sport and group interactions. Another strength of the Sport Education model is that students get high levels of activity time and have motivation to work hard and improve their skills. For a full description please use the *Complete Guide to Sport Education* (Siedentop, Hastie, and van der Mars, 2004, Human Kinetics).

An abbreviated version of the Sport Education model will be described here. The Sport Education model can be used with almost any activity. It is best to begin by using a simplified version of the model and then add elements as you are ready for them. In the simplest model, students in the class are put into groups for the unit. Ideally, students are grouped into three or six teams. Each team is given a designated section of the playing area to meet in and conduct their practice. All players are asked to sign a teamwork and sportsmanship pledge indicating their agreement with standards of behavior. Each team decides on a coach, a manager, and a statistician. The coach is responsible for organizing the team, and the manager is responsible for organizing the equipment. The statistician deals with any scorekeeping or personal records. These students are used as leaders in the class. They help lead practice drills for their group, get out equipment, and so on. Each day of the unit is run as a team practice. Warm-up and conditioning drills are decided on by the team (within parameters you have provided) and then led by the coach of each team.

Figure A.3 Small-sided 4-on-4 games teaching grid.

You should provide a clinic (short lesson) every day for the class on a needed skill or strategy and an activity for practicing that skill. Teams then return to their areas, and their captain leads them in practicing that drill. Each day there is also some form of competition between teams. Players from two teams compete while a member of the third team (called a duty team) keeps the score or officiates if needed. After each competition a different team becomes the duty team and the other two teams compete. These competitions start as small-sided games (1-on-1, 2-on-2, etc.) and build to larger games (5-on-5). This is similar to the grid teaching unit explained earlier.

An example of a five-day unit in pickleball using the Sport Education model is provided next.

DAY 1

1. Once the teams have grouped together, each player signs the player's pledge, and the team decides on their coach, manager, and statistician (takes volunteers and votes if there's more than one volunteer).

2. Provide a warm-up and basic skill clinic that addresses the roles and behaviors of leaders and players, racket grip, and ball control activities (ups, downs, flip-flops).

3. Have teams return to their areas and complete the warm-up and then begin to practice ball control.

4. Competition: One player from each team gets together to form a group of three.

Each player attempts to go through a routine of 10 ups, 10 downs, and 10 flip-flops while the other two count the number of hits. The person with the highest score gets three points for his or her team, the one with the second highest score gets two points, and the one with the third highest score gets one point.

5. Have players return to their teams and report their scores to the statistician. (A discussion of honesty is valuable here.)

6. Encourage students to reflect on the good aspects of the day and celebrate team totals.

DAY 2

1. Have managers help get out equipment for their teams. Managers help set up nets lengthwise across the gym or across each side of the tennis courts while the teams are beginning warm-ups and practice.

2. Offer a teacher clinic on hitting back and forth over a net, including moving to the ball and hitting gently.

3. Have teams do warm-up routines and practice among themselves, hitting back and forth with feedback from the coach.

4. Competition: One player from each team gets together in a group of three. Two players hit the ball across the net, and the third player counts the number of hits in a row. Players rotate positions until each has had a turn in each role. Players add their top scores with each player and report them to their team statisticians at the end of the competition. The statisticians add up all points.

5. Celebrate team scores by writing them on the chalkboard or posting them as the daily record for each team, and compliment students on their good sporting behavior.

DAY 3

1. Meet with the coaches while the managers get out and set up equipment.

2. Have the teams practice.

3. Offer a clinic on serving in pickleball.

4. Have teams return to their areas and warm up and practice serving.

5. Competition: Students get into groups of three, with one student from each team in the competition group. Each person gets 10 serves. The other two in each group count the number of serves that go into the service box.

6. Have competitors return to their teams, and have the statistician add up the scores of all the players from their team.

7. Celebrate team scores and compliment students on their good sporting behavior.

DAY 4

1. Meet with coaches while managers help set up practice time for teams.

2. Hold a teacher clinic on player positions, rules, and scoring in pickleball.

3. Have the teams warm up and practice.

4. Captains divide their teams into pairs to play pairs from other teams. Create groups of six players including two from each of three teams. (If you have three teams set up in the class with 12 players on each team, this would result in six groups being formed with two players from each of the three teams in each

group. Each group of six would participate in a different mini-game, creating six mini-games going on simultaneously during the competition time.) In each group, have the partners from two teams play each other while the third pair officiates and keeps score (acts as the duty team). Have each pair play the other two pairs in a round robin format. Winners of each game get 2 points and the losers earn 1 point, so a pair could finish the competition with 2 to 4 points, depending on how many games they win.

5. Have students return to their teams, and have the statisticians add up scores from all their pairs.

6. Celebrate team scores and compliment students on their sporting behavior.

DAY 5

1. Meet with the coaches while the managers set up.

2. Because this is the last day of the unit, there is no clinic (if you are doing a 10- to 15-day unit, clinics continue).

3. Have coaches lead team warm-ups and practice.

4. Competition: Captains divide their teams into pairs to play against pairs from other teams. As on day 4, have a pair from each team get together so that there is a group of six—including two from each team. Have two pairs play while the third pair officiates and keeps score. Have each pair play the other two pairs in their group. Winners of each game get 2 points and the losers earn 1 point, so a pair could finish the competition with 2 to 4 points, depending on how many games they win.

5. Have players return to their teams, and have the statisticians add up scores from all their pairs.

6. Celebrate team scores and compliment students on their good sporting behavior.

In the full Sport Education model, scores and team standings are kept, but it is often better when starting off to use the model for a couple of units before adding that complexity to the situation. When the class is ready, set up a "sport season" in which points for all aspects of the class (e.g., teams having everyone appropriately dressed, doing warm-ups properly on their own, showing good sporting behavior during games, getting in place to play on time, points scored in competition) are added into the team score. Season standings are posted and celebrations planned just as in professional sport seasons.

Other roles can be added to each team such as a publicity manager, who can take pictures of the group or write up reports of team strengths. These roles help each student on the team be involved as a valuable team member.

This Sport Education format can be used for any activity. In dance, the teacher clinics can be specific steps or dances that the teams go back and practice and then come together at the end of class to perform together. Although the Sport Education model is most appropriate for a competitive format in which points are given for some aspect of learning the skill or playing a sport, it can also be used as a way for students to take leadership responsibilities and to practice in smaller groups. If the class has become a community, it works very well.

If the class has students who are always on task, sometimes the points are used to reinforce this behavior and motivate other students to stay on task because they can earn points for their team. Points are awarded to the group if everyone in their group is ready on time or participates fully in the warm-ups. Although this works for many students, it can be very discouraging if there are unmotivated players on your team who do not care about the team getting points. For this reason, this aspect must be used carefully.

Teacher Tip

Getting middle school students connected with resources and opportunities in the community through networking and physical activity promotion efforts is an important part of a physical educator's role. Find experts in your community who can introduce students to physical activity opportunities outside of school. Invite these local experts into your classroom to deliver a unit of instruction. These experiences can be exciting, fun, and educational for your students and for you.

Appendix B: Scheduling Options

Many different scheduling options for *Fitness for Life: Middle School* were described on pages 14 to 18, but only three schedules were provided: the basic plan, the basic plan with organizational lessons (10 weeks) and the integrated semester plan (18 weeks). This appendix contains the schedules for the remaining options.

Week	Student Text content	MONDAY	TUESDAY	WEDNESDAY	THURSDAY	FRIDAY
1	Ch. 1	Organizational lessons	Organizational lessons	1.1	1.2	1.3
2	Ch. 2	2.1	2.2	2.3	2.4	2.5
3	Ch. 3	3.1	3.2	3.3	3.4	3.5
4	Ch. 4	4.1	4.2	4.3	4.4	4.5
5	Ch. 5	5.1	5.2	5.3	5.4	5.5
6	Ch. 6	6.1	6.2	6.3	6.4	6.5
7	Ch. 7	7.1	7.2	7.3	7.4	7.5
8	Ch. 8	8.1	8.2	8.3	8.4	8.5
9	Ch. 9	9.1	9.2	9.3	9.4	9.5

If you don't have extra time before the program begins, run organizational lessons during the first week by cutting lessons 1.4 and 1.5.

Classroom lesson days are shaded.

Figure B.1   Basic plan with organizational lessons (9 weeks).

Week	Student Text content	MONDAY	TUESDAY	WEDNESDAY	THURSDAY	FRIDAY
Before program	—	—	—	Organizational Lesson 1	Organizational Lesson 2	Organizational Lesson 3
1	Ch. 1	1.1	1.2	Skill unit 1	Skill unit 1	Skill unit 1
2	Ch. 1	1.3	1.4	1.5	Skill unit 1	Skill unit 1
3	Ch. 2	2.1	2.2	Skill unit 2	Skill unit 2	Skill unit 2
4	Ch. 2	2.3	2.4	2.5	Skill unit 2	Skill unit 2
5	Ch. 3	3.1	3.2	Skill unit 3	Skill unit 3	Skill unit 3
6	Ch. 3	3.3	3.4	3.5	Skill unit 3	Skill unit 3
7	Ch. 4	4.1	4.2	Skill unit 4	Skill unit 4	Skill unit 4
8	Ch. 4	4.3	4.4	4.5	Skill unit 4	Skill unit 4
9	Ch. 5	5.1	5.2	Skill unit 5	Skill unit 5	Skill unit 5
10	Ch. 5	5.3	5.4	5.5	Skill unit 5	Skill unit 5
11	Ch. 6	6.1	6.2	Skill unit 6	Skill unit 6	Skill unit 6
12	Ch. 6	6.3	6.4	6.5	Skill unit 6	Skill unit 6
13	Ch. 7	7.1	7.2	Skill unit 7	Skill unit 7	Skill unit 7
14	Ch. 7	7.3	7.4	7.5	Skill unit 7	Skill unit 7
15	Ch. 8	8.1	8.2	Skill unit 8	Skill unit 8	Skill unit 8
16	Ch. 8	8.3	8.4	8.5	Skill unit 8	Skill unit 8
17	Ch. 9	9.1	9.2	Skill unit 9	Skill unit 9	Skill unit 9
18	Ch. 9	9.3	9.4	9.5	Skill unit 9	Skill unit 9

If classroom time is limited, run the organizational lessons, and then break up the lessons with skill units so that you run only one classroom lesson per week.

Classroom lesson days are shaded.

Figure B.2   Integrated semester plan II (18 weeks).

Week	Student Text content	MONDAY	TUESDAY	WEDNESDAY	THURSDAY	FRIDAY
Before program	—	—	—	Organizational lesson 1	Organizational lesson 2	Organizational lesson 3
1	Ch. 1	1.1	1.2	1.3	1.4	1.5
2	—	Skill unit 1	Skill unit 1	Skill unit 1	Skill unit 1	Skill unit 1
3	—	Skill unit 1	Skill unit 1	Skill unit 1	Skill unit 1	Skill unit 1
4	—	Skill unit 1	Skill unit 1	Skill unit 1	Skill unit 1	Skill unit 1
5	Ch. 2	2.1	2.2	2.3	2.4	2.5
6	—	Skill unit 2	Skill unit 2	Skill unit 2	Skill unit 2	Skill unit 2
7	—	Skill unit 2	Skill unit 2	Skill unit 2	Skill unit 2	Skill unit 2
8	—	Skill unit 2	Skill unit 2	Skill unit 2	Skill unit 2	Skill unit 2

Repeat the above pattern (lesson plan for one week, skill units for three weeks) for chapters 3 through 9 of the student textbook.

Teach a lesson plan for one week followed by three weeks of skill units.

Classroom lesson days are shaded.

Figure B.3   Year plan I (36 weeks).

Week	Student Text content	MONDAY	TUESDAY	WEDNESDAY	THURSDAY	FRIDAY
1	Ch. 1	Organizational Lesson 1	Organizational Lesson 2	1.1	Skill unit 1	Skill unit 1
2	Ch. 1	Skill unit 1	Skill unit 1	1.2	Skill unit 1	Skill unit 1
3	Ch. 1	Skill unit 1	Skill unit 1	1.3	Skill unit 1	Skill unit 1
4	Ch. 1	Skill unit 1	Skill unit 1	1.4	Skill unit 1	1.5
5	Ch. 2	Skill unit 2	Skill unit 2	2.1	Skill unit 2	Skill unit 2
6	Ch. 2	Skill unit 2	Skill unit 2	2.2	Skill unit 2	Skill unit 2
7	Ch. 2	Skill unit 2	Skill unit 2	2.3	Skill unit 2	Skill unit 2
8	Ch. 2	Skill unit 2	Skill unit 2	2.4	Skill unit 2	2.5
Repeat the above pattern for chapters 3 through 9 of the student textbook.						

Run one or two lessons per week, and run skill units on the other days of the week.

Classroom lesson days are shaded.

Figure B.4 Year plan II (36 weeks).

Week	Student Text content	MONDAY	TUESDAY	WEDNESDAY	THURSDAY	FRIDAY
Before program	—	—	—	Organizational lesson 1	Organizational lesson 2	Organizational lesson 3
1	Ch. 1	1.1	—	1.2	—	1.3
2	Ch. 1	—	1.4	—	1.5	—
3	Ch. 2	2.1	—	2.2	—	2.3
4	Ch. 2	—	2.4	—	2.5	—
Repeat the above pattern for chapters 3 through 9 of the student textbook.						

If your class meets only every other day for 18 weeks, simply stretch the Basic Plan out over the semester.

Classroom lesson days are shaded.

Figure B.5 Semester plan (18 weeks).

Week	Student Text content	MONDAY	TUESDAY	WEDNESDAY	THURSDAY	FRIDAY
Before program	—	—	Organizational lesson 1	—	Organizational lesson 2	—
1	Ch. 1	1.1	—	1.2	—	1.3
2	Ch. 1	—	1.4	—	1.5	—
3	—	Skill unit	—	Skill unit	—	Skill unit
4	—	—	Skill unit	—	Skill unit	—
Repeat the above pattern for chapters 2 through 9 of the student textbook.						

If your class meets only every other day for 36 weeks, alternate two weeks of lessons with two weeks of skill units.

Classroom lesson days are shaded.

Figure B.6 Year plan (36 weeks).

Week	Student Text content	MONDAY	TUESDAY	WEDNESDAY	THURSDAY	FRIDAY
1	Ch. 1	1.1	—	1.2	—	—
2	Ch. 1	1.3	—	1.4	—	—
3	Ch. 1/2	1.5	—	2.1	—	—
4	Ch. 2	2.2	—	2.3	—	—
5	Ch. 2	2.4	—	2.5	—	—
6	Ch. 3	3.1	—	3.2	—	—
7	Ch. 3	3.3	—	3.4	—	—
8	Ch. 3	3.5	—	Unit wrap-up	—	—
Repeat the above pattern for unit 2 (chapters 4 to 6) and unit 3 (chapters 7 to 9) of the student textbook.						

If your class meets only twice per week, deliver each unit of the program over eight weeks.

Classroom lesson days are shaded.

Figure B.7 Unit plan (class twice per week).

Week	Student Text Content	MONDAY	TUESDAY	WEDNESDAY	THURSDAY	FRIDAY
1	Ch. 1	Class A: 1.1	Class A: 1.2	Class A: 1.3	Class A: 1.4	Class A: 1.5
			Class B: 1.1	Class B: 1.2	Class B: 1.3	Class B: 1.4
2	Ch. 2	Class A: 2.1	Class A: 2.2	Class A: 2.3	Class A: 2.4	Class A: 2.5
		Class B: 1.5	Class B: 2.1	Class B: 2.2	Class B: 2.3	Class B: 2.4
3	Ch. 3	Class A: 3.1	Class A: 3.2	Class A: 3.3	Class A: 3.4	Class A: 3.5
		Class B: 2.5	Class B: 3.1	Class B: 3.2	Class B: 3.3	Class B: 3.4
4	Ch. 4	Class A: 4.1	Class A: 4.2	Class A: 4.3	Class A: 4.4	Class A: 4.5
		Class B: 3.5	Class B: 4.1	Class B: 4.2	Class B: 4.3	Class B: 4.4
Continue the above pattern until both classes have completed all lesson plans.						

If your class (Class A) and another class (Class B) share the same room, have Class B start the program one day later so the two classes don't need the room at the same time.

Class A classroom lesson

Class B classroom lesson

Figure B.8 Staggered classes.

Appendix C: Computer Programs

The *Fitness for Life: Middle School* computer programs for review and reinforcement—Mount Fitness and Tour de Fitness—were described in "High-Tech Options" on pages 40 to 41. This appendix explains how you can use the programs to teach strategy and tactics and to supplement lessons with supporting physical activities.

Your first step is to become familiar with Mount Fitness and Tour de Fitness. Visit the *Fitness for Life: Middle School* Web site (www.fitnessforlife.org/middleschool) and click on the "Teacher Information" button to go to the page of additional teacher resources. There, you'll find complete instructions for

▶ accessing each program,
▶ setting up before class begins, and
▶ playing each program with students.

Suggestions for Teaching Strategy and Tactics

Physical education standards for middle level students (both national and state) require teaching of game strategy and tactics. After familiarizing yourself with the setup and organizational details on the *Fitness for Life: Middle School* Web site, you will realize that Tour de Fitness provides an excellent opportunity to teach the meaning of the terms *strategy* and *tactics* and to apply them in a game setting. Before beginning the Tour de Fitness game, define the terms for students:

▶ **Strategy**—A comprehensive plan to do one's best in a game or sport; a strategy often involves combining several tactics.
▶ **Tactics**—Decisions to use one's skills or abilities to best advantage in a game or sport; several tactics are used to carry out a strategy.

The goal of Tour de Fitness is to solve as many puzzles as possible and to accumulate more kilometers (a better score) than other teams. A good general strategy for Tour de Fitness is to accumulate as many points as possible early before trying to solve the puzzle. If you try to solve the puzzle too soon you score few points (kilometers). Even if you know the answer to a puzzle you may not want to solve it if you have accumulated few points.

Tactics that can be used to carry out your strategy include:

▶ Select consonants to build up points.
▶ Select letters that are common to many puzzles such as R, S, T, and L.
▶ When you have accumulated many points but do not yet know the answer to the puzzle, consider buying a vowel for 25 points. It can help you solve the puzzle.
▶ If you have accumulated less than 50 points and know the answer to the puzzle, you may want to continue to spin and select letters you know are in the puzzle.

- ▶ If you know the answer, select letters that appear more than once in the puzzle because you get kilometers for each letter in the puzzle.
- ▶ When you have accumulated 50 or more points and you know the answer to the puzzle, you may want to solve the puzzle so that you do not risk losing all of your kilometers by landing on "Leg Cramp" or "Restart."

Exercises and Activities

After reading the setup and organizational instructions, you will know that you have the option of showing exercises or not. If you choose to have students do exercises while playing the games, you may want to review the activities listed next. This will help you show students how to perform activities and exercises properly.

Classroom Exercises

Classroom exercises are the same for both Mount Fitness and Tour de Fitness.

Chapter 1

Jog in place: 10 steps with each foot (cardiovascular fitness)

Calf stretch: Stand with one foot forward and the other foot back. Keep the back heel on the ground to stretch the back leg's calf muscle. Do the same with the other foot back. (flexibility)

Book curl: Hold a book in one hand with the arm lowered. Bend the elbow to lift the book to the shoulder. Lower to the side. (muscle fitness)

One leg stand: Stand on one foot for a count of 10. (balance)

Heel click: Jump in the air and use foot speed to click your heels together. (speed)

Vertical jump: Stand on one foot, jump as high as you can, and repeat with the other foot. (power)

Coin drop: With the upper arm held parallel to the floor and the lower arm bent back so that the hand is by the ear, place a coin on the elbow so that it doesn't slide off. Quickly straighten the arm and catch the coin before it drops. (reaction time)

Zipper: Reach over the shoulder and down the back with one hand, reach behind the back and upward with the other hand, and try to touch hands. (flexibility)

180 degree jump: Jump into the air and turn around so that you land facing the opposite way. (agility)

Paper ball bounce: Crumple a piece of paper into a ball. Volley the ball in the air using your hands. Try to keep it up for 10 hits. (coordination)

Chapter 2

Jump shot: Practice shooting a basketball 5 times with an imaginary ball. (skill)

Heel click: Jump in the air and use foot speed to click your heels together. (speed)

Vertical jump: Stand on one foot, jump as high as you can, and repeat with the other foot. (power)

Volleyball block: Jump in the air to block an imaginary volleyball 5 times. (skill)

Paper ball juggle: Practice juggling with three paper balls. (skill)

Jump ball: Jump in the air 5 times to tip an imaginary ball. (skill)

One foot 180 degree jump: Jump off one foot into the air and turn around so that you land facing the opposite way. (agility)

One knee balance: Kneel on the ground, then lift one knee and balance on the other. (balance)

Paper ball bounce: Crumple a piece of paper into a ball. Volley the ball in the air using your hands. Try to keep it up for 10 hits. (coordination)

Coin drop: With the upper arm held parallel to the floor and the lower arm bent back so that the hand is by the ear, place a coin on the elbow so that it doesn't slide off. Quickly straighten the arm and catch the coin before it drops. (reaction time)

Chapter 3

Walk in place: 5 steps with each foot (lifestyle activity)

Walk in place: 10 steps with each foot (lifestyle activity)

One-foot stork stand: Stand like a stork on one foot, and hold the other foot bent with the foot near the knee of the supporting leg. (stability)

One-foot stork stand: Repeat on the other foot. (stability)

Lift an imaginary box: 3 times with a half squat (lifestyle activity)

Defensive stance: Defensive-stance run in place 5 times. (stability)

Chapter 4

Jog in place: 10 steps (5 with each foot) (active aerobics)

Jog in place: 20 steps (active aerobics)

One foot hop: Hop 10 times on one foot. (active aerobics)

Other foot hop: Hop 10 times on the other foot. (active aerobics)

Two foot hop: 10 steps (active aerobics)

Straddle hop: 10 steps (alternate apart/together 10 times); start with feet together, hop and move feet apart, continue. (active aerobics)

Forward/backward jump: 10 steps (jump forward 5 times, then backward 5 times) (active aerobics)

Chapter 5

Jump ball: Jump in the air 5 times to tip an imaginary ball. (active sports)

Volleyball block: Jump in the air to block an imaginary volleyball 5 times. (active sports)

Track sprint in place: 5 times (active sports)

Swim: 5 crawl strokes with each arm (active sports)

Football drill: Defensive-stance run in place 5 times. (active sports)

Canoe row: 10 times (active recreation)

Hiking: 10 steps (5 with each foot) (active recreation)

Rock climb: Reach 5 times with each arm. (active recreation)

Chapter 6

Zipper: Reach over the shoulder and down the back with one hand, reach behind the back and upward with the other hand, and try to touch hands. (flexibility)

Calf stretch: Stand with one foot forward and the other foot back. Keep the back heel on the ground to stretch the back leg's calf muscle. Do the same with the other foot back. (flexibility)

Cross-leg squat: Stand with the legs crossed just above the ankles. Sit down without moving the feet. Then stand without moving the feet. The goal is to complete the squat without losing your balance. (flexibility)

Archery stretch: Imagine shooting a bow, and reach back with the bent arm. (flexibility)

One-arm side bend: Reach down your side with one arm, and reach over your head and to the same side with the other arm. (flexibility)

Other-arm side bend: Repeat in the other direction. (flexibility)

Arm stretch in place: Clasp your hands behind your back, and raise your arms as high as you can. (flexibility)

Standing one-leg hug: Stand on one leg. Raise the other leg and hug the knee toward the chest. (flexibility)

Standing other-leg hug: Do the standing one-leg hug on the other leg. (flexibility)

Trunk twist: Keeping the feet planted, twist to the left and the right. (flexibility)

Chapter 7

Two-leg half squat: Squat until your upper leg is parallel to the ground 5 times. (muscle fitness)

One-leg half squat: Squat as low as you can (up to half squat) 3 times. (muscle fitness)

Other-leg half squat: 3 reps (muscle fitness)

Book press: Press a book from shoulder level to above the head 5 times. (muscle fitness)

Isometric hand press: Press hands together in front of the chest, elbows out, for 10 seconds. (muscle fitness)

Isometric hand pull: Hook the fingers of both hands together across the chest, elbows out, and pull for 10 seconds. (muscle fitness)

Book curl: Hold a book with one arm lowered, and bend the elbow to lift 5 times. (muscle fitness)

Left hand grip: Make a fist and squeeze hard for 10 seconds. (muscle fitness)

Right hand grip: Repeat with the other hand for 10 seconds. (muscle fitness)

Upward row with book: Lean over so that the upper body is parallel to the floor and the arm is hanging down. Hold a book in the hand. Bend the arm and lift the book to the trunk. Repeat 5 times. (muscle fitness)

Chapter 8

Walk in place: 10 times each foot (lifestyle activity)

Jog in place: 10 times each foot (active aerobics)

Canoe row: 10 times (active recreation)

Two-leg half squat: 5 reps (muscle fitness)

Zipper: 5 seconds with each arm (flexibility)

Calf stretch: 5 seconds with each leg (flexibility)

Jump ball: 10 times (active sport)

Two foot hop: 10 hops (active aerobics)

Volleyball block: 10 times (active sport)

Hiking: 10 steps (5 with each foot) (active recreation)

Book press: 5 times (muscle fitness)

Chapter 9

Walk in place: 10 times (lifestyle activity)

Jog in place: 10 times (active aerobics)

Jump ball with imaginary ball: 10 times (active sport)

Canoe row: 10 times (active recreation)

Two leg half squat: 5 reps (muscle fitness)

Zipper: 5 seconds right arm up (flexibility)

Calf stretch: 5 seconds with each leg (flexibility)

Two foot hop: 10 hops (active aerobics)

Volleyball block: 10 times (active sport)

Hiking: 10 steps (5 with each foot) (active recreation)

Book press: 5 times (muscle fitness)

Gym Activities

If you decide you would rather have students do more vigorous gym activities while using the computer programs, set up the programs to show "No Exercises." Before each question in Mount Fitness or before pedaling the bicycle in Tour de Fitness, have students perform an activity of your choice. The activities should correspond to the topic of the chapter—for example, you would want to select an active aerobics activity for a question or puzzle related to chapter 4.

About the Authors

Guy C. Le Masurier, PhD, is a professor of physical education at Malaspina University-College, British Columbia, Canada. He has published numerous articles related to youth physical activity and physical education and coauthored the National Association for Sport and Physical Education (NASPE) *Physical Activity Guidelines for Children.* Dr. Le Masurier has given more than 30 research and professional presentations at national and regional meetings. Dr. Le Masurier reviews research for numerous professional journals and has contributed to *Fitness for Life, Fifth Edition,* and the *Physical Best Activity Guide.* Dr. Le Masurier is a member of AAHPERD, NASPE, ACSM, and Canadian AHPERD.

Dolly D. Lambdin, EdD, is a senior lecturer in the department of kinesiology and health education at the University of Texas at Austin. She has 16 years experience in public and private schools and 30 years in teacher preparation at the university level, much of it simultaneous. This required her on a daily basis to teach curriculum theory and teaching methods and actually teach hundreds of 5- to 14-year-olds. She has supervised over 100 student teachers, visiting thousands of public school classes and learning from scores of fabulous "cooperating teachers." Dr. Lambdin served as NASPE President (2004-05), on the NASPE Board of Directors (2000-2006), and on the writing teams for the Texas Physical Education Essential Knowledge and Skills, the NASPE Beginning Teacher Standards, the Texas Beginning Teacher Standards, NASPE Online PE Guidelines, and the NASPE Appropriate Practices Revision. She has been an invited keynote speaker at state and national conferences, and she has been honored as the Texas AHPERD Outstanding College and University Physical Educator of the Year and for distinguished leadership by the CSLPE.

Charles B. Corbin, PhD, is a professor emeritus in the department of exercise and wellness at Arizona State University. He has published more than 200 journal articles and has authored or contributed to more than 70 books, including *Fitness for Life,* an award-winning book now in its fifth edition. An internationally recognized expert in physical activity, health and wellness, and youth physical fitness, he has keynoted more than 35 state AHPERD conventions and made major addresses and prestigious lectures in more than 15 countries. He is past president and fellow of the American Academy of Kinesiology and Physical Education, an American College of Sports Medicine (ACSM) fellow, and a life member of AAHPERD. Among his awards are a Healthy American Fitness Leaders Award, an AAHPERD Honor Award, a Physical Fitness Council Honor Award, a COPEC Hanson Award, and the Distinguished Service Award from the President's Council on Physical Fitness and Sports (PCPFS). Dr. Corbin was named an AAHPERD Alliance Scholar and a NAKPEHE Distinguished Scholar and was recently inducted into the NASPE Hall of Fame.

How to Use the CD-ROM

System Requirements

You can use this CD-ROM on either a Windows®-based PC or a Macintosh computer.

Windows

- IBM PC compatible with Pentium® processor
- Windows® 98/2000/XP/Vista
- Adobe Reader® 8.0
- Microsoft® Word
- 4x CD-ROM drive

Macintosh

- Power Mac® recommended
- System 10.4 or higher
- Adobe Reader® 8.0
- Microsoft® Word
- 4x CD-ROM drive

User Instructions

Windows

1. Insert the *Fitness for Life: Middle School Teacher's Guide* CD-ROM. (Note: The CD-ROM must be present in the drive at all times.)
2. Select the "My Computer" icon from the desktop.
3. Select the CD-ROM drive.
4. Open the file you wish to view. See the "Start.pdf" file for a list of the contents.

Macintosh

1. Insert the *Fitness for Life: Middle School Teacher's Guide* CD-ROM. (Note: The CD-ROM must be present in the drive at all times.)
2. Double-click the CD icon located on the desktop.
3. Open the file you wish to view. See the "Start.pdf" file for a list of the contents.

Note: OSX users, to open the "Start.pdf" file, you must first open Adobe® Reader®, then select the file from your CD-ROM drive and open the file from within Adobe® Reader®.

For customer support, contact Technical Support:

Phone: 217-351-5076 Monday through Friday (excluding holidays) between 7:00 a.m. and 7:00 p.m. (CST).

Fax: 217-351-2674

E-mail: support@hkusa.com

Contents of the CD-ROM

The *Fitness for Life: Middle School Teacher's Guide* CD-ROM contains materials for teachers to use in delivering the *Fitness for Life: Middle School* program. The materials are ready to be printed and used as is. However, teachers can also customize the materials for a particular class, unit, or school, or to meet any specific need. (Customized files can't be saved to the CD-ROM, but they can be saved to another source, such as a hard drive or a separate writeable disc.)

The materials on the CD-ROM are listed below, along with page numbers in this book that contain information about using the materials.

- ▶ Worksheets and resources for the lesson plans (pages 8, 32)
- ▶ Rubrics for assessment of students (pages 32, 34-36)
- ▶ Web site resources (Mount Fitness answer cards) (page 40)
- ▶ Classroom quotes related to lesson reading (page 8)
- ▶ Quiz and answer key for each chapter of the student textbook (page 35)
- ▶ Quiz and answer key for each unit of the student textbook (page 35)
- ▶ Quiz and answer key for all student textbook material (page 35)
- ▶ Answer key for unit reviews found on the Web site (page 35)
- ▶ Answer key for chapter reviews found in the student textbook (page 35)